To Don Cupitt

*who through his books has taught me the importance
of 'getting theology right'; and who now reckons that
he is 'going to shut up'
after four decades of thought-provoking writing!*

Table of Contents

Preface

Religion is back, but perhaps for all the wrong reasons! Whilst its repositioning in the consciousness of humankind as *"spirituality"* might be a reaction to full-blown secularism and the accompanying search for "something more," it is also true that religion has of late been widely greeted with fear and suspicion. More recently yet, it has returned with a few positive images; but disturbingly most descriptions have been overwhelmingly negative. Three scenes from Australia will suffice to illustrate this situation.

First, a few days before Christmas more than 50,000 people crammed into the Domain at Sydney for "Carols by Candlelight"—a syrupy melange of modern non-religious songs and traditional carols that intersperses the Christian story with appearances by Santa Claus and television personalities. Such were the crowds that the authorities issued warnings six hours before the starting time for no more people to attend as the venue had already reached its full capacity! "If only people would flock to their local church for the *real* Christmas," moaned ecclesiastical officials. Second, in Melbourne the "Global Atheist Convention" was sold out months in advance; and participants who had flown from many parts of the world loudly applauded speakers who rejected "the absurd and wicked claims of the religious" and who now sought "for answers in the marvels and complexities of science, as well as in the higher and deeper riches of literature."[1] Third, a group of local residents successfully protested against the construction of a mosque in Perth, citing as one of the reasons for their objection that "extremists would use the mosque to incite hatred and violence towards non-Muslims."

These scenes could, of course, be replicated in many Western countries. Christian priests are convicted of the crime of pedophilia; and televangelists are charged over fraudulent and immoral practices. The building of minarets is banned in Switzerland; and France officially outlaws the burqa. The wearing of a cross as Christian jewelry is deemed inappropriate for airline staff in the United Kingdom; and large crowds gather to try out the latest spiritual techniques at the "Mind, Body, Soul" exhibition. Religion is under attack on many fronts!

This book's title began as that of a lecture delivered to conferences in Perth and Sydney in which the only focus was the attacks that "the new atheists" had launched on religion. Indeed, I well remember expressing my concerns in a conversation with Bishop John Shelby Spong that no one seemed to understand *what* their objections were nor why those who were religious needed to respond in a reasonable way. He replied: "Then you must write about *how* we might respond." No sooner that I had written my first chapter than I realized that religion was facing more than one attack. It was being bombarded from every quarter—scientists, spiritualists, agnostics, ex-believers, non-believers and those who had never bothered with religion in the first place. Moreover, that hostility towards religion was not only aimed at my own religious tradition, Christianity, but in particular, at Islam as well. As I investigated further I came to realize that the two crucial questions facing those who peddled their religion to others were these: "Why is your religion worth bothering with?" and more pointedly, "What kind of God do you want me to worship if I follow your religion?" These interrogations led me to wonder whether, and at last to suspect that, the current predicament of religion derives from the God it proclaims. That is the central thrust of this book.

My thanks once again go to all those associated with Polebridge Press for their unstinting help in the production of this book: Larry Alexander, Char Matejovsky, Robaire Ream and Tom Hall, wordsmith *par excellence*. I am also indebted to those whose "voices" can be heard beneath the surface of the text: Don Cupitt, Lloyd Geering, John Shelby Spong and Peter Carnley. These are the visionaries who have been prepared to be the Socratic gadflies urging those within the church to get serious about their theology. I am also beholden to Robert Semes for the gracious theological sparring at The Jefferson Center in Oregon together with his and Harvey Ray's wonderful hospitality—true friendship indeed! Likewise, I would like to acknowledge the wonderful theological banter with Steven Ogden and the warm reception from the staff and students of Saint Francis Anglican Theological College, Brisbane, especially Clarry White and Greg Jenks; together with the theological openness of Saint John's Anglican Cathedral ably led by its Dean, Peter Catt. It is good to have found a milieu in which theology can be explored honestly and with an enquiring spirit.

Above all, heartfelt thanks and love go to my wife Julie and son Sebastian for their support during this project. Julie has helped me in so many ways, but especially by urging me to be true to myself. Sebastian is still amazed that on a visit to a bookstore in the United States a young assistant recognized my name and gushed, "So, you wrote that wonderful book *The God Problem*." We dined out on that story for some time. I hope that *Religion Under Attack* adds to the debate over the future of religion, for without a decent theology, then I fear religion will only decline still further.

1. Christopher Hitchens, *The Portable Atheist*, xi.

Nigel Leaves
Brisbane, 2011

Introduction

The resilience of religion
the resurgence of atheism
the popularity of spirituality
the rise of progressive faith

> We are at a moment as epochal as the Reformation itself:
> a reformation moment not only for Catholics but for the
> entire Christian world. Christianity as a whole is growing
> and mutating in ways that observers in the West tend not
> to see (and) it is Christianity that will leave the deepest
> mark on the 21st Century.[1]

This sanguine assessment of the Church's future imag-
ines a second reformation marked by a new flowering of
Christian faith and practice. Christendom will reemerge in
the Third World as a dominant force, exhibiting many different manifestations and all but redefining the Church in
the West. The message is loud and clear: Christianity isn't
going to disappear. Of course, other major world religions
have proved themselves equally robust. Islam has shown a
surge of influence; Buddhism is touted as the most popular religion amongst Westerners; and Hinduism remains
numerically strong on the Indian sub-continent. Moreover,
newer forms of spirituality—often subsumed under the label
"New Age"—have emerged to compete in the religious supermarket. Indeed, the spiritual landscape of most countries
is replete with a veritable smorgasbord of options for those
seeking religious self-definition. In 1998 the philosopher
John Caputo asserted that many postmodern academics

talk about "the other," but have side-stepped religion, since the subject seems "just too, too other for them, too 'tout autre.'"[2] That is not the case today, and we may now agree with another philosopher of religion, Graham Ward, that "it no longer seems necessary to argue for postmodernism's fascination with things religious."[3] An increasing number of spiritual pathways are sufficiently attractive that politicians and leaders of nations are sometimes eager to avow religious affiliations![4] Every year the President of the United States of America presides at the National Prayer Breakfast in Washington and commends others to pray for God's favor on the nation. Even sporting triumphs and disasters are attributed to religious beliefs: Zach Johnson, the surprise winner of the Masters golf tournament at Augusta in 2007 thanked Jesus for his victory, while in that same year the Pakistan cricket team's shockingly early exit from the World Cup in the West Indies was blamed on their fixation with preaching and praying instead of concentrating on training. Johnson felt that God had helped him win the tournament because he was a devout Baptist. P. I. Mir (the Pakistan media manager) blamed the negative influence of religion on the Pakistan cricket team's poor performance. In particular, overt displays of religiosity were inappropriate for a national team and instead of praying privately had made it a public spectacle. This display of religiosity had distracted the team from its main concern: winning the competition.

Of course, things weren't supposed to pan out this way! In the 1950s and '60s social scientists such as Anthony F. Wallace and Peter Berger advanced what became known as "the secularization theory"—the notion that modernization would lead to a decline of religion both in society and in the minds of individuals. As the Enlightenment became increasingly internalized, it was assumed, people would lose their religious beliefs and become ever more secular. The main opponent of the secularization theory was David Martin of the

London School of Economics, with his magisterial *A General Theory of Secularization* (1978) in which he questioned the inevitability of the demise of religion and the rise of secularism. Martin argued that secularization was complex and differed from country to country and required detailed comparative analysis. Martin's caution concerning secularization has been shown to be accurate. As a matter of fact, religion has proved extremely resilient and has emerged in diverse forms ranging from various fundamentalisms to the spate of new spiritualities that has flooded the marketplace.[5] Clearly, the announcement of "God's funeral" that began in the nineteenth century with Thomas Hardy, and was spectacularly proclaimed by Friedrich Nietzsche in his celebrated parable of the madman, was rather premature.[6]

Religion Under Attack

But even as religion has regained its voice, it has come under attack from many quarters. A number of differing individuals and groups have been lumped together as "the new atheists" and several media personalities have been singled out as representatives of the attack against religion. But the argument of this book is that the attack on religion comes from a much larger consistency than atheists. It is my aim to show that religion is being challenged not only by atheism but on many other fronts as well. Ranging from the popular cry that religion is responsible for most of the armed conflicts in the world to the sophisticated arguments of evolutionists, a whole chorus of voices is making the case "against religion." In recent years a flurry of books has attacked religious belief from every conceivable angle: psychological, scientific, mathematical, ethical, secularist, and philosophical.[7] Even the film industry has been drawn into the debate with the screening of *The Golden Compass* (an adaptation of the first volume of Philip Pullman's trilogy: *His Dark Materials*) because some allege it to represent an attack on the dogmatism of the Roman Catholic Church (The Magisterium). Some even view Pullman's trilogy as a direct rebuttal of C. S. Lewis and the implicit Christian message of his *Narnia* series. Whilst Pullman officially remains agnostic on the existence of God, there can be no doubt that he is critical of dogmatic religion and its unsavory record of oppression.[8]

To these negative factors must be added the growing host of the faithful who view with alarm the increasing conservativism within their organizations and are determined to present another "face" of religion. Indeed, religious factions are engaged in a struggle for the heart and minds of the faithful. Likewise, a growing band of "agnostics" remain on the margins of religious belonging or have left altogether, still unsure of the existence of a divine being, but not completely wanting, as they say, "to throw the baby out with the bathwater." It is my premise that, in view of all these factors, the challenge to religion is far more diverse than is often presented.

Atheism

Of course it is clear that atheism, having been widely and colorfully promoted, has captured the imagination of the media and in recent years has become more acceptable—or even fashionable! Rather than remain unobtrusive academics, such atheists as Richard Dawkins, Sam Harris, Daniel Dennett, David Mills, Richard Carrier, Walter Sinnott-Armstrong and Robert Price have publicly challenged the validity of religious belief.[9] They have been joined by such writers as Christopher Hitchens, Martin Amis, Polly Toynbee, Susan Jacoby and media personality Julia Sweeney.[10] Outspokenly dismissive of religious creeds and observances, they promote atheism as the only *reasonable* theological position for people today. Indeed, this new approach has been labeled "evangelistic atheism" or "missionary secularism." When challenged by a journalist that he was mimicking the zeal of traditional religions, all of which have at their core an urge to convert nonbelievers to their worldview, Dawkins astutely replied: "You called me an outspoken atheist, but you didn't call the Pope an outspoken Christian."

Moreover atheists have insisted on subjecting religious belief systems to the same intellectual scrutiny that applies to other disciplines. If the head of a religious group demands or outlaws certain articles of apparel or teaches that their exalted founder will soon return to judge the world, they insist that these claims must be investigated and openly debated. So, outlandish statements such as that by the Sunni Muslim cleric, SheikTaj Aldin al-Hilali, that Australian girls who dressed immodestly were "uncovered meat" and thus responsible for enticing men to commit rape must be condemned. Likewise the claims by many fundamentalist Christian groups that Jesus will return soon in an apocalyptic firestorm that will destroy the earth and carry off the "redeemed" to heaven should be regarded as nonsense. All special pleading on behalf of religions or religious beliefs, all attempts to exempt them from accepted social, academic, and scientific norms must be actively opposed. Religions must be held accountable for what they teach their followers:

> I take it to be self-evident that ordinary people cannot be moved to burn genial old scholars alive for blaspheming the Koran, or celebrate the violent deaths of their children, unless they believe some improbable things about the nature of the universe. Because most religions offer no valid mechanism by which their core beliefs can be tested and revised, each new generation of believers is condemned to inherit the superstitions and tribal hatreds of its predecessors.[11]

Even in the United States atheists have effectively marshaled their forces. This is despite the fact that "there is still a deep prejudice against atheists in this country, and this prejudice is expressed in the ridiculous notion that belief in God is some sort of qualification for public office."[12] Although atheists in the USA are outnumbered and politically ostracized, they are now a force to be reckoned with. Moreover, according to a survey in 2008 of religious affiliation by the Pew Forum on Religion and Public Life the group that had the greatest net gain was the "unaffiliated." More than 16 percent of American adults say that they are not part of any organized religion which makes them the country's fourth largest grouping. Whilst obviously not all of this 16 percent will be "full-blown" atheists it shows that there are far more "unbelievers" than often admitted in the USA. Joined by their European counterparts headed by Michel Onfray—and in a strange turn of events by disillusioned or ex-Muslims such as Ibn Warraq, Ayaan Hirsi Ali, Taslima Nasrin, Shirin Ebadi, Mina Ahadi, Nawal al-Saadawi and Wafa Sultan— atheists have mounted a fierce campaign for the liberation of the public mind.[13] A new phenomenon is emerging—the zealous disbelief in God—and there is no shortage of converts. Therefore it is premature, if not fallacious, to propose with Alister McGrath that we are living in an era of "the fall of disbelief" and "the twilight of atheism."[14] Like those who proposed the secularization thesis, the advocates of the death of atheism are misjudged and ill-informed.

In this book I intend to show that atheism is a force to be reckoned with, and that this new phenomenon has its sights on all religions. I will counter Tina Beattie's claims in *The New Atheists* that the debate is "dominated by a small clique of white English-speaking men";[15] that it is "primarily a British and American phenomenon";[16] and that there "must be a more courteous and respectful exchange of ideas."[17]

First, I find it quite surprising that, although she claims to be a feminist theologian concerned to promote the female voice, she has remained silent on the feminist critique of

Islam by women who were not born in the West. This goes to the heart of a debate in feminist theology about how much the critique of women's experiences are fundamentally written by white, middle and upper class women who represent the Academy. Although there is now recognition that Asian and African women's experience of oppression might be different from Western women there is still the issue of the marginalization of women who are not included in the dominant discourse of feminist theology. This then becomes a "power issue" and the exclusion of "minority women" who oppose the prevailing social structures. Thus, there is not just one feminist understanding of oppression, but following the insights of post-structuralism there are multi-variant understandings (readings) of what oppression means!

So, when Beattie wonders if Muslim women "might have something different to say if they were permitted to contribute to this debate," which Muslim women is she referring to? She seems to imply that all Muslim women will share the same voice! She has totally ignored those "caged virgins" who are outraged by the status of women in Islam. Likewise, she fails to give any examples of feminist Muslim voices in her book that portray what "women themselves say in different cultural and economic contexts."[18] By her silence on these matters, it strengthens the atheist assertion that religions purposely suppress women and that the female voice is never heard. Indeed, despite her plea for feminism she ends up privileging conservative Christian male theologians (in particular Keith Ward, Alister McGrath and Francis Collins). Then in a contradictory note she also claims that these same conservative males have excluded women from the debate![19] In short, it is my aim to widen the debate and show that the new atheists come from a wide variety of backgrounds and that it is **not** solely a Western phenomenon aimed at the downfall of Christianity. Islam too is under attack from those who consider that its "God is not great."

Second, whilst Beattie's concern for generosity of spirit towards opponents ("kindness") is admirable, it deflects from the serious debate that is being waged. To offer a measured critique of a religious belief is an important part of the necessary discourse. True dialogue is more than a polite listening to another person's point of view; it can occur only when people are willing to admit that their own religious or intellectual positions ("faiths") may be flawed and that they could change in the course of the exchange. As the Indian philosopher R. Sundarara Rajan puts it:

> If it is impossible to lose one's faith as a result of an encounter with another faith, then I feel that the dialogue has been made safe from all possible risks.[20]

The cut and thrust of intellectual arguments cannot be watered down to avoid the risk of offending someone's belief. Likewise, participants in such debates must be prepared to admit the validity of an opponent's position and the possibility of learning from the encounter with someone of a differing view. Whilst at the end of a debate people may "agree to differ," they must be allowed to put forward their views in a reasoned way without fearing that they will be reviled, condemned, or even killed.

Beattie seems to have underestimated the violence that is taking place in the name of religion and the potential risk to those who dare to question religious beliefs. Having personally been vilified, received "hate mail" (both letters and e-mail) and verbally abused by fellow Christians for writing a book that simply *explored* alternative understandings of the term "God," I can testify to the irrationality and hostility of many who claim to be religious. Why are people ostracized for questioning sacred texts and representatives of religious traditions? Why do religions dread scrutiny and debate? On what grounds should someone like Dawkins be considered to have "betrayed everything that the Western intellectual tradition stands for, with its privileging of informed scholarship based on the study of texts"?[21] If religious claims are true, those who make them should not fear requests for clarification about how those claims are consistent with the latest scientific research. The challenge laid down by atheists is that religions be more transparent about their beliefs and ask whether the world they promote is more loving or brutal than the existing one. Indeed, many have *already* decided on the aptness of the latter characteristic, and therefore voted to reject religion altogether.

Non-religious and Postmodernity

Another factor to be considered in this book (and one that is surprisingly overlooked by most commentators) is the increasing percentage of those in the "Western world" who now *openly* declare themselves "non-religious." This is in no small part linked to the decline in adherence to mainstream Christianity and to the changes that have taken place in society as people have moved from the "modern" to embrace the present era of "postmodernity."

Richard Holloway aptly describes the decline of religious faith in the Western world and the erosion of the plausibility of belief in God:

> Faith has become an implausible minority option, indulged for historical reasons, at best tolerated, sometimes treated with amused disdain, sometimes with dismissive contempt.[22]

He argues that there are intellectual and moral reasons why people have rejected religions. Intellectually, religions have become faith systems that rely on plugging the gaps left by scientific knowledge. However, those gaps have increasingly diminished leaving religions high and dry. Once the intellectual gap is filled by science there is seemingly no need for God or religion. Morally, religions have been culpable, the cause of evil and the source of human suffering. Religions have been rejected because they have been the cause of human misery and conflict. This is corroborated by statistics from the *World Christian Encyclopaedia* which show that the number of those without any religion has climbed from 3.2 million in 1900 to 697 million in 1970 and on to 918 million by 2000. It is estimated that 8.5 million people per year join the non-religionists and that there is close to one billion who now do not practice any recognized religion. These figures from the *World Christian Encyclopaedia* also reveal that nearly 18 percent of the world's population are nonreligious and the growth of secularism is unparalleled. Indeed, the only increase in adherents from religions comes from Islam which is due, not to conversions, but by the high birth rate amongst its followers.[23] Researchers, Gregory Paul and Phil Zuckerman claim that religious faith prospers only in "comparatively primitive social, economic and educational disparities and poverty characteristic of second and third worlds and the US." When a nation advances in terms of democratic, egalitarian education and prosperity it will lose its faith. Supernatural props are not needed when a nation improves the lot of its people and the disparity between rich and poor is lessened. For Paul and Zuckerman it is economics, not ideas that produce the best way of eradicating faith. For them, the decline of religion is assured:

> Disbelief now rivals the great faiths in numbers and influence. Never before has religion faced such enormous levels of disbelief, or faced a hazard as that posed by modernity. How is organized religion going to regain the true, choice-based initiative when only one of them is growing, and it is doing so with reproductive activity rather than by convincing the masses to join in, when no major faith is proving able to grow as they break out of their

ancestral lands via mass conversion, and when securely prosperous democracies appear immune to mass devotion? In the end what humanity chooses to believe will be more a matter of economics than of debate, deliberately considered choice or reproduction. The more national societies that provide financial and physical security to the population, the fewer that will be religiously devout. The more that cannot provide these high standards the more that will hope that supernatural forces will alleviate their anxieties.[24]

Despite this intriguing neo-Marxist suggestion that the answer to religious fundamentalism lies in economic policy and the bettering of socio-economic conditions, it is in the world of ideas that the battles are being fought. As Daniel Dennett points out in *Breaking the Spell* there are "many ideas to die for" and countless religious and secular people are prepared to risk their lives for an idea. Many devote their entire lives "to further the interests of an *idea* that has lodged in their brains" whether this be Democracy, Allah, Jesus or Evolution.[25] What is more, all parties are intent on winning the hearts and minds of ordinary people. A war of ideas is being fought in conference venues, television debates, newspaper articles, best-selling books, and on the internet. Samuel Huntingdon's famous prediction of a clash of civilizations has come true: we are now witnessing a clash of *intellectual* civilizations. The worlds of science and religion are on a collision course, with each intent on eliminating the other because one asserts that "God is a delusion" while the other condemns "scientific naturalism" as evil. The forces of naturalism/scientific materialism are pitched against those who argue that matter and the body are not the totality of existence. Notable scientists either openly disavow any credence in supernatural beings or assert their belief in a "Something More" by affirming "the God hypothesis."[26] And a similar division separates religious scholars; some theologians cast doubt on the validity of Darwin's theory of evolution, while others assert that the Universe is unsupported and "outsideless."[27] In spite of occasional calls for moderation, champions of religion and atheism are becoming more shrill and hostile towards each other. As their voices become more acrimonious, the combatants grow increasingly confrontational. Consider these two statements; the first from an atheist:

> My faith has been a faith of fear. My relationship with Allah was like this: as long as He left me in peace, I was happy. Certainly, I prayed when I was in pain; I begged Him to stop my mother from beating me. But like any child who, sooner or later, realizes at the back of his mind that Santa Claus does not exist, I accepted that I should not expect much from Him. I think that most people who call themselves religious are essentially atheists. They avoid thinking about whether they really believe in God and allow themselves to be distracted by details. We should have a debate . . . about the source of our moral standards: did we people invent them, or were they the work of God? Can we believe that the world was created in six days? That Eve was created from Adam's rib? That simply cannot be true. Scientists are unbelieving.[28]

And the second from an evangelical Christian:

> *While a schoolboy*, I had once, like Dawkins believed that natural sciences demanded an atheist worldview. . . . I was naturally interested to see what kind of arguments Dawkins would develop in support of this interesting idea. What I found was not particularly persuasive. He offered a few muddled attempts to make sense of the idea of "faith," without establishing a proper analytical and evidential basis for his reflections.[29]

Clearly, neither atheists nor believers are overly generous in their estimation of one another. The result is that they operate out of parallel universes with both claiming the intellectual high ground. Moreover, those who advocate accommodation are dismissed as lightweight liberals. "You can't have it both ways," insist the true believers on both sides for whom irreconcilable differences demand epistemological monism. To use a colloquial expression, "It's my way or the highway!" When viewpoints become this polarized, people are told they must sign up for one belief system or the other. There is seemingly no middle or common ground for dialogue or conversation.

This disturbing state of affairs reveals a growing intransigence in what should be a tolerant era. Postmodernity was supposed to be characterized by discourses forged from dialogue and choice. People were to be "ironists" or "constructivists" in either case acknowledging that beliefs are made "on the shifting ground of our own socially-constructed cultural worldviews." No one style in art, culture or religion would prevail and everyone would be content to improvise and combine traditions to create unique lifestyles. If there is one animal that best represents postmodernity it would be the Australian platypus. Combining webbed feet and a bill that resembles a duck it has a broad furry body and flat tail. The bizarre appearance of this semi-aquatic mammal fooled naturalists when it was discovered in 1799: it was thought to be a hoax and that somebody had deliberately sewn a duck's beak onto the body of a beaver-like animal. Like postmodernity the platypus defies categorization having characteristics of many different species: it shares genes found in birds yet it is a mammal. So, in postmodernity people freely mix religious and cultural allegiances. They pick and choose from a wide variety of what might have been perceived in previous generations to be conflicting options. You can be an atheist lesbian Muslim, an agnostic pagan Christian, a secular Marxist who is fascinated by the Occult or a Zen tarot reading Calvinist who drives a Ferrari! You create your own lifestyle and *personal* belief system and no one has the right to say that what you have chosen is wrong, inconsistent or unacceptable. You *are* what you are. What emerges is a global civilization where multi-variant discourses vie among the several fields of knowledge and religions.

Progressive Religionists

Religion has been forced to respond to what has happened since the turn of the new millennium. The events of 9/11 in New York, 3/11 in Madrid, 7/7 in London, 10/12 in Bali and elsewhere confirmed to the non-believer that religion was a threat to all civilized and humane people. Likewise, when Muslim fanatics, urged on by their clerics in Northern Nigeria and Pakistan, slaughtered doctors in an attempt to halt polio immunization causing the paralysis of hundreds of infants because they believed it was a plot to reduce the world's Muslim population, then religion was viewed as inhumane and barbaric. And, when a Romanian Orthodox priest was convicted of the death of a twenty-three-year-old nun after an exorcism at an isolated hilltop monastery, religion was understandably castigated as medieval. Moreover, when writers, artists, film-makers, cartoonists, abortion doctors, and gay and lesbian communities are attacked and even killed by religious zealots, then God is discredited. The result is that religion comes to be seen and feared as anti-life, fanatical, and disturbingly irrational:

> Those atheists looking for a surefire way to increase their appeal need only to hope . . . for harsh, vindictive, and unthinking forms of religion to arise in the West, which will so alienate Westerners that they will rush into god-lessness from fear and dislike of its antithesis.[30]

It is this polarization of *all* followers of religion as terrorists prepared to don suicide vests replete with explosives that has prompted progressive religionists to promote a different understanding of their religion. Indeed, following 9/11 politicians in many countries called upon religious believers not only to condemn the attacks perpetrated in the name of religion, but to advocate a different set of beliefs. It was assumed that radical extremists had hijacked religion; and that other less belligerent forms of faith should be endorsed:

> When I was able to isolate Islam from the images and rhetoric that have become commonplace in our society and on TV, I found a religion that was simple, that stood for justice, that placed the utmost importance on revering God and tolerating other faiths. . . . Far too often, the word "jihad" has been misused and taken out of context. Jihad is not another word for terrorism. Jihad is a term that refers to a person's struggle to uphold justice. . . . What is clear is that armed struggle cannot target innocent people—that is just plainly against Islam. Terrorism is no way justified or condoned in Islam. It's as simple as that.[31]

The liberalization of religion is perhaps one of the most difficult undertakings for followers of religion. In this book I will outline some of the personal costs that those who have dared to reform their own faith have had to endure. The most vociferous and courageous attack on her own faith tradition has come from Irshad Manji in *The Trouble with Islam Today*. In what she describes as an "open letter" to her fellow Muslims she proposes that they revive the Islamic concept of "ijtihad"—the tradition of independent thinking and questioning. Indeed, by making small shifts in thinking the present-day fundamentalist manifestation of Islam would be replaced by a reasonable faith that could dialogue with other faiths. Likewise Reza Aslan, in *No god but God* makes the case that Islam itself is not uniform but consists of many differing voices. Currently unfolding in Islam, then, is a struggle over what kind of Islam will triumph—conservative or liberal.

It is a similar story in Christianity where progressive religionists such as John Shelby Spong, Marcus Borg, Richard Holloway, the late Robert Funk, Lloyd Geering, Don Cupitt, Michael Morwood, Gretta Vosper and Karen Armstrong have championed the cause of a less dogmatic and authoritarian faith. The work of transforming an inadequate and antiquated faith into a new radical vision is not easy and for those who attempt such an undertaking there is much hostility from those who wish to keep the status quo. Spong painfully recounts how even at his first wife's funeral he was physically assaulted:

> While seated with my daughters in the first pew of St. Paul's Church beside Joan's pall-draped coffin, I was amazed to feel myself being struck across the back and shoulders with a cane in a manner that was clearly not accidental. My assailant was an elderly woman. I turned instinctively to respond to this blow. The woman then said in a voice audible to anyone within ten yards, "You son of a bitch." Continuing her journey down the aisle, she went through the side door where the pallbearers, all but one of them who were priests of our diocese, were waiting to come into church. To them she said, "I've been waiting to tell that bastard what I think of him for a long time, and I finally got the chance."[32]

In order to provide support and a milieu in which difficult questions of faith can be discussed many have organized themselves into networks, institutes and organizations dedicated to fostering an inclusive and intellectually robust Christianity. At local, national and international conferences, planned by such bodies as The Center for Progressive Christianity, Common Dreams, the Westar Institute et al., people gather to discuss openly what they see as the failings of the Church and to share dreams and promote "progressive religion as a transforming agent."[33] Moreover, there has been a spate of books by clergy and laity who have decided that they can no longer belong to churches that are intellectually and spiritually bankrupt. Some have lost faith in the Church, though still affirm belief in God. Others, like Barbara Brown Taylor in her book, *Losing Faith*, find spiritual fulfillment in teaching rather than the pulpit. Michael Hampson, an ex-episcopalian priest, reveals the rate of clergy drop-out in the Church of England:

> When I left after thirteen years, I was behind the game. Only a quarter of my college leavers' year completed those thirteen years in parish ministry. Another quarter left and then went back, with varying degrees of reluctance and varying plans for the future. The rest have left with no intention of going back. They have worked for charities as front line service providers, and for the prison service and health service as chaplains and managers. They have bluffed on their CVs to cover up their history. They have been unemployed and early-retired. They go to church rarely or not at all.[34]

To prevent further decline, progressive religionists are committed to find answers to such questions as: should not religion enhance human life rather than diminish it? Can people of good will forge reasonable and tolerant religious traditions that will foster productive public discourse? What is the future faith in the light of the latest critical and scientific thinking?

In conclusion, then, I will argue in this book that religion is under attack from a wide range of combatants and they are marshalling their forces effectively. Atheists, agnostics and progressive religionists have reacted to the growth of fundamentalism and violence perpetrated in the name of religion. They are no longer prepared to remain silent and submissive when religion threatens not only their own personal well-being, but the human race as a whole. Moreover, ordinary people in the twenty-first century have reached a point of maturity where they will choose whichever spiritual path (or none) that best suits them. They will not be persuaded by uncritical thinking or by rhetoric lifted from the pages of ancient sacred texts. For many the non-religious option is the most viable. For them, it is possible to be ethical and live in harmony with one another without any recourse to religion. They don't need a god to tell them how to live. There is only one life and this liberates them from fear about the next one and makes them content to live this life as best they can.

Despite their protestations, the main monotheistic religions are feeling the heat from a collusion of forces. To begin, then, let us examine the recent rise of atheism . . .

Notes

1. Angela Shanahan quoting Philip Jenkins, "The Next Christendom," in *The Australian*, 13–14 January 2007: 21.

2. Edith Wyschogrod, and John D. Caputo. "Postmodernism and the Desire for God: an e-mail exchange." *Cross Currents* 48, no. 3 (Fall 1998).

3. Graham Ward, "Theology and Postmodernism," *Theology* 100 (November/December 1997): 435.

4. The list of leaders of nations who have declared their allegiance to a particular faith is quite exhaustive. For a good account of the rise of the Christian religious right in Australia and its influence over conservative politicians see Maddox, *God Under Howard*.

5. See Leaves, *The God Problem*, chap. 5.

6. Nietzsche, *The Gay Science*, section 125. For a discussion of this passage, see Leaves, *The God Problem*, 69ff.

7. Tamas Pataki, *Against Religion*, Richard Dawkins, *A Devil's Chaplain*, Steven Pinker, *The Blank Slate*, Michael Shermer, *Why Darwin Matters*, Erik Wielenberg, *Value and Virtue in a Godless Universe*, Louis M. Antony, *Philosophers without Gods*.

8. In a question and answer session in the Guardian newspaper on-line, Pullman replied that whilst he could see no evidence for God's existence, he could not rule out the possibility that God might

exist. However, some like the conservative British columnist Peter Hitchens view Pullman as a militant atheist seeking to undermine Christianity. Others, including Rowan Williams, argue that he is criticizing destructive forms of religion. The North American Catholic League urged a boycott of *The Golden Compass*. For an insightful article on Philip Pullman see Laura Miller, "Far From Narnia," *The New Yorker*, December 26, 2005.

9. Richard Dawkins, *The God Delusion*, David Mills, *Atheist Universe*, Sam Harris, *Letter to a Christian Nation*, *End of Faith*, Robert M. Price, *The Reason Driven Life*, Daniel C. Dennett, *Breaking the Spell*, Richard Carrier, *Sense and Goodness without God*, William Lane Craig and Walter Sinnott-Armstrong, *God: A debate between a christian and an atheist.*

10. Julia Sweeney is a well known cast member on the satirical USA show *Saturday Night Live*. She has produced an autobiographical monologue, *Letting Go of God*, in which she rejects the Roman Catholic faith in which she was raised and promotes her new found atheism. Christopher Hitchens, *God is not Great*, Martin Amis, "The Age of Horrorism," Susan Jacoby, *The Age of American Unreason*. Polly Toynbee is a journalist for the Guardian newspaper and was appointed President of the British Humanist Society in 2007.

11. Harris, *The End of Faith*, 31.

12. Susan Jacoby, "On Faith," Blog on Washington Post.com.

13. Michel Onfray, *Atheist Manifesto*, Ibn Warraq, *Why I am not a Muslim*, Ayaan Hirsi Ali, *The Caged Virgin*, *Infidel* and *Nomad*, Taslima Nasrin, *Shame* and *Meyebela,* Shirin Ebadi, *Iran Awakening*, Nawal al-Saadawi , *Walking Through Fire*. Wafa Sultan is working on a book to be called 'The Escaped Prisoner: when God is a monster.' Mina Ahadi founded the Council of Ex-Muslims in Europe.

14. Title of book by Alister McGrath.

15. Beattie, *The New Atheists*, 10.

16. Beattie, *The New Atheists*, 5.

17. Beattie, *The New Atheists,* 17.

18. Beattie, *The New Atheists*, 67; See Hirsi Ali, *The Caged Virgin.*

19. Beattie, *The New Atheists*, 9. Her attitude to Keith Ward in particular is contradictory, for example contrast page 9 with her encounter with Ward on page 16.

20. Quoted in Hunter, *Christianity and Other Faiths in Britain*, 10.

21. Beattie, *The New Atheists*, 16.

22. Holloway, *Dancing on the Edge,* 8.

23. Gregory Paul and Phil Zuckerman, "Why the gods are not winning," *Edge*, 1 May 2007. http://www.edge.org/3rd_culture/paul07/paul07_index.html

24. Paul and Zuckerman, "Why the gods are not winning." They suggest that people in the USA are still outwardly religious because of the ever-present fear of economic failure: "It is the great anomaly, the United States, that has long perplexed sociologists. America has a large, well educated middle class that lives in comfort—so why do they still believe in a supernatural creator? Because they are afraid and insecure. Arbitrary dismissal from a long held job, loss of health insurance followed by an extended illness, excessive debt due to the struggle to live like the wealthy; before you know it a typical American family can find itself financially ruined. . . . In part to try to accumulate the wealth needed to try to prevent financial catastrophe, in part to compete in a culture of growing economic disparity with the super rich the typical American is engaged in a Darwinian, keeping up with the Jones competition in which failure to perform raises levels of psychological stress. It is not, therefore, surprising that most look to friendly forces from the beyond to protect them from the pitfalls of a risky American life, and if that fails to compensate with a blissful eternal existence."

25. Dennett, *Breaking the Spell,* 4.

26. Scientists opposed to belief in God include Taner Edis, *The Ghost in the Universe*, Matt Young, *Why Intelligent Design Fails* and Jerry Coyne, *Why Evolution is True*. Those who assert the existence of God include Owen Gingerich, *God's Universe* and Francis Collins, *The Language of God*.

27. Creationist theologians such as William Dembski and Dinesh D'Souza together with anti-evolutionist scientists William Behe and those affiliated to the Discovery Institute oppose Darwin's findings. Those theologians who regard "God" as a human construct include Don Cupitt and Lloyd Geering, see Leaves, *The God Problem*, chap. 3.

28. Ali, *The Caged Virgin*, 79–80.

29. McGrath, *Dawkins' God,* 2 (my italics). Note the disparaging comment "while a schoolboy" which is the ultimate put-down in academic circles.

30. McGrath, *Twilight of Atheism*, 278

31. Ingrid Mattson, "Finding the Voice of Islam" in *From the Ashes*, 145.

32. Spong, *Here I Stand*, 365.

33. Title of Common Dreams Conference organized by The Center for Progressive Religious Thought in Australia in Sydney 2007. For a list of progressive religious/institutes/networks see Leaves, *The God Problem*, 91.

34. Hampson, *Last Rites*, 13.

Chapter 1

The Rise of Atheism: The "New Atheists"

The Typical Atheist?

The Oscar-nominated Australian film *Little Miss Sunshine* features a young man named Dwayne who admires the most famous atheist of all—Friedrich Nietzsche—and proudly wears a t-shirt with Nietzsche's face printed on it. He reads Nietzsche's *Thus Spake Zarathustra*, as other youngsters would read a magazine. Yet it is made very clear that reading Nietzsche does not bring Dwayne happiness. Although Dwayne belongs to a very chaotic family he is portrayed as the most dysfunctional of them. His liking for Nietzsche is linked to his rejection of oral communication and to his general air of depression. For two-thirds of the film he remains mute and confused, totally immersed in his own thoughts and indisposed to speak to anyone. The message is unambiguous: reading Nietzsche is a clear sign of an introverted, angst-riddled existence. Espousing atheism is certain to prove hazardous to one's health and well-being. This negative attitude towards atheists is reinforced by conservative evangelicals as evidenced by the Reverend Pat Robertson's advice on

the internet to a born-again Christian lady who happened to
have a long-standing relationship with an atheist man:

> There is no fellowship between an atheist and a fol-
> lower of God . . . You've got to **go find somebody
> else**. . . . You'll be serving God and he'll be serving the
> Devil.[1]

Philosophical and Historical Factors

Historically and philosophically, atheists have been viewed
with suspicion and disdain. Philosophically, academics have
scoffed at those who are defined "by what they do not
believe" and inquired suspiciously, "How can you prove a
negative?" Moreover, atheism is perceived as hastening the
slide into moral decay. Without the controlling influence of
religion there can be no objective ethics: the result is law-
lessness. This viewpoint was famously expressed by Fyodor
Dostoevsky in his novel, *The Brothers Karamazov*, through
his character Ivan Karamazov: "if God does not exist, everything is permissible." Atheists are lampooned as anarchists
and nihilists; and, as Walter Sinnott-Armstrong succinctly
suggests, "Who would want to befriend or hire or vote for
anyone with no morals?"[2] The philosopher, Don Cupitt, asserts that atheism is a "word which historically has been used
as a quasi-political smear word to brand innovators—including (ironically) at one time the early Christians."[3] Thus if you
wish to discredit someone then you call them an atheist. In
describing his own radical position of a Christian who does
not believe in an objective God he prefers "Christian non-
realist" to "Christian atheist," as the latter would never be
taken seriously. To admit that you are an "atheist" is to be
judged before you have had the chance to state your case.

To counter the negativity surrounding atheism and weary
of being dismissed censoriously as "godless," "unbelievers"

or "immoral," long-term atheist activists Paul Geisert and Mynga Futrell, coined the word "Bright." Their aim was to promote a more positive image for those opposed to a supernatural or mystical worldview and to bring together atheists, secularists, humanists and rationalists in a worldwide "community of reason." In 2003 they launched their Bright website (www.the-brights.net) where people from around the globe could sign up to belong to a movement that endorsed a naturalistic understanding of the origins of the universe, ethics and morality. Brights do not need gods or spirits: everything was (and is) to be understood as having natural causes. Brights have campaigned for the civic right to hold such an opinion without fear or condemnation. It is estimated that by 2007 more than 35,000 people in one hundred and forty nations had signed up on the website to become Brights.

There has been a mixed reaction from atheists to the appellation "Bright." Daniel Dennett has actively promoted the word and urged others to use it:

> The time has come for us brights to come out of the
> closet. We brights don't believe in ghosts or elves or the
> Easter bunny—or God. We disagree about many things,
> and hold a variety of views about morality, politics and
> the meaning of life, but we share a disbelief in black
> magic—and life after death.[4]

Richard Dawkins, whilst not rejecting "Bright," prefers to retain the original word (atheist) and wear it with pride: you can purchase a t-shirt from his website which has a scarlet-colored capital "A" emblazoned on it. Many, especially philosophers, favor "humanist" as it links them with "thinkers like Aristotle, Descartes, Hume, Kant and Marx, who were awed and inspired by human capacities: for thought, for creation, and for sympathy."[5] Humanists are perceived as those who by their kindly actions promote a more compassionate world. Yet again, others adopt the nomenclature "secular" or "rationalist" whilst Christopher Hitchens calls himself an "anti-theist." This latter epithet neatly sums up the position of anyone who uses these various labels, that is, someone opposed to belief in a supernatural God.

Historically, atheism has been a risky undertaking with many incurring the wrath of the Church or the opprobrium of their fellow human beings. For example, it was not until the late seventeenth century that the death penalty for questioning the Christian doctrine of the Trinity was repealed; and not until 2008 that the United Kingdom Parliament finally abolished the common law of blasphemy and blasphemous libel. The latter because it was a common law offence had no limit on punishment and was invoked in earlier centuries to great effect to silence opponents. It resulted in executions and imprisonments with hard labor for people who wrote and said things that would be considered trivial today. The freedom of human beings *even* to debate religious dogmas has been a very hard-fought victory. The celebrated writer Thomas Hardy was condemned in the nineteenth century by the ecclesiastical authorities and the Anglican Bishop of Wakefield, William Walsham How, burnt a copy of his last novel *Jude the Obscure* because he considered it "obscene" in that it dealt with religious doubts and attacked the institution of marriage.[6] In 1559 the Roman Catholic Church began publishing the *"Index Librorum Prohibitorum"* (List of Prohibited Books) and did not cease its prohibition of the reading of certain books until 1966. The avowed aim of the list was to protect the faith and morals of Catholics by preventing the reading of what were classed as "immoral" books or works containing theological errors. Many atheist writers such as David Hume, Auguste Comte, Ernest Renan and André Gide were included in the *Index*. The various editions also contained the rules of the Church relating to the reading, selling and censorship of books. Books that passed inspection were printed with *"nihil obstat"* (nothing forbids) or "*Imprimatur*" (let it be printed) on the title page. It is no wonder that atheists more often than not erred on the side of caution to conceal their true beliefs.

Many of them deliberately fudged their credentials preferring the appellation "agnostic" coined by Thomas Huxley in 1869, which was more acceptable and not likely to cause offence. It might be argued that Charles Darwin himself adopted this policy. Whilst atheism was the logical outcome of his theory of evolution by natural selection because it removed the need to posit a Prime Mover as the origin of life on earth, Darwin probably settled on "agnosticism" for a mixture of emotional and personal reasons. Michael Shermer suggests that Darwin's celebrated statement that "an Agnostic would be the more correct description on my state of mind" was a deliberate move in that he preferred not to upset his wife, Emma, who held orthodox Christian views and whom he dearly loved and adored.[7] It was only in late 1881 with his approaching death (19 April 1882) that Emma realized the full implications of her husband's scientific studies:

> The talks she (Emma) and Charles had had back at Maer, so long ago, had never really salved her fears. Although Charles had done as much as he could to protect her sensibilities, he had never been able to look her in the eye and say he believed in the gospels, the Christian faith or the existence of an after-life. He remained convinced that death was the end whilst Emma wholeheartedly believed the opposite. The problem was, she was also convinced that if he did not believe, he would never make it to heaven and she would lose him forever.[8]

Throwing-off the disapproval surrounding atheism has been a difficult task. This is nowhere better shown than with Nietzsche himself. It is probably true to say that he was haunted by the thought that he was the "murderer of all murderers" and that his declaration of the "death of God" significantly contributed towards his decline into insanity in his later years. To openly espouse atheism was a lonely undertaking and many did not have the required strength of character to rebut "the claims of the rabbis and priests and imams."[9] To challenge the power of the church and sing God's requiem required extraordinary courage. There were, of course, notable exceptions: theologians like Ludwig Feuerbach, philosophers such as Bertrand Russell and poets like Algernon Swinburne. However, atheism was not widely touted with many, as Wilson correctly notes, "being so terrified of the implications of scientific materialism and Unbelief, they huddle(d) for shelter beneath the arms of Orthodoxy."[10] The classic example is Thomas Hobbes (1588–1679) who proclaimed himself Christian, yet many historians of philosophy assert that he was in fact an atheist, arguing that by the use of irony and other subtle rhetorical devices, Hobbes sought to undermine his readers' religious beliefs. Whatever the truth of the matter, we should agree with Edwin Curley that "when the cost of candor is high, we should not be surprised to find people not practicing it."[11]

Some atheists described themselves as "mystics" whilst others preferred obscurity to the pain of confrontation. History is strewn with the names of those who were persecuted for challenging the Church's teaching and although a few brave souls dared to speak out, many decided anonymity was the best option.[12] Whilst Wilson describes this as a "dishonorable position" it was an understandable one, as in many cases being an atheist meant social ostracism which could lead to financial ruin. Throughout history, pragmatism has taken precedence over intellectual honesty with scientists, theologians and philosophers erring on the side of caution and appearing to espouse Christian orthodoxy whilst secretly embracing ideas that conflict with church dogma. Scholars have found ingenious ways to reconcile personal religious beliefs with their scholarship practiced in academia. They have masked, dissembled, or otherwise avoided these conflicts for a wide variety of reasons, not the least of which was their own personal safety. Intellectual sincerity usually means risk and not all are "honest" enough like Don Cupitt and Robert Funk to publish the results of their scholarship. Indeed, even in the case of Cupitt, he waited until his university position was secure before he wrote a controversial book in which he repudiated the existence of an objective God:

> When *Taking Leave of God* appeared there was a hell of a row and I realized that it had finished my career as an academic and in the church. . . . It was known that I had "come out" in a big way. The Cambridge system meant that I got a University assistant lectureship in 1968 and I got tenure in 1976, by which time I was over forty. Then I was reasonably safe. I couldn't actually be kicked out, so I started the disclosing publications.[13]

In *The Twilight of Atheism*, Alister McGrath argues that atheism is a movement that from the seventeenth century has attempted to eliminate religion as an outmoded superstition. He ascribes quasi-mystical qualities to atheism, as if it were a force being blown through history. But, this is to state the case too forcefully. McGrath is right to point to the communist parties in charge of (the former) Soviet Union and China (until the Cultural Revolution of the late 1970s) who officially politicized atheism and tried to discourage their citizens from practicing religion. He is also correct to note that these regimes committed innumerable atrocities on their own citizens. But, he neglects to mention that those atheists repressed others in the name of *communism*, not atheism. It was *political ideology* that was the driving force of their evil deeds.

He is also accurate in observing that secular ideas that took root in Western societies as a result of "The Enlightenment" encouraged people to question the teachings of the church. In particular, theism (belief in a personal god) was challenged by deism (belief in an impersonal first cause) or skepticism (belief that there was no god). But again, what McGrath fails to take into account is that it was *only* the Christian religion that could be interrogated because its effects had "penetrated intellectual life, social life, political life, daily life."[14] Christianity was all pervasive, so those who gained new insights by way of scientific, philosophical or social analysis, had to meet head-on the Church's teaching. The Church was the custodian of knowledge and had imposed it upon Western societies. New (secular) ideas had to spar with the Church's official decrees that had reached into every facet of life. So, divine revelation was confronted by human endeavour, discovery and scientific enquiry. New virtues of personal freedom, free-thought and equality jousted with the received dogmas of Christianity.

However, McGrath is plainly wrong to argue that as a result of The Age of Reason the Western World gradually slid into godlessness. The situation is far more complex than a simplistic notion of a clash between religion and secularism. In fact, secularism has not eradicated religion. Rather, the opposite has occurred.

It is true that secularism weakened the grip of Christianity (which McGrath as an evangelical Christian obviously deplores) but at the same time it fostered societies that included a *plurality* of religious options. Christianity became *one of many* religious options, not necessarily the only or preferred option of all people. Likewise, Christendom has not been replaced by "non-religious" or "irreligious" communities, but we have seen the emergence of multiculturalism, diverse spiritualities and innumerable lifestyle choices. Secularism, far from limiting people's religious options, has actually increased them and has defended the right of every person to follow *their* own particular religious or spiritual path. Religion has been taken out of the public sphere and privatized—it is *my* choice to be a Christian, Hindu, Baha'i, practice Transcendental Meditation or venerate the Flying Spaghetti Monster! Moreover, post-Christian secular society will *defend* my right to worship in the way that *I* choose. The liberty to worship in the manner I consider best for me flows from the Enlightenment ideals of individual human rights, autonomy and human equality. Atheism is simply an intellectual option: to choose not to believe in any god. Western societies are not, as McGrath alleges, a conflict between "the attractions of a world without God" (atheism) and the "presence of God" (Christianity).[15] Rather, in the Western world there is now a smorgasbord of spiritual options which goes beyond "Christianity versus unbelief." People's spiritual identities traverse religious boundaries and defy easy categorization. Today people often "pick and mix" their religious beliefs: you can be a Jewish Buddhist, a Wiccan Christian, a Muslim who practices reiki or an atheist who sings in a church choir. The list is endless. Whereas in the past Christendom preached theological monism, today secularism encourages spiritual pluralism. Thus atheism implies no political or even spiritual agenda and is not in itself a worldview:

> Zen Buddhists, Taoists, metaphysical naturalists, and Platonic materialists can be described as atheists. Being an atheist does not require a person to subscribe to any one, particular overall worldview. **At the minimum, atheists simply deny the existence of God or gods.** . . . Atheists disagree about economics, politics, art, morality, and science itself. But each atheist has her own particular worldview. While you'll find pockets of atheists who agree with each other on the broad lines of the same worldview, depending on sociological, economic, racial, moral, and political factors, you cannot predict in

advance what an atheist believes about other things simply because she is one.[16]

Intellectual and Emotional Reasons for Atheism

I would contend that, in general, atheism has lacked orga-
nizational structure, being more akin to private dissent by
individuals who have undergone what is often erroneously
dubbed: "a crisis of faith." This has been due to two factors—intellectual and emotional. Intellectually, people become atheists because they reach a point where they reject
the existence of a supernatural, omniscient, omnipotent and
all-loving deity who created and watches over the world.
Belief in God adds nothing to their view of the cosmos and
humanity's place within it. Science can explain the origins
and workings of the cosmos: there is no divine plan and no
divinity that interferes in people's daily lives. There is no
need for a consoling figure from beyond the skies to assuage
fears of our own mortality. This life is all that we have and
we must take responsibility for ourselves, our fellow humans
and our planet. Belief in God becomes redundant: a figment
of our imaginations that can be discarded. Intellectual honesty takes precedence over any comfort that might be gained
from religious adherence. It must not be underestimated the
price that this break with the religious faith of their up-bring-
ing has on many atheists. Whilst admitting that unbelief is a
liberating experience it is also a costly one, as Joseph Levine,
a former orthodox Jew, explains:

> I do think one loses something significant when one
> loses belief in God. I admit that the idea that my life was
> somehow a matter of concern for the ultimate power of
> the universe provided me with a sense of my own signifi-
> cance that I lost when I lost that belief. I also miss the

comforting thought that however dark the world seems, the bright light of redemption may be just around the corner. . . . Once we rid ourselves of the veil imposed by religious ideology, we face formidable challenges. We must face our own death without comfort of an afterlife; we must endow our projects with significance from within; we must find it in ourselves to fight for justice though the odds may be against us; and we must self-consciously build a new sense of community based on recognition of our and others' autonomous choices. Can we succeed? I don't know, that's the whole point. Still, it's all we have, and it's a noble project to try.[17]

Emotionally, people become atheists because they have experienced the ill-effects of religion. The damage perpetrated in the name of religion has been most fiercely laid at the doors of Christianity and Islam.

From novels such as James Joyce's *A Portrait of the Artist as a Young Man* to autobiographies such as Frank McCourt's *Angela's Ashes* to recent films such as Amy Berg's *Deliver us from Evil* to the numerous allegations of wanton "cover-ups" of sexual perpetrators the Roman Catholic Church has been shown to be the opposite of what its purports to proclaim. Instead of a God of compassion and love, it has promoted an evil and capricious deity. This has been highlighted not only by deviant priests within various parishes but has been shown to be systemic in many of its organizations, especially those supposedly concerned with the education and well-being of children.

Similarly, the Protestant Churches have been condemned for a range of offences. These have included permitting corrupt, money-fleecing televangelists to pray on people's insecurities, the condemnation of gay and lesbians, and the killing of abortion doctors. The Protestant emphasis that people are "fallen sinners" and its pessimistic attitude towards sex and sexuality has had a negative impact on the lives of some of its followers. Many of these churches have been guilty of "thought-control," unwilling to allow their constituents to challenge their core beliefs. Those who threaten the received faith are often cowed into submission, or if unresponsive to calls to "mend their ways" ("repent") are ostracized and excluded. Tanya Levin in her exposé of Hillsong, the Assemblies of God mega-church in Australia, recounts how her whole existence was dominated by the belief that the end of the world (the Rapture) would soon eventuate:

> I had grown up knowing that the Rapture could come at any minute. Since there were 2000 years from Adam to Moses, and 2000 years from Moses to Jesus, we knew there would be 2000 years until the Rapture when, after a trumpet call from the skies, all Christians get caught up in a cloud in the twinkling of an eye. . . . I could always hear the clock ticking. I was terrified and stayed terrified. When you are working in the end-times framework, planning is difficult. It feels like you have a terminal illness for Jesus. I had never expected to see the end of school, or to be around long enough to get married and have children. Why were we spending our days studying, working, if Jesus was due any minute? It seemed for most of my life that nothing mattered and everything mattered at the same time.[18]

Islam too has been targeted as a domineering religion that especially oppresses women. It is clear that religion has been used in most Muslim countries not to liberate but to entrench inequality. The most extreme is the Taliban, with its fanatical subjugation of the female sex, yet it belongs on a continuum that includes Saudi Arabia, Kuwait, Pakistan and the relatively moderate states of Egypt and Jordan. Those countries where women are granted the greatest degree of equality, for example in Turkey, it is because Islamic principles have been deferred to secular law. Thus, "the way Islam has been practiced in most Muslim societies for centuries has left millions of Muslim women with battered bodies, minds and souls."[19] The imposition of "purity" laws that forbid women to choose their own sexual partner, subordinate their desires to that of their husband and be submissive to him, have been questioned by a growing band of ex-Muslim women. These criticisms have been reinforced by media reports of Muslim women being raped by male family members because they have supposedly "dishonored them"; or women being harassed and arrested by members of the commission for the promotion of virtue and prevention of vice (Saudi Arabian religious police) because they have been seen alone in a coffee shop with a male work colleague who is not a member of her family! Women have been browbeaten into submission in the name of religion. The furor sparked by the Archbishop of Canterbury's affirmation of the possibility of introducing some elements of (Islamic) Shari'a Law into the United Kingdom, highlights the perceived threat to human freedom that religions pose. Indeed, as one female commentator noted, the plight of many Muslim women in the United Kingdom is *already* desperate:

> As soon as you look at the actual operation of religious law in this country, the picture looks less rosy. Even if the Archbishop didn't have in mind barbaric punishments such as stoning women to death for adultery, there is plenty of evidence that shari'a courts are a means of consolidating patriarchal power in societies where Muslim women have begun to demand the same rights as men. The Department for Work and Pensions recently made an astonishing decision to pay state benefits to Muslim men for each of their wives, as long as the marriages were contracted legally abroad. Bigamy is illegal in Britain and the spectacle of the Government colluding in the practice

of polygyny—not polygamy, for Muslim women cannot have four husbands—is a signal that ministers are losing their moral compass on the subject of women's rights. If a woman is running away from her parents or a violent husband, mosques and shari'a courts are not the obvious place for her to turn to get justice. The Centre for Social Cohesion study contains a startling insight into attitudes in one British mosque, reported by Mohamed Baleela, a team leader at the Domestic Violence Intervention Project in Hammersmith, west London. "Last time I talked about marital rape in a mosque," he said, "I nearly got beaten up. Because we said that the law makes it illegal to rape your wife, someone got up and hit me because he was ignorant of the law."[20]

Tamas Pataki goes even further by suggesting that "bullying has been one of the most conspicuous forms of monotheism."[21] In fact, monotheistic religions cannot operate without some form of violence towards others. A religion needs to assert itself in two ways. First it must compete against another religion in order to survive: it must have a message that is better than another religion. It must shout loudly in the religious market-place and stake its claims to have an exclusive message which in a nutshell is: "my God is greater than yours." Secondly, it must police its own adherents: they must abide by the rules of the religion. There may be sanctions (anything from mild reprimands to expulsion or more violent punishments) against any of its own group members who defy its beliefs/leadership. This results in aggressive, bullying tactics fed by group narcissism and insecurity. There is no room for infidels, heretics or those who flout the rules. Simply put, believe in our God and obey His (always His) commands, or else! Eventually, some of those who have been harmed or abused by religion flee its embrace. Many of them (though not all) discard God along the way as well.

The lesbian feminist Irshad Manji who still retains her belief in Allah eloquently expresses the potential harm inflicted by religious leaders upon their followers:

> Why tolerate violent bigotry? Amin Maalouf, a French-Arab novelist, nailed this point when he wrote that "traditions deserve respect only insofar as they are respectable—that is, exactly insofar as they themselves respect the fundamental rights of men and women." Allow me to invoke a real-life example of what can't be tolerated if we're going to maintain freedom of expression for as many people as possible. In 1999, an uproar surrounded the play "Corpus Christi" by Terrence McNally, in which Jesus was depicted as a gay man. Christians protested the show and picketed its European debut in Edinburgh, a reasonable exercise in free expression. But Omar Bakri Muhammad, a Muslim preacher and a judge on the self-appointed Shari'a Court of the United Kingdom, went further: he signed a fatwa calling for Mr. McNally to be killed, on the grounds that Jesus is considered a prophet by Muslims. (Compassion overflowed in the clause that stated Mr. McNally "could be buried in a Muslim graveyard" if he repented.) Mr. Bakri then had the fatwa distributed throughout London. Since then, Mr. Bakri has promoted violent struggle from various London meeting halls. He has even lionized the July 7 bombers as the "fantastic four."[22]

Thus the failure of religions to deliver on their core message of peace, love and justice has caused some to grasp atheism firmly by the hand.

However, until recently, atheism has remained the provenance of philosophers, academics or literary figures, together with those who have been labeled "free-thinkers."[23] Most of the forty-seven notable atheists selected by Christopher Hitchens in *The Portable Atheist*, which he regards as essential readings for non-believers, fall into one of these categories. Whilst admittedly this is only a selection of those opposed to God and religion throughout history, by and large the number of those espousing atheism is tiny compared to those who have been "believers." Indeed, as Louise Antony points out, atheism is still "a minority position in today's world."[24] Lloyd Geering makes the pertinent point that in Western culture atheism was not really viewed by ordinary folk as an attractive proposition until the end of the twentieth century because people prior to that time had an inviolable understanding of God as creator. Whilst many, including his own parents, might not have attended church they sent their children each week to Sunday School and believed that there was a God who had started everything:

> Perhaps of greatest significance within the changing character of Western culture has been the changing conception of God. At the beginning of the twentieth century nearly everyone in the Western world conceived of God as the creator of everything. God was the eternal reality upon whom everything depended. God was all-powerful and all-knowing. This God was the same for everybody, whether they knew it or not. *For the majority of Western people this seemed to be a self-evident fact, and only a very few dared to call themselves atheists.* God was the solid rock upon which everything stood. But by the end of the century we were beginning to see that even God had a story. Karen Armstrong made a daring and important contribution in 1993 when she attempted to tell that story in her bestseller, *A History of God.* [25]

Thus, the typical atheist was the solitary Nietzschean individualist who from a darkened room denounced Christianity as "the will to nothingness sanctified." It was not until existentialist writers like Sartre and Camus and the 1960s "Death of God" theologians (Thomas Altizer et al.) that atheists began to "come out," although they still tended to be viewed with suspicion. Atheists were contemptuously dismissed as French intellectuals, communists, off-beat radicals or university college chaplains who should be sacked from their positions. That has all changed in the last few years.

The New Atheists?

Today, most atheists declare openly that the God hypothesis is redundant and that people can develop effective ethics and create a common humanity without recourse to religion. Belief in God is not necessary for people to be good. Objective morality is independent of God's existence. Atheists are increasingly organized, confrontational and unafraid to go public with their grievances against religion. The 2007 survey by the Pew Forum on Religion and Public Life indicates that 16 percent of Americans are atheist, agnostic or have no religious preference. They have emerged from their foxholes and are encouraging others to declare their allegiance to what has been dubbed: "the church of the non-believers." There has been a surge in the number of former Christians and Muslims who have written books that describe how they have left the faith of their birth. It is no longer the sole responsibility of Prometheus Publishing to promote atheism. Atheists from across many academic disciplines are joining forces to challenge religious people about their ideas of God, faith and the workings of the cosmos. They are committed to weakening religion's hold on people's minds and hearts. They exhibit the same fervor that is commonly ascribed their opponents, preaching an alternative gospel that we can be content in this world without the need of a divine Being. By appealing to non-believers and joining forces with humanists, skeptics, and secularists, atheists are on the march in the fight against religion. They have challenged people to admit that they are atheists too and join the movement to dispense of the need for God or gods. They have pressurized people to take a stance on one fundamental issue, neatly summarized by Hitchens: "either one attributes one's presence here to the laws of biology and physics, or one attributes it to a divine design."[26] It is an either/or scenario and one must sign up for either side. Science and belief in a creator God are incompatible. Religion is indefensible and its harmful effects are plainly visible. Religions are the "root of all evil" and "licensed insanities" responsible for untold horrors:

> Religion is as much a living spring of violence today as it was at any time in the past. The recent conflicts in Palestine (Jews versus Muslims), the Balkans (Orthodox Serbians versus Catholic Croatians; Orthodox Serbians versus Bosnian and Albanian Muslims), Northern Ireland (Protestants versus Catholics), Kashmir (Muslims versus Hindus), Sudan (Muslims versus Christians and animists), Nigeria (Muslims versus Christians), Ethiopia and Eritrea (Muslims versus Christians), Sri Lanka (Sinhalese Buddhists versus Tamil Hindus), Indonesia (Muslims versus Timorese Christians), Iran and Iraq (Shiite versus Sunni Muslims), and the Caucasus (Orthodox Russians versus Chechen Muslims; Muslim Azerbaijanis versus Catholic and Orthodox Armenians) are merely a few cases in point. In these places religion has been the explicit cause of literally millions of deaths in the last ten years.[27]

Those advocating such a stance have acquired the epithets "militant atheists" or "the new atheists." Their detractors accuse them of being "radical" and "combative," as if atheists should keep their ideas to themselves. Tina Beattie even goes so far as to describe it as "the emergent **cult** of new atheism." She is scathing in her assessment of the new atheists admonishing them as "showing all the hallmarks of some of the twentieth century's most destructive ideologies in its intolerance of difference and its labeling of its enemies with the language of malevolence, vermin and pestilence."[28] Yet, Beattie's vitriolic attack reinforces the new atheists' cause. By her empty rhetoric she perpetuates the view that religious people are irrational and are unable to debate in an orderly fashion. Moreover she commits a grave error in classifying this movement as "new." She inexplicably fails to acknowledge atheism's protracted history. Ian McEwan correctly notes that *there is nothing new* about the new atheists:

> I am a little baffled as to why it is called the "new Atheism." There is a very long tradition of free thinking, and the arguments made against religion tend to be the same but made over and over again. But I think what has happened is that there have been a number of good, articulate books—Hitchens, Dawkins, Dennett, Sam Harris, and so on. What they have discovered to their own great surprise is that in the United States, and right across the South too, there are an enormous number of people who also think this way. I don't think they have suddenly been persuaded by this rash of books—the feelings were there anyway—but they didn't have a voice, they didn't have a focus. When Hitchens took his book across the Bible Belt and debated with Baptist ministers in churches, there were huge audiences, most of whom, it seems, from when they spoke to him afterwards, were somewhat irritated that the place in the United States that they lived in was called the Bible Belt. I think there was something there that people had not taken into account. Quite heartening really, given that America is meant to be a secular republic with a strong tradition of upholding all freedom of thought.[29]

It is thus preferable to drop the appellation "new" and acknowledge the continuity between atheists of the past and now. Perhaps all that needs to be conceded is that in the twenty-first century two "new" events have occurred. First, as McEwan points out, there has been the publication of a few articulate books promoting the atheist cause. Second, the global communication revolution (the internet and personal computers) has meant that people in so many countries now have instant access to what might once have been considered heretical views. The influence of websites that distribute an atheistic viewpoint cannot be underestimated. Despite, for example, Pakistan in 2008 attempting to censor viewing of the promotional video of Dutchman Geert Wilder's film, *Fitna*, hostile to Islam aired on the popular site "YouTube," the atheist message was received. Freedom of speech overrides concerns of blasphemy. Indeed, for unbelievers how can something be blasphemous if you do not believe in God?

The question that this section leads into is: so why has there been this sudden rise in interest in atheism? Why *now*?

Two Reasons for the Rise of Atheism

1. Violent Religions

The philosopher A. C. Grayling identifies two main reasons for the rise of atheism. First, all major religions have become more assertive and demanding in defense of their belief systems. They have protested, often violently, against any criticism of their beliefs and values, most notably by imposing *fatwas* upon and even murdering those they consider blasphemers. Not only individuals but religious writers, artists, cartoonists, film-makers, abortion doctors, as well as gay and lesbian communities have felt the wrath of extremists whose God needs protecting.

Sam Harris notes that the defining moment for the resistance to religious extremism came on 11 September 2001 with the four suicide strikes by Islamic jihadists in the United States that killed more than three thousand people from over eighty countries. That attack spurred him to begin writing *"the very next day"* his best-selling *The End of Faith* in which he decries the irrationality of all belief systems. It is fashionable within Western thought to follow Harris to redefine history in terms of pre- and post-9/11. However, I would suggest that the modern seeds of discontent with religion began earlier on February 14, 1989 when the former Iranian spiritual leader Ayatollah Khomeini condemned the author Salman Rushdie to death for writing *The Satanic Verses*. The "Rushdie Affair" (as it came to be known) also proved to be the catalyst for one of the most forthright attacks on Islam by one of its former believers. Ibn Warraq began his indictment against Islam with a book in the style of the atheist Bertrand Russell entitled *Why I am not a Muslim* precisely because of the treatment of Rushdie by the Muslim world.[30]

Whilst, as I have previously indicated, there had been attempts by Christians to ban the reading of books, the emergence of the modern era had privatized religion and people were now free to read at will. Indeed, the landmark ruling in Britain almost thirty years earlier in 1960 in favor of the publication of D. H. Lawrence's *Lady Chatterley's Lover* meant that religions could not interfere with freedom of thought and writing. They might urge their followers not to read a particular book, but they could not prohibit its publication. That lay with the secular laws passed by a secular government. The publication of *The Satanic Verses* was different in that it angered not Christians, but Muslims, many of whom had been born in a non-secular country. They had no concept of the privatization of religion and the division between mosque and state. By imposing a *fatwa* upon its author the Iranian authorities were directly questioning the Western Enlightenment Project. For them individual freedom must be subject to religious dogma. Religious beliefs were exempt from interrogation. Non-believers must be subject to blasphemy laws. Thus the furor over *The Satanic Verses* was the beginning of the West's clash of civilizations. But, what exactly was the objection from Muslims?

It must be admitted that there were quite a few insensitive and problematic allusions to the Prophet's wives and the names and adventures of some of his principal characters would have incurred offense to strict believers if interpreted as the rewriting of historical facts. However, it should be remembered that this was a work of "fiction" and so the complaint that Rushdie was dishonoring the origins of Islam were unsubstantiated. The main concern was the book's central theme.

The "Satanic Verses" refer to two lines of disputed text that were supposedly spoken by Muhammad as part of the original Qur'an and then subsequently withdrawn on the grounds that the devil had sent them, deceiving Muhammad into thinking they came from God. The story is that when Muhammad and his community came under severe persecution, eighty-three of his followers who had no protection emigrated from Mecca to Abyssinia (modern day Ethiopia), taking refuge in that ancient Christian country. Under increasing boycotts and pressure, Muhammad went through a time of weakness and compromised with the Meccans by acknowledging the existence of three goddesses Lat, Uzza, and Manat alongside belief in Allah. The Arabian goddesses are mentioned in Sura an-Najm (Star) 53:19–22. When the inhabitants of Mecca heard Muhammad confess the importance of the ancient goddesses inside the Ka'aba, they immediately revoked their ban on him. Those who had immigrated to Abyssinia started to return home after hearing Muhammad's confession and his acceptance in Mecca. But when they arrived, they were shocked to hear that Muhammad had retracted his confession and admitted that he had fallen prey to the "whispering of Satan." Thus, today Islam considers Sura an-Najm (Star) 53:19–22 to be related to the time when Muhammad spoke the Satanic Verses. In

Sura Hajj (Pilgrimage) 22:52–53, Muhammad confessed his mistake, alleging that all prophets were tempted by Satan who inspired them with demonic verses, as if they were actually revealed by God. But later on Allah abrogated those Satanic Verses with new revelations and instructed his prophets with new verses. This called into question the purity of the Qur'an by suggesting that at least for a period of time unholy verses were included in its text. For many Muslims it was simply inconceivable that Satan somehow could "whisper" his thoughts into the substance of God's holy Word.

Rushdie spent many years in hiding, protected by British security police. In July 1991, Hitoshi Igarashi, the novel's Japanese translator was stabbed to death and in 1993 his Norwegian publisher William Nygaard was wounded in an attack outside his house. In February 1999 Ayatollah Hassan Sanei promised a US$2.8 million reward for killing the author. The Iranian government has both rescinded (1998) and reaffirmed the *fatwa* (2006), and Rushdie is now living openly in the United States. However, the controversy surrounding *The Satanic Verses* was never fully resolved. Both sides in the debate were left wondering whether they had won or lost. The Islamic world was content that Rushdie had been forced into hiding but still disappointed that the book was published. The Western world thought it had defused Muslim anger whilst still upholding the right of an individual to freedom of expression. However, the resultant calm was an illusion, a time-bomb waiting to explode.

The central issue that most commentators fail to mention is that of "tolerance." This was one of the new values to emerge from the Enlightenment. Tolerance for the Western world was the ability to include all forms of expression. But tolerance was seen by religious people as a form of moral weakness, an unjustifiable compromise with falsehood and the secular world. Instead of condemning violence as a form of protest the West in some Muslims' eyes capitulated.

Violence was perceived to be an effective way to silence secularists who dishonored the name of the Prophet. The secular world sowed the seeds of discontent by not more vociferously supporting Salman Rushdie. When Muslims used exactly the same tactics at a later date in the case of 9/11, Theo van Gogh, Ayaan Hirsi Ali and Danish cartoons lampooning their faith (see Chapter 3) then secularists, especially atheists, began to fight back.

Moreover some Christian groups have joined their Muslim counterparts in targeting the Western world's toleration of diverse lifestyle choices. In particular, it is homosexuals that are the constant targets of both Christian and Islamic fundamentalists. It is estimated that since 1979 the Islamic Republic of Iran has executed four thousand lesbians and gays for "the crime of homosexuality." Similarly, the infamous Westboro Baptist Church in the USA apportions all the ills of American society on its toleration of homosexuals. Indeed, there were Christian leaders who saw the 9/11 attacks and even Hurricane Katrina's destruction of New Orleans as divine punishment on a society that condones homosexuality. Following 9/11 preacher Jerry Falwell argued that it was "pagans, secularists, abortionists, feminists, gays, lesbians and those who are actively trying to make that an alternative lifestyle" who had "helped this happen." Fellow evangelist Pat Robertson concurred with his sentiment. After heavy criticism, Falwell apologized, though he later said that he stood by his statement, stating "If we decide to change all the rules on which this Judeo-Christian nation was built, we cannot expect the Lord to put his shield of protection around us as he has in the past."[31]

In response to the intransigence of religious authorities, atheists have begun to fight back, claiming that the influence of religious bodies threatens the de facto secular arrangement that allows a huge diversity of lifestyles and worldviews.

Religions, they opine, are dangerous to the health of society; in fact, many atheists are now beginning to assert that society would be better off without religion. Why should we trust religious believers when we see their beliefs producing violence, hostility, and irrationality? The emergence of a global, humanistic, secular society is perceived to be under threat from religion and many intellectuals have decided it is too precious to lose. If religions assault the secular world then they must expect a backlash from secularists and a fierce interrogation of their beliefs. *No longer* is "criticizing a person's ideas about God and the afterlife thought to be impolitic."[32]

2. Religions Are Intellectually Bankrupt

Second, atheists view religious people as unreflective, unwilling to question their own belief systems, and resistant to intellectual or academic scrutiny of their creeds, scriptures and dogmas. This lack of objectivity was especially clear in the Rushdie case. The widespread and vitriolic outpouring of anti-Rushdie sentiment was remarkable in that it completely overlooked the important fact that the tale of the "Satanic verses" derived from the work of a Muslim biographer of the Prophet, al-Tabari, in his *Tarikh al Umam wal Maluk*. As a Bangladeshi commentator, Zeeshan Hasan, explains:

> Why have conservative Muslims largely refused to discuss al-Tabari's account of the "Satanic verses?" The simple reason seems to be that it presents a messy picture of the Prophet as fallible, and a Qur'an capable of being temporarily distorted by his human inclinations to win over his tribe. More importantly, the immense body of Islamic Law is based upon the reports (Hadith) of the Prophet's life and teachings. However, if even the Qur'an, which is held to be pure divine revelation, was subject to the fallibility of the Prophet, then the Hadith are even more

so, since they are explicitly his words and not God's.
The Qur'anic verses regarding abrogation can in fact be
seen as a divine guarantee of the revelation; in spite of
the fallibility of the prophet, God ensures the correctness
of the Qur'an by replacing incorrect verses. However,
there is no such guarantee of abrogation for the Hadith.
Conservatives find such questioning of the Hadith and
Islamic Law to be unacceptable.[33]

The implication is that admitting that there is flimsy element
to support one cornerstone of the faith might result in the
whole house tumbling down. All religions are protective of
their doctrines and dogmas and tend to package them as
a unified product. You can't be selective about what you
believe. However it is also true to say that some Islamic
scholars have questioned the validity and historical accuracy
of the satanic story pointing out that its source is unknown
and that just because al-Tabiri included it in his biography of
Mohammed does not necessarily make it historically true.[34]
Moreover, the phrase "satanic verses" was probably coined
at a much later date by the Victorian Scottish Orientalist, Sir
William Muir, who spent much time in India with the Bengal
civil service and wrote books on the life of Mohammed and
the composition of the Qur'an with a Western bias shaped
by European imperialism. In short, it might be argued that
Rushdie has used a highly dubious story to suggest that that
the Qur'an is tainted by satanic influence.

Whatever the authenticity of the "satanic verses," it was
the *reaction* by religious zealots that created the backlash
from atheists. Grayling points out that in societies founded
upon secular values, religious beliefs do not merit special
status, and religious claims must be scrutinized and held up
to literary, historical, and philosophical criticism. Religious
leaders cannot claim immunity from the satire of writers,

cartoonists, and comedians who refuse to privilege their founders, clergy, or sacred texts. Religious people cannot peddle highly speculative and even irrational beliefs without expecting those ideas to be interrogated:

> The absolute certainty, the unreflective credence given to ancient texts that relate to historically remote conditions, the zealotry and bigotry that flow from their certainty, are profoundly dangerous: at their extreme they result in mass murder, but long before then they issue in censorship, coercion to conform, the control of women, the closing of hearts and minds. Thus there is a continuum from the suicide bomber driven by religious zeal to the moral crusader who wishes to stop everyone from seeing or reading what he himself finds offensive. **The fact makes people of a secular disposition no longer prepared to be silent and concessive.**[35]

Religions have become too assertive and too unreflective and must not be surprised to be treated accordingly. Atheists are no longer willing to allow their lives and societies to be hijacked by religious extremists. They are not only fighting back but asking others to declare their support:

> This is the challenge posed by the New Atheists. We are called upon, we lax agnostics, we noncommittal nonbelievers, we vague deists who would be embarrassed to defend antique absurdities like the Virgin Birth or the notion that Mary rose into heaven without dying, or any other blatant myth; we are called out, we fence-sitters, and told to help exorcise this debilitating curse; the curse of faith. The New Atheists will not let us off the hook simply because we are not doctrinaire believers. They condemn not just belief in God but respect for belief in God. Religion is not only wrong; it's evil. Now that the battle has been joined, there's no excuse for shirking.[36]

The Non-believers

It is normal for commentators to list Richard Dawkins, Sam Harris, Daniel Dennett, Christopher Hitchens, Michel Onfray and Anthony Grayling as the commanders of this new army, but they tend to overlook a much wider community of non-believers. In these next chapters I will broaden the scope of atheism to include not only the scientific community but renegade Muslims, disenchanted intellectuals and mainstream readers who have propelled their books to bestselling status. While scientists are traditionally assumed to be the main opponents of religion, it is perhaps religious deserters, disaffected intellectuals and ordinary folk who will have the greatest effect on taming religion. Their inside knowledge of religion and its damaging effects are often more effective in swaying people's opinions than acerbic scientists. It should be remembered that the most effective missionary for Christianity began as a rabid persecutor representing the enemy community. The zealous *Jew*, Saul of Tarsus, became the *Christian* Paul. His "inside" knowledge of Judaism proved invaluable in converting many members of his former faith. Likewise today many new unbelievers were once believers.

This last point has been grossly neglected. Whilst it is generally assumed that in Europe, Australia and New Zealand the number of those who now openly declare that they have "No Religion" is increasing, the United States is touted as an exception. It is commonly assumed that only a very small percentage of Americans admit to not believing in God and that secularists, agnostics and atheists are just a small blip on the landscape. One is told: just wander through a typical American city or town on a Sunday morning and you will find God being worshipped by 90 percent of the population. But is that assertion true? Having spent a few Sundays in the United States my observation was that people were inclined to spend the Sabbath on many tasks other than attending a

holy place. Whilst this may be dismissed as the usual disparity between "believing, but not belonging" (i.e., belief in God
is strong, but attending Church might be infrequent) I would
contend that there is far more unbelief than is often acknowledged, as Ronald Aronson explains:

> How many unbelievers are there? The question is difficult
> to assess accurately because of the challenges of con-
> structing survey questions that do not tap into the pre-
> vailing biases about religion. According to the American
> Religious Identification Survey, which interviewed more
> than 50,000 people, more than 29 million adults—one in
> seven Americans—declare themselves to be without reli-
> gion. The more recent Baylor Religion Survey ("American
> Piety in the 21st Century") of more than 1,700 people,
> which bills itself as "the most extensive and sensitive
> study of religion ever conducted," calls for adjusting
> this number downward to exclude those who believe in
> a God but do not belong to a religion. Fair enough. But
> Baylor's own Gallup survey is a bit shaky for at least
> two reasons. It counts anyone who believes in a "higher
> power" but not God as believing in God—casting a vast
> net over adherents of everything from spirit to history to
> love. Yet the study allows unbelievers only one option:
> to not believe in "anything beyond the physical world,"
> leaving no space for those who regard themselves as ag-
> nostics or skeptics, secularists or humanists. Contrast this
> with a more recent and more nuanced Financial Times/
> Harris poll of Europeans and Americans that allowed
> respondents to declare agnosticism as well as atheism: 18
> percent of the more than 2,000 American respondents
> chose one or the other, while 73 percent affirmed belief
> in God or a supreme being. A more general issue affects
> American surveys on religious beliefs, namely, the "social
> desirability effect," in which respondents are reluctant

to give an unpopular answer in a society in which being religious is the norm. What happens when questions are framed to overcome this distortion? The FT/H poll tried to counteract it by allowing space not only for the customary "Not sure" but also for "Would prefer not to say"—and 6 percent of Americans chose this as their answer to the question of whether they believed in God or a supreme being. Add to this those who declared themselves as atheists or agnostics and, lo and behold, the possible sum of unbelievers is nearly one in four Americans.[37]

It is obvious that atheist writers have struck a chord with many Americans and they have avidly devoured their books. There may also be a significant percentage of intellectuals within American society who have been waiting for someone to articulate their abhorrence of religious fundamentalism and the conservative Christian takeover of the political agenda. When Daniel Dennett promises to "break the spell" of religious belief revealing that it is a human creation and Sam Harris preaches "the end of (irrational) faith" atheists begin to come out of the closet. When Richard Dawkins marshals leading scientists at a national conference that discusses "Beyond Belief, science, religion, reason and survival," the scene is set to decry belief in God as a "delusion." Likewise in France when Michel Onfray urges non-believers to fight against "theological hocus-pocus" and to reassert the principles of the Enlightenment he has a ready audience at his experimental educational college in Caen (Université de Caen).

Religion is under attack from a wide range of opponents who are marshalling their forces openly and effectively. Let us now examine the challenge from the scientists . . .

Notes

1. http://www.youtube.com/watch?v=7Zv9AgwKAE0: "Pat Robertson gives relationship advice about atheist fiancé."

2. Walter Sinnott-Armstrong, "Overcoming Christianity," in Antony, *Philosophers without Gods*, 78.

3. Cupitt, *The Sea of Faith*, 224.

4. Daniel Dennett, "The Bright Stuff," *New York Times*, 12 July 2003.

5. Antony, "For the Love of Reason" in Antony, *Philosophers without Gods*, 57.

6. Wilson, *God's Funeral*, 4.

7. Shermer, *Why Darwin Matters*, 118–119.

8. White and Gribbin, *Darwin*, 277.

9. Hitchens, *The Portable Atheist*, xxii.

10. Wilson, *God's Funeral*, 289.

11. Curley, "On becoming a heretic" in Antony, *Philosophers without Gods*, 85.

12. Leaves, *The God Problem*, 9–10.

13. Leaves, *Odyssey on the Sea of Faith*, 27.

14. Garber, Religio Philosophi' in Antony, *Philosophers without Gods*, 33.

15. McGrath, *The Twilight of Atheism*, 278–79.

16. Loftus, *Why I Became an Atheist*, 64, n.37 (my bold).

17. Levine, "From Yeshiva Bochur to Secular Humanist," in Antony, *Philosophers without Gods*, 30–31.

18. Levin, *People in Glass Houses*, 92–93.

19. Riffat Hassan quoted by Beyer, "The Women of Islam," *Time*, 25 November 2001.

20. Joan Smith, "British women are already suffering from Islamic Law," *The Independent*, 10 February 2008.

21. Pataki, *Against Religion*, 84.

22. Irshad Manji, "Why tolerate the hate?" *New York Times*, 9 August 2005.

23. For an excellent introduction to freethinkers see, Jacoby, *Freethinkers*.

24. Antony, *Philosophers without Gods*, ix.

25. Geering, *Wrestling with God*, 8 (my italics).

26. Hitchens, *A Portable Atheist*, xxi.

27. Sam Harris, "An Atheist Manifesto," http://www.truthdig.com/dig/item/200512_an_atheist_manifesto. *Licensed Insanities* is a title of a book by John Bowker.

28. Beattie, *The New Atheists*, 14.

29. Interview with Ian McEwan, in *The New Republic*, 11 January

2008. http://tnr.com/politics/story.html?id=2cee28d1-869d-447a-8e83-4e046f5ad6df.

30. Warraq, *Why I am not a Muslim,* chap 1.

31. For a good discussion on how Christians have used the Bible to justify hatred of homosexuals see Spong, *The Sins of Scripture,* 111–142.

32. Harris, *The End of Faith,* 13.

33. *New Age* (Bangladesh), 2 November 2003. http://www.liberal-islam.net/satan.html.

34. M. S. M. Saifullah et al., "Those are the high flying claims" http://www.islamic-awareness.org/Polemics/sverses.html.

35. A. C. Grayling, "Believers are away with the fairies." http://www.telegraph.co.uk.

36. Gary Wolf, "The Church of the Non-Believers." http://www.wired.com/wired/archive/14.11/atheism.html.

37. Ronald Aronson, "The New Atheists," *The Nation,* June 2007.

Chapter 2

Scientists Against Religion (1)

The Gradual Evolution of Disbelief

If there really is a Supreme Being who is concerned about how his name is worshipped on earth, these days He may be wishing he had put a caveat in His scriptures: Please don't irritate the scientists.[1]

From the medieval Galileo Galilei to the Victorian Charles Darwin, to the twentieth-century Albert Einstein and today's Richard Dawkins, scientists have challenged religious assumptions about how the world was created and whether a supernatural God can suspend its internal "laws" to intervene in the lives of His creatures. The scientific method of inquiry—empirical observation and experimental prediction—has pitted itself against mystical and metaphysical speculation. Indeed, as Paul Kurtz bluntly puts it: "scientific progress can only occur when the theological and philosophical authorities (have been) discarded."[2] It is not my aim in this chapter to provide a detailed analysis of all the conflicts that have occurred throughout history between scientists and theologians. That particular story has been covered extensively elsewhere by more competent historians of science.[3] Rather, I will discuss a few of the disputes that have triggered the alleged dissonance between religion and science; and examine how they have informed the *current* attacks upon religion from scientists. It is my aim in this chapter to show that the attack on religion from science is a most serious one. For those who wish to promote an intelligible religion in the twenty-first century they must demonstrate that it is consistent with what is known about the universe and our place within it. Taner Edis neatly sets out the challenge laid down by scientists:

> Among believers of all stripes, it is commonplace that science is unable to answer ultimate questions about human origins, meanings and destiny. This is at best an overly narrow view of science. In fact . . . we can say quite a few things without the benefit of religion. We come from accidents, not design. Our lives have no cosmic meaning. And our destiny is dust, not immortality. Many of us find such answers profoundly unappealing. Nevertheless, I believe that they are correct.[4]

It is that claim by some scientists that they have a better and more cogent understanding of the cosmos than anyone else that now characterizes the debate. Theologians have been thrown a challenge: respond to the specter of a godless universe by describing how belief in a divine being might "fit" the prevailing scientific worldview. How can religion speak intelligibly about a "creator and sustainer of the cosmos" when the scientific establishment has banished the need for such a god? Are science and religion incompatible? If so, does that make religion redundant and must we agree that it "spoke its last intelligible or noble or inspiring words a long time ago"?[5]

The Accommodation of Science and Religion

Taner Edis makes the salient point that there have *always* been nonbelievers, but they have been rare. In Greek societies atheism was almost non-existent with most people worshipping the local gods. Scientific studies could not be separated from religion with the "real" world lying beyond this one. This cosmology was derived from the writings of Plato (c. 428–348 BCE), Aristotle (c. 384–322 BCE) and Ptolemy (c. 83–161 CE). The soul's home was in heaven and religions revealed how you might get to the next world of the immortals. Edis argues that Greek science had a distinctly "astrological flavor" that was adopted by the monotheistic religions. Priests were considered the best people to explain how you fitted into the Aristotelian universe and how you might ascend through the various planetary spheres to arrive at the motionless empyrean heaven, inhabited by God and the elect.[6] Thus there was little conflict between science and religion:

> The science of antiquity was not substantially associated with religious doubt. Even with hindsight, finding echoes of a conflict between science and religion is difficult. The precursors of natural science were usually little more than narrow areas of practical knowledge, with only a modest role in overall intellectual life. Where science was more ambitious, it was also spiritualized and absorbed into a religious perception of the world.[7]

Before the seventeenth century, religion was usually accommodated when a major skirmish arose as a result of scientific enquiry. For example, investigations by Johannes Kepler (1571–1630) into the heliocentric cosmos were motivated by his desire to discern the mathematical ordering of the Universe. Upon discovering elliptical orbits, he proposed that planets were attempting to reach the divine ideal. He employed science not to disprove God's existence but to reveal the geometrical pattern by which God had rendered the cosmos beautiful. Likewise Sir Isaac Newton (1643–1727) studied the Scriptures as assiduously as he did the motions of celestial bodies, and viewed science as a means of reinforcing belief in a Christian God. Despite his many private doubts *publicly* he "committed his science to the service of orthodoxy, and Newtonian natural philosophy quickly became the basis for a powerful new synthesis of science and Christianity."[8]

Originally that unity of science (natural theology) and revelation (the Bible) had been due to Thomas Aquinas (c. 1225–1274) rediscovering the works of Aristotle, which in a strange twist of history Islamic scholars had preserved when they were lost to the West. The Thomist-Aristotelian system of thought reinforced the notion that there was a "book of Nature" (discovered by observation and experiment of the world) and a "book of Religion" (the scriptures). Both "books" had been written by God and were complimentary accounts of God's wondrous handiwork.

The Beginnings of the Separation of Science and Religion

However that accord was to change as science began to loosen its grip from religion in the sixteenth century. Ironically, most of these scientists were devoutly religious. Many commentators herald the burning at the stake of Giordano Bruno (1548–1600) and forced recantation of Galileo (1564–1642), because following the insights of Copernicus they advocated a heliocentric universe (the sun as opposed to the earth being at the center), as the beginning of enlightened thought and the weakening of the authority of the Church. Bruno and

Galileo are portrayed as "free spirits" who were snuffed out by an obscurantist Church. Indeed, one commentator goes so far as to describe Bruno as a "martyr to human hysteria expressed ecclesiastically."[9]

Margaret Wertheim presents a useful corrective to that analysis in her book *Pythagoras' Trousers*. She points out that Bruno was far more interested in magical hermeticism and wanted to replace Christianity with the ancient Egyptian religion of the magician, Hermes Trismegistus. Bruno favored heliocentricism, not for its "scientific" worth but, "because he saw Copernicus' cosmological diagram as a magic symbol of the world."[10] He hoped to usher in a new age of "magical" religion. It was this that brought him into conflict with, not only the Church, but other scientists. Likewise, Wertheim considers that Galileo's downfall was not due so much to his scientific discoveries but more the way that he had bullied and belittled his opponents. She points to the context of "patronage dynamics" where in providing amusement for his patron, Cosimo di Medici, Galileo had alienated the leading Jesuit scientists of the day. Combined with a crude attack on Pope Urban VIII (calling him "Simplicio") in *Dialogue on the Two Chief World Systems,* Galileo was not the most favored scientist by the Church. The fact that he got off relatively lightly with house arrest and wrote his most influential book during his final years reveals a more conciliatory Church (and Pope) than is often credited. Wertheim downplays the far reaching impact of Galileo's views insisting that the Church was being reasonable in discrediting Galileo because he, like Copernicus, had no proof: heliocentricism was merely a hypothesis. And why should theologians listen to scientists, who had no right to question the authority of sacred texts?

Whilst Wertheim's insights into the Bruno and Galileo "affairs" brings out the many cultural factors that were operating at that time, the fact remains that these clashes began to drive a wedge between science and religion. Although the main proponents might not have been conscious of the ramifications of their discoveries, the foundations of future clashes between scientists and theologians had been laid:

> Very great issues were and still are at stake, although it is the nature of such cases that the antagonists at the time are never fully aware of them. For example, it is clear in retrospect that the revolution in cosmology whose success Galileo ensured was to have enormous social implications, because from now on great institutions like kingship, religion and the moral order could no long claim the sort of cosmic backing that they always had in previous societies. In the long run people would begin to perceive authority and order as coming up from below rather than down from above, from within the human community rather than from a higher world above; and it is a significant fact that the first successful democratic revolution in modern history was actually getting under way in England during the last years of Galileo's life. But at the time nobody either could or did formulate this thought clearly. It was too new, and people were not to become conscious of it for some generations yet.[11]

Charles Darwin

That consciousness of the revolutionary nature of the discoveries in science came to a head in the nineteenth century with the findings of a British naturalist, Charles Darwin. In *On the Origin of Species* he proposed and provided evidence for the scientific theory that at all species evolved over time. Darwin at first suggested that "animals have descended from at most four or five progenitors" but then became more confident in declaring that "all organic beings have descended from one primordial form," a common ancestor through the process of natural selection.[12] Darwin's life and theory of evolution have been extensively covered in countless books, but it is worthwhile here just reminding ourselves of the salient points of his premise. This is set out neatly by John Maynard Smith:

1. There exists a population of entities (units of evolution) with three properties
   - Multiplication (one can give rise to two)
   - Variation (not all entities are alike)
   - Heredity (like usually begets like during multiplication)
2. Differences between entities will influence the likelihood of surviving and reproducing. That is, the differences will influence their "fitness."
3. The population will change over time (evolve) in the presence of selective forces.
4. The entities will come to possess traits that increase their fitness.[13]

Darwin's "descent with modification through natural selection" challenged the teachings of the Church and its literal interpretation of the Bible. Simply put, the process of natural selection called into question the need for a Creator. Human beings were not created in the image of God (Genesis 1:27) but like all organic beings had "descended from one primordial form." Humankind was just one animal species among many. Moreover, the Biblical account of creation was seriously compromised together with the then fashionable "argument from design" proposed by Archdeacon William Paley (1743–1805) that God's handiwork (design) could be seen in nature. As Darwin famously commented in his autobiography:

> The old argument of design in nature, as given by Paley,
> which formerly to me seemed so conclusive, fails, now

that the law of natural selection has been discovered. We can no longer argue that, for instance, the beautiful hinge of a bivalve shell must have been made by an intelligent being, like the hinge of a door by a man.[14]

There is fierce debate as to whether Darwin was an atheist, agnostic, Christian believer, theist or mixture of all four! It is still held by some that Darwin remained an orthodox Christian believer. There are even fanciful stories that Darwin underwent a death-bed conversion and renounced evolution. The best known is that attributed to Lady Hope, a Victorian evangelist who claimed she had visited a bedridden Darwin at Down House in the autumn of 1881. She alleged that when she arrived he was reading the Book of Hebrews, that he became distressed when she mentioned the Genesis account of creation, and that he asked her to come the next day to speak about Jesus to a gathering of servants, tenants and neighbors in the garden summer house. This story first appeared in print in an American Baptist journal and was reprinted in many books, magazines and Christian tracts. However, Darwin's family dismissed these stories as fanciful fabrications. Francis Darwin wrote to Thomas Huxley on February 8, 1887, that a report that Charles had disowned his theory of evolution on his deathbed was "false and without any kind of foundation." Lady Hope's story has been shown to be uncorroborated by James Moore in his book *The Darwin Legend*.

The claim that Darwin remained a Christian believer rests on the closing words of *On the Origin of Species*:

There is grandeur in this view of life, with its several powers, having been originally breathed [by the Creator] into a few forms or into one; whilst this planet has gone cycling on according to the fixed law of gravity, from so simple a beginning endless forms most beautiful and most wonderful have been, and are being evolved.

The inclusion of the words: "by the Creator" in the second (1860) edition of the book (they did not appear in the first edition of 1859) are often cited as evidence that Darwin did not abandon the idea of God as a First Cause or Prime Mover; and that his theological outlook was close to deism. God provided the initial "ingredients" for the Universe to come into existence and then had let it run its course through the process of evolution by natural selection. There is almost an echo of the second account of creation in the book of Genesis 2:7 of God "breathing" life into humankind. Whether this was intentional by Darwin is unknown but the connection to the Old Testament would have been easily made by Victorians who were steeped in the Scriptures.

The case for agnosticism has been made by Alister McGrath who suggests that Darwin believed that "certain things simply cannot be known" and that his doubts concerning the Christian God were due to the failure and inadequacies of nineteenth-century theology and its inept theologians. In particular, he cites the well-documented idea that Darwin rejected the "damnable doctrine" promulgated by countless Victorian preachers that hell was "eternal punishment for unbelievers." Moreover in his private autobiography Darwin is critical of Christianity because if one believes in such a notion this would mean that his father, brother and many of his best friends would be consigned to eternal suffering. Similarly, the death of one of his daughters Anne at the tender age of ten destroyed his belief in divine providence: God's special intervention in the lives of humans. God had not intervened to save her and thus Christianity and its God are blatantly false. McGrath suggests that Darwin rejects Christianity on "moral, not scientific grounds." The Christian God was popularly presented as a tyrannical and unprincipled deity and Darwin like many other sophisticated thinkers of his day, rejected that crude amoral god. The implication is that if only Darwin had been conversant with better theology his faith in the Christian God would probably have survived.[15] It is an ingenious suggestion but lacks credibility.

Whilst there may be some truth that Darwin had moral qualms about some of Christianity's doctrines, the main thrust of his rejection of Christianity was because of his scientific discoveries. Indeed, he abandoned churchgoing in 1849 when he was deeply engrossed in working through the implications of his theory of natural selection; and it was a year prior to the death of his daughter. Moreover, when Anne died "he could not draw any solace from an afterlife or salvation."[16] He was also very conversant with more liberal theology having read popular Unitarian writings by James Martineau, John James Taylor and Francis Newman that were in opposition to adherence to the dogmas outlined in the 39 Articles of the Church of England.

It would seem that he appropriated the nomenclature "agnostic" ("an Agnostic would be the more correct description of my state of mind") for very *pragmatic* reasons. Darwin's agnosticism was more nuanced than McGrath proposes. As I have shown in chapter 1, Darwin's agnosticism was probably a convenient label to shield him from too much hostility. Adrian Desmond and James Moore convincingly reveal in their detailed biography of Darwin that he was a "tormented evolutionist" who although a freethinker was fearful of being seen as an anarchist and becoming socially ostracized.[17] He was genuinely distressed by the upheaval that would be caused by the publication of his research, to his family and especially Emma, his wife. Realizing the reaction he was likely to receive he held back for years from airing and then publishing his theories on the principle of natural selection. In the end he was stampeded into action by news that Alfred Russel Wallace (1823–1913) had reached the same conclusions from completely different observations and was about to publish his findings. Both Wallace's and Darwin's papers were read to the Linnean Society of London on 1 July 1858.

Darwin's fears were proved to be justified. He was pilloried by the scientific and religious establishment of the time. One famous caricature depicted him with the body of a monkey, so angered were people by the suggestion that humans and apes might have a common ancestor rather than having been the special creation of God. He was also a very emotional man and tears came easily. He was a "family" man who despite his travels was more comfortable being at home with his beloved wife and ten children, even setting aside scientific research to accompany one of the girls to a seaside retreat to recuperate from sickness. It is well known that he suffered from a debilitating illness (gastro-intestinal in nature) almost his entire adult life which restricted him from public debates. Thus his later addition of "by the Creator" in *On the Origin of Species* were probably a ruse because he was genuinely fearful of the reaction of Victorian society and the effect it might have upon his family and especially his wife who was a devout Christian.[18] Like many, before and after him, he was cautious and determined to lessen the impact his writings would have upon his family.

It is extremely difficult to know the complete truth as to what *exactly* was Darwin's own theological standpoint. A detailed analysis of all his writings reveals varied and often contradictory ideas about whether there was a God or not. Sometimes he asserted the concept of God as a primary cause and even spoke of natural laws as "the secondary means" by which God created. At other times he was less certain falling back into agnosticism and even admitted that "disbelief crept over me at a very slow rate but was at last complete" and he wondered how "anyone ought to wish Christianity to be true."[19] Perhaps, all that can be said with certainty is that Darwin's writings drove a wedge between science and religion. Darwin had overthrown the Biblical view that there were fixed species and proposed natural causes for the evolution of life. There was no need for the Biblical account of creation and religion's influence was relegated to the moral sphere. In evolution by natural selection, Darwin had given a rival account of the origins and development of the species to that proposed by religion. A question remained unanswered: "Was religion redundant?"

It is interesting to note that up to the end of the nineteenth century 70 percent of the Fellows of the most prestigious scientific establishment in Britain—the Royal Society—were members of the established churches. Likewise, many clergy were what we might label "scientific naturalists" who had an interest in the natural sciences and actively encouraged scientific exploration of the natural world. Many of them were, of course, sons of the landed gentry and so were of the educated elite with both the inclination and the finances to dabble in a pastime studying biology or astronomy. Was the subsequent drop-off in clergy interest in the scientific endeavor due to Darwin's insights and the seeming incompatibility of science and religion? Or was it due to the beginning of the major societal changes that overtook Britain from the mid to latter parts the nineteenth century—industrialization and the slow but inevitable disintegration of social classes? Likewise, there was the growth of specialization with the professionalization of scientists (science became a subject taught at Universities from 1850 onwards) and eventually of the clergy with ministers not necessarily coming from the same privileged establishment classes. The reasons behind the gradual severance of science and religion are probably a combination of all these factors. What can be said with confidence is that by the end of World War I in 1918 Britain had changed so significantly that science and religion had come to be viewed as separate enterprises. Thus it is true to say that *after* the publication of *On the Origin of Species* atheism gained academic credibility. As Dawkins neatly explains: "although atheism might have been logically tenable before Darwin, Darwin made it possible to be an intellectually fulfilled atheist."[20]

Non-Overlapping Magisteria

The gradual rise of science and its classification into various methodologies—biology, physics, chemistry etc.—posed a grave threat to religion. Every part of the Universe including human origins was investigated, dissected and classified according to new categories—from cellular structure to genetic make-up. New ways of understanding the body, the mind and the physical cosmos competed with religion's ancient holy books. It soon became a "conflict about which institutions would have authority in defining reality."[21] Religion retreated from defining "what is" to "how we ought to live" and was regarded as more concerned with ethics than defining reality. Religion was not competent to pass comment on the inner workings of the cosmos and should confine itself to the moral and spiritual realms.

Moreover the newer disciplines of the social sciences (sociology and psychology) utilizing the insights of Emile Durkheim, Sigmund Freud and Carl Jung viewed religions as natural phenomena that could be analyzed as having human origins and were culturally conditioned. Religions could be explained as "social systems" that "are transmitted culturally, through language and symbolism."[22] These systems could be described and their teachings investigated as to how they benefit humanity. Indeed, Daniel Dennett fears

> That if we *don't* subject religion to such scrutiny now,
> and work out together whatever revisions and reforms
> are called for, we will pass on a legacy of ever more toxic
> forms of religion to our descendants.[23]

In order to keep science and religion separate then the theory of "non-overlapping magisteria" (NOMA) was proposed by the late Stephen Jay Gould in his book *Rocks of Ages*. For Gould there can be no synthesis of religion and science but both operate from a different domain of authority (magisterium)—science the empirical realm and religion "the realm of human purposes, meaning and values."[24] Gould, an agnostic Jew, was keen to limit the influence of creationism and to resist its repackaging as "creation **science**." To label it "science" was to accord it a status that it did not deserve. Creationism could not masquerade as science. Its proponents could only propose a *religious* account of the world's origins (i.e., that there was a God somehow involved) and not a scientific explanation. Thus, let scientists take care of explaining how the world was created and let the followers of religion explain how we might live in the world.

> I believe, with all my heart, in a respectful, even loving concordat between our magisteria—the NOMA solution. NOMA represents a principled position on moral and intellectual grounds, not a mere diplomatic stance. NOMA also cuts both ways. If religion can no longer dictate the nature of factual conclusions properly under the magisterium of science, then scientists cannot claim higher insight into moral truth from any superior knowledge of the world's empirical constitution. This mutual humility has important practical consequences in a world of such diverse passions.[25]

Whilst there might be meaningful dialogue ultimately there is separation of the magisteria and people "must live the fullness of a complete life in many mansions."[26] I shall analyze this claim later in this book. Gould's specific aim was to decrease hostility between science and religion by the central principle of "respectful non-interference." This is neatly expressed by Michael Rees:

> The preeminent mystery is why anything exists at all.
> What breathes life into the equations of physics, and ac-
> tualized them in a real cosmos? Such questions lie beyond
> science, however, they are the province of philosophers
> and theologians.[27]

However, today most of his scientific colleagues have not
heeded Gould's call for restraint and mutual respect. In 2006
there began a yearly conference when scientists called into
question the need for any religion and the quest for a time
when we could go "Beyond Belief." At the first gathering at
the Salk Institute for Biological Studies in La Jolla California
thirty of the world's leading scientists gathered for a sympo-
sium entitled: "Beyond Belief: science, religion, reason and
survival." Its participants addressed three questions:

1. Should science do away with religion?
2. What would science put in religion's place?
3. Can we be good without God?

Despite some conciliatory remarks about the value of
religion expressed by scientists such as Michael Shermer,
Lawrence Krauss and Steven Weinberg, the overwhelming
consensus was that in answer to questions 1 and 3 science
should contribute to the overthrow of religion and morality
was not dependent on belief in a God. For many participants
science could either replace religion or lead to its downfall
(question 2). This was expressed well by Neil deGrasse
Tyson, director of the Haydn Planetarium in New York:

> Referring to a recent poll of US National Academy of
> Science Members which showed 85 per cent do not
> believe in a personal God, he suggested that the re-
> maining 15 per cent were a problem that needs to be
> addressed. "How come the number isn't zero?" he
> asked. . . . DeGrasse Tyson clearly found it hard to swal-
> low the idea that a scientist could be satisfied by revela-
> tion rather than investigation.[28]

Likewise, Carolyn Porco, the head of the imaging team for the Cassini space probe to Saturn argued that the grandeur of the cosmos was much more satisfying than anything that religion could offer. Images taken of earth from beyond Saturn by Cassini were far more awe-inspiring than ancient myths offered by religion. Moreover, even a "comforting" religious doctrine like life after death can be more accurately explained by the scientist:

> To the promise of immortality, she counters with the proposition that all the atoms of our bodies will be blown into space in the disintegration of the solar system, to live on forever as mass or energy. That's what we should be teaching our children, not fairy tales about angels or seeing grandma in heaven. "If anyone has something to replace God," she says, "I think scientists do."[29]

It is this more aggressive attack on religion and the assertion that science can provide answers to the mysteries of life which are far more cogent than those proffered by religions that has hit the headlines. The former accommodationism that gradually over the centuries turned into separation and then eventually to the peaceful co-existence of "power sharing" (science-facts: religion-ethics) is now contested by a scientific monism that asserts that there are not two distinct areas of discourse, but *only* one. Instead, for Sam Harris, science can tell us how to live. Morality can be derived from science.[30]

In the next chapter I will examine the claims of those for whom religion is not only an outmoded superstition but also a dangerous phenomenon that must be *replaced* by the scientific enterprise.

Notes

1. Christopher Dreher, "When the ain'ts go marching in," *The Globe and Mail*, 10 March 2007.

2. Kurtz, *Science and Religion*, 11.

3. The "classic" book is Ian Barbour's 1989–91 Gifford lectures reprinted in 1997 as *Religion and Science*. There is also an excellent and very extensive annotated bibliography in Edis, *Science and Nonbelief*, 245–73.

4. Edis, *The Ghost in the Universe*, 16.

5. Hitchens, *God is not Great*, 7.

6. Edis, *Science and Nonbelief*, chap. 1. See also Cupitt, *The Sea of Faith*, 41–44.

7. Edis, *Science and Nonbelief*, 8–9.

8. Wertheim, *Pythagoras' Trousers*, 126

9. Spong, *A New Christianity*, 222.

10. Wertheim, *Pythagoras' Trousers*, 90.

11. Cupitt, *The Sea of Faith*, 46.

12. See White and Gribbin, *Darwin*, 217–18.

13. As quoted in Peters and Bennett, *Bridging Science and Religion*, 70.

14. Darwin, *The Autobiography of Charles Darwin with original omissions restored*, 87.

15. McGrath, *Twilight of Atheism*, 104–5.

16. Browne, *Charles Darwin Voyaging*, 502.

17. Desmond and Moore, *Darwin*. In a later book, *Darwin's Sacred Cause,* Desmond and Moore argue that Darwin was not a dispassionate scientist, but a passionate humanitarian who was driven by the great moral crusade of his day: opposition to slavery. Indeed, by advocating his belief in the common descent of all humans he was opposing the prevailing supposition of the slave traders that different races of humans were different species. If it could be shown that everyone had a common ancestor then slavery must be immoral.

18. Emma's religious convictions straddled the Unitarianism of her birth (the Wedgwood family were Unitarians) and Anglicanism that she embraced when she married Charles. However, it is reported that she still favored Unitarianism even refusing to turn to the altar at Divine Service at Downe Church at the recitation of the Creed. For a fascinating account of the relationship between Emma and Charles and how they managed to live together for 43 years whilst holding conflicting views about science and religion see Heligman, *Charles and Emma.*

19. Howard, *Darwin*, 9.

20. Dawkins, *The Blind Watchmaker*, 6.

21. Edis, *Science and Nonbelief*, 14.

22. Dennett, *Breaking the Spell*, 9, 24.

23. Dennett, *Breaking the Spell*, 39.

24. Gould, *Rocks of Ages*, 4.

25. Stephen J. Gould, "Nonoverlapping magisteria," *Natural History* 106 (March 1997), 19.

26. Gould, *Rocks of Ages*, 4.

27. As quoted in John Cornwall, *Darwin's Angel*, 153. There is no reference in the book to the origin of the quotation.

28. As quoted by Michael Brooks, "Beyond Belief," *The New Scientist*, 18 November 2006, 10.

29. Jerry Adler, "Atheists discuss the benefits of faith," *Newsweek*, 12 November 2006.

30. Sam Harris, *The Moral Landscape*.

Chapter 3

Scientists Against
Religion (2)

Militant Atheism

"We've got to come out," urged chemist Harry Kroto of
Florida State University, Tallahassee. Dawkins also used
the same phrase, and compared the secular scientists'
position to that of gay men in the 1960s. If everyone was
willing to stand up and be counted, they could change
things. . . . Kroto certainly declared himself ready to fight
the good fight. . . . His answer is to launch a coordinated
global effort at education, media outreach and campaign-
ing on behalf of science. Such an effort worked against
apartheid and the internet now provided a platform that
could take science education programs into every home
without being subject to the ideological and commercial
whims of network broadcasters. He has schools run by
religious groups firmly in his sights too. "We must try to
work against faith schooling" he said.[1]

In the last few years atheist scientists have become media
stars, appearing on television and touring the world in an

endless whirl of conferences and debates. Two of the biggest celebrities span the Atlantic Ocean—one a neurobiologist, the other a zoologist. Sam Harris and Richard Dawkins have become household names, with their books at the top of worldwide best-sellers lists. Their writings have elicited both hostility and rapturous applause. They have become representatives of what has been labeled: "new atheism" or "militant atheism." Yet, as I mentioned in the introduction to this book, this is rather a misleading nomenclature. In the case of Dawkins it is a belated claim, for he has been openly advocating an atheistic worldview since the publication of *The Selfish Gene* in 1976. The aim of this chapter is to catalogue the scientific arguments behind these attacks on religion, and to use the writings of Dawkins as a template for the atheistic scientific worldview. Dawkins is but the tip of the iceberg comprised of a large group of atheist scientists who are becoming increasingly well-organized and vocal in their opposition to religion, as the opening quotation above, taken from the first in a series of annual *Beyond Belief* conferences, reveals.

Of course, it must also be stated that (a) not all scientists are atheists and (b) not all those who are atheists demonstrate open hostility towards religion. The former group includes thinkers like Simon Conway Morris, John Polkinghorne and Francis Collins, authors who have written books that attempt to accommodate their religious beliefs with the insights of science.[2] My present purpose, however, is not to analyze these attempts at synthesis, but rather to focus on those who are antagonistic to religion, and to explicate the reasons for their hostility. The recent literature from religious writers against "militant atheism" is sadly lacking in any real understanding of *why* the attack on religion has been so fierce. I will address these reasons in this chapter.

Moreover, as much of the most recent literature about him fails to mention, Dawkins is but one participant in an acrimonious debate that has taken place *within* the scientific community, a controversy that has been described as "the Darwin Wars" or "the battle for science."[3] Most of those who make up this latter group of atheist scientists are more sympathetic towards religious belief and are critical of the strident approach taken by Dawkins and those of his persuasion. I will make a slight detour in order to outline this debate, for if one has little or no acquaintance with the scientific context within which Dawkins is working, then his dramatic rise to fame and his attack on religion may make no sense at all. It is quite astonishing that so many critics of Dawkins make no reference to *how* he has become embroiled in a scientific dispute that has preoccupied the best evolutionary theorists since 1975. That disagreement, to put it as briefly as possible, is over how to evaluate the scope and importance of Darwin's evolutionary theory and to determine the extent to which it can be applied to humankind.

The Scientific Battle: Sociobiology

In 1975 the Harvard zoologist, Edward O. Wilson published a coffee-table sized scientific monograph. At first sight it was hardly a publisher's dream, being over five hundred pages long. Even more intimidating, perhaps, it contained twenty-seven chapters, twenty-five of which discussed animals, with only brief opening and closing chapters that offered descriptions of how evolutionary theory might apply to humans. It is fair to say that most of the controversy about the book has centered on those first and last chapters. In *Sociobiology: the new synthesis* Wilson set out the case that "evolutionary biology can at last put the study of human nature on a scientific basis."[4] He viewed evolutionary biology as the foundation of the social sciences and proposed that human behavior could be explained by evolutionary biology:

> Sociobiology is defined as the systematic study of the biological basis of all social behavior. For the present it focuses on animal societies, their population structure, castes and communication, together with all the physiology underlying the social adaptations. But the discipline is also concerned with the social behavior of early man [sic] and the adaptive features of organization in the more primitive contemporary human societies. . . . Taxonomy and ecology, however, have been reshaped entirely during the past forty years by integration into neo-Darwinist evolutionary theory—the "Modern Synthesis," as it is often called—in which each phenomenon is weighed for its adaptive significance and then related to the basic principles of population genetics. It may not be too much to say that sociology and other social sciences, as well as the humanities, are the last branches of biology waiting to be included in the Modern Synthesis. . . . This book makes an attempt to codify sociobiology into a branch of evolutionary biology and particularly of modern population biology.[5]

Whilst *Sociobiology* was at first warmly received within the Academy, it began to be savaged by a group calling itself "The Sociobiology Study Group of Science for the People" that was led by Stephen J. Gould, Richard Lewontin and Richard Levins. The debate that soon raged can be epitomized by the polarizing formula, "Nature versus Nurture"; and the implications of Wilson's book amply fed that dispute. The question, simply put, was whether *culture* or *genetics* was the primary determinant of how we behaved. To the opponents of *Sociobiology,* Wilson seemed to be proposing that our genetic make-up was the best or perhaps the *only* explanation. Biology was being touted as the premier science, a single discipline that could adequately explain the human condition. The approach was labeled "reductionist" and Wilson decried as a "genetic determinist," "political reactionary," "racist," and "sexist." On one memorable occasion in 1978, he was assaulted by having a pitcher of iced water poured over his head as he was preparing to lecture at a meeting of the American Association for the Advancement of Science.

But apart from the hysteria and irrationality surrounding Wilson's book there were genuine emotive reasons for the opposition. His principal adversaries—Gould, Lewontin, and Levins—were all Jewish, and their concern stemmed from a mixture of memories of the Nazi holocaust, the specter of eugenics (the study and practice of *selective breeding* applied to humans with the aim of "improving" the species) and distrust of any suggestion of scientific determinism. Moreover, they called for the formulation of *proper limits to what the scientist could say about humans.* Evolutionary biology might be important, they agreed, but insisted that humans represented something more than the mere sum of evolutionary processes.

It is open to conjecture whether Wilson was actually advocating genetic determinism. Ullica Segerstråle argues that he was misunderstood and that ironically he actually thought "Nurture" more important than "Nature." Nonetheless, she insisted, he wanted people to take "Nature" into account when describing human behavior:

> His book was a plea for taking biology seriously in explaining humans too—not exempting our species because of such things as language, culture, and learning. Accordingly, to demonstrate this point he provided bits and pieces of suggestive research in his last chapter. Wilson's larger concern was the future of humankind (as part of life on this planet): it was important to know human nature for adequate social planning. What he

wanted was to start a discussion about human nature and the future of humankind. What he got was the socio-biology debate.[6]

In her book, *Defenders of the Truth*, Segerstråle insight-fully outlines all the combatants in the sociobiology im-broglio. Like most academics, Wilson did not operate in a vacuum. He underwent a significant change in thinking after reading a short paper that summarized the findings of the British zoologist, William D. Hamilton. This study, written in 1963 and eventually printed as a two-part paper in 1964 was entitled "The Genetical Evolution of Social Behavior."[7] It produced a "paradigm shift," as Thomas Kuhn expressed it, since it represented an acknowledgement of "the evolution of altruism, that most selflessly social of behaviors, by which animals assist others even to the point of self-sacrifice."[8]

The problem Hamilton set was easy to understand but had until then been difficult to resolve. If natural selection as out-lined by Darwin favors the survival and reproduction of the "fittest" individual, then how can we explain behaviors such as the bee dance, in which a sterile bee worker informs an equally sterile bee sister about the nature and whereabouts of a source of food? Hamilton's answer concentrated on bees, wasps and ants. These have a peculiar genetic system that results in a female having more genes in common with her sisters than with her daughters, a state of affairs which, Hamilton noted, "is very favorable to the evolution of re-productive altruism." This means that a gene that causes an individual to act so as to favor the survival of a relative will increase in frequency if on average more copies of the gene are transmitted to future generations by the individual or its relatives. Hamilton's brief paper in 1963, argued that if there is a gene G, which causes its carrier to act altruistically, then "the ultimate criterion which determines whether G will spread is not whether the behavior is to the benefit of the behaver but whether it is to the benefit of the gene G." *The crucial insight from Hamilton was to see the world from the point of view of genes, rather than creatures.* As I shall show later, this awareness that what ultimately mattered was the "gene's eye view" was what spurred Dawkins to write *The Selfish Gene.*

It is reported that when T. H. Huxley first saw Darwin's theory of evolution by natural selection, he remarked "how stupid not to have thought of that"; and many biologists had the same reaction when they read Hamilton's paper, offering as it did a whole new way of thinking about evolutionary questions. Dawkins neatly sums up Hamilton's contribution to the advancement of biological knowledge:

> This work became the basis of a continuing attempt to explain altruistic behavior in terms of relatedness, not only in social insects, but at all levels of the living world, from the origin of life to the origin of human beings. Although first developed to explain self-sacrificing behavior in animals, Hamilton's ideas became the basis of sociobiology, an attempt to reduce the social sciences to a branch of biology, and the later and less naive evolutionary psychology. Hamilton was sympathetic to these attempts to apply Darwinian ideas to human society, but his own work remained grounded in natural history. For his doctoral work he proposed a difficult mathematical model with a simple conclusion now known as "Hamilton's Rule." It states that a gene for altruistic self sacrifice will spread through a population if the cost to the altruist is outweighed by the benefit to the recipient devalued by a fraction representing the genetic relatedness between the two. Hamilton's original paper was so difficult and innovative that it almost failed to be published, and was largely ignored for a decade. When finally noticed, its influence spread exponentially until it

became one of the most cited papers in all of biology. It is the key to understanding half the altruistic cooperation in nature. The key to the other half—reciprocation among unrelated individuals—is a theory to which Hamilton was later to make a major contribution, in collaboration with the social scientist Robert Axelrod.[9]

Hamilton thus proposed that what Darwin referred to as "the survival of the fittest" meant "the survival of the fitness of the whole group of relatives because they also carry the individual's genes."[10] Thus, "it does make evolutionary sense for an animal to risk its own life by saving a whole bunch of relatives" and Hamilton's (mathematical) Rule can be employed to work out the likelihood of such an act.[11] Hamilton coined the term "inclusive fitness" to describe his new way of thinking and this was further elaborated by the British zoologist John Maynard Smith, who named it "kin selection" which was "the evolution of characteristics which favor the survival of close relatives of the affected individual, by processes which do not require any discontinuities in the population breeding structure." It is at this point and with this biological background that Dawkins enters the scientific scene.

Richard Dawkins

The Selfish Gene

It was as an inheritor of this sociobiological tradition that had its antecedents in Wilson, Hamilton, and Maynard Smith, that Dawkins wrote *The Selfish Gene*. He took up Hamilton's demand that we view events in terms of genetic success. Since what matters most in evolution is the transmission of genes, why not take a "gene's eye view" and analyze what strategies they adopt for their survival? As Segerstråle explains:

Developing the gene's eye view as a pedagogical tool for understanding such concepts as inclusive fitness and parental investment, Dawkins provides a window also on population genetics. In the process Dawkins' heuristic device becomes a conceptual glue for keeping the different ideas of sociobiology together.[12]

In *The Selfish Gene* he described, in non-technical language and with a very liberal use of metaphor, a world where all life is simply a conveyor belt for the gene. Darwin's theory of natural selection underpinned the argument of the book. All species "are machines created by our genes" and "the predominant quality expected in a successful gene is ruthless selfishness."[13] Thus each gene has one specific purpose: to survive by replicating itself. Each gene must attempt to hitch a ride on the "fittest" organism possible, i.e., the one most likely to mate and reproduce. The gene is the most selfish entity one could imagine, and for the successful gene to survive it must be utterly pitiless. Each gene must be viewed as "pursuing its own self-interested agenda against the background of other genes in the gene pool."[14]

As Dawkins himself notes, his "gene's eye view" of all life was not universally appreciated. In the course of reviewing the book for its thirtieth anniversary edition, he recounts some disturbing responses. An Australian reader expressed the wish that he had never read the book, as it was responsible for "a series of bouts of depression" that lasted almost a decade. Similarly, the book's "cold, bleak message" caused a foreign publisher three sleepless nights. Others wondered "how Dawkins could get up in the mornings," and a teacher reported that after reading the book, one of his students considered her life "empty and purposeless." For many the book reinforced the idea that the Darwinian approach to life was nihilistic and lacking in hope.[15]

These negative responses somehow missed the essential point of the book and Hamilton's above-noted insights on altruism. Dawkins' analysis of genes was intended simply to explain how the evolutionary process happens: the behavioral characteristics of genes are such that they act selfishly *in order to enhance their own and their relatives' prospects of survival*. This does not mean that in Dawkins' view we should base our own sense of morality on our how our genes behave. Rather we are animals who have evolved to a point that we have the capacity to transcend our genes. As he states explicitly in the opening chapter:

> Let us try to *teach* generosity and altruism, because we are born selfish. Let us understand what our own selfish genes are up to, because we may then at least have the chance to upset their designs, something that no other species has ever aspired to.[16]

Dawkins' scientific detractors included both those who had attacked Wilson and some new voices. Gould and Lewontin were joined by Leon Kamin and the philosopher Mary Midgely. Their criticisms were identical to those that had been hurled at Wilson; especially the claim that Dawkins was a "reductionist" who was peddling "genetic determinism." Midgley was scathing in her attack, rounding on Dawkins for linking the notion of a gene's emotional nature with that of humans in order to argue for the selfishness of humans. Her celebrated remark: "Genes cannot be selfish, or unselfish, any more than atoms can be jealous, elephants abstract or biscuits teleological" has passed into folklore and is still quoted by commentators.[17] The spat between Dawkins and Midgley continues to this day with both combatants wary of the other; and has been described in adequate detail elsewhere.[18] What needs to be said here is that Midgley misunderstood Dawkins completely. First, she failed to understand Dawkins' distinction between the analytical and the functional concept of the gene. For Dawkins, following G. C. Williams, "a gene is defined as a chromosomal material that potentially lasts for enough generations to serve as a unit of natural selection."[19] A gene is a replicator with "high-copying-fidelity."

Midgley's second error was one that has been perpetrated by many who have not read *The Selfish Gene* in much depth: she makes the mistake of equating how genes behave with how humans might behave. It is extremely surprising that the classic *is/ought* moral dilemma should evade such a celebrated philosopher! Indeed, apart from the controversial final chapter on memes, humans are seldom mentioned at all, and even in his conclusion Dawkins is crystal-clear:

> The point I am making now is that, even if we look on the dark side and assume that individual man is fundamentally selfish, our conscious foresight—our capacity to stimulate the future in imagination—could save us from the worst selfish excesses of the blind replicators. We have at least the mental equipment to foster our long-term selfish interests rather than merely our short-term selfish interests. . . . We have the power to defy the selfish genes of our birth. . . . We can even discuss ways of deliberately cultivating and nurturing pure, disinterested altruism—something that has no place in nature, something that has never existed before in the whole history of the world. We are built as gene machines, but we have the power to turn against our creators. We, alone on earth, can rebel against the tyranny of selfish replicators.[20]

Perhaps, as Dawkins reflects in the thirtieth anniversary edition of the book, "selfish" was the wrong word to use. It had too many negative connotations. A publisher friend, Tom Maschler, had suggested the title *The Immortal Gene* and Dawkins grants that Maschler "may have been right."[21] The emphasis in the title should be on "gene" more than "selfish"; after all, the book is concerned with how and why *genes* survive or are destroyed through the process of natural selection, and how genes attempt to become immortal, i.e., to survive forever. And although one of its strategies is to appear to be selfish, Dawkins (following Hamilton) is at pains to point out that altruism is also a trait of genes. Indeed, in the first two chapters of his next book, *The Extended Phenotype*, he reiterates the co-operative nature of genes in their fight for survival. Incidentally, it is interesting to note that most commentators ignore Dawkins' second book, and far from achieving the popular success due in part to the controversy sparked by his maiden offering, it is often sidelined because no one is disturbed by its title! Indeed, most would be hard-pressed to know what an "extended phenotype" is!

But the selfishness debate has continued unabated, and in 1984 Kamin and Lewontin were joined by the English neurobiologist Steven Rose in writing a response to Dawkins, one they aptly titled *Not in our Genes*. The authors argue that scientists always work from within political and cultural biases; and that sociobiologists have become so linked with the cause of right-wing conservatism as to raise the specter of the sinister world of eugenics. In the worst case scenario, they suggest, by insisting on the primacy of genes, sociobiology means the acceptance of biological determinism with the resultant dehumanizing reductionism that could lead to Nazi-style abuses such as racial/ethnic cleansing, human experimentation and genetic modification. They encourage instead a "dialectical" approach to "human nature," in which a number of wide-ranging scientific fields are taken into account and integrated appropriately. They regard the "nature versus nurture" label given to the debate as misleading. Obviously, this did not cut much ice with Dawkins, who in a review in *New Scientist* was particularly scathing, accusing the authors of a "bizarre conspiracy theory of science," characterizing their critique as a combination of lies and idiocy, and concluding that it is a "silly, pretentious, obscurantist and mendacious book."

Unweaving the Rainbow

Dawkins' response to the perceived "cold, bleak message" of *The Selfish Gene* was *Unweaving the rainbow: science, delusion and the appetite for wonder*.[22] His starting point is the most famous anti-scientist of the Romantic poets, John Keats (1795–1821). While a poet like William Wordsworth revered Sir Isaac Newton and was able to reconcile Newton's discoveries with his own mystical view of nature, Keats accused Newton of having destroyed the beauty of the rainbow by reducing it to its scientific description: sunlight spread out into its spectrum of colors and diverted to the eye of the observer by water droplets. With its mystery dispelled, he argued, our sense of wonder at the rainbow is diminished. In *Lamia* (1819) he included a metaphorical portrait of Newton as an evil and destructive figure:

> There was an awful rainbow once in heaven
> We know her woof; her texture; she is given
> In the dull catalogue of common things.
> Philosophy will clip an Angel's wings,
> Conquer all mysteries by rule and line,
> Empty the haunted air, and gnomed mine—
> Unweave a rainbow, as it erewhile made
> The tender-person'd Lamia melt into a shade.

By "philosophy" Keats obviously meant "natural philosophy," which was the name given to what today we call "science." Dawkins counters Keats and all those who view science in negative terms, arguing that engaging in the scientific enterprise leads to more, not less, of a sense of awe and wonder at the world of nature. Indeed, by "unweaving the rainbow" scientists do not have to rely on the bizarre myths of religions or spiritualities, but can find pleasure in deciphering how the cosmos works:

> After sleeping through a hundred million centuries we
> have finally opened our eyes on a sumptuous planet,

sparkling with color, bountiful with life. Within decades
we must close our eyes again. Isn't it a noble, an enlightened way of spending our brief time in the sun, to work
at understanding the universe and how we have come
to wake in it? . . . To put it the other way round, isn't
it sad to go to your grave without ever wondering why
you were born? Who, without such a thought, would not
spring from bed, eager to resume discovering the world
and rejoicing to be part of it?[23]

It is in this context that we should understand Dawkins'
use of the word "delusion" in the book's subtitle, for the
word is aimed not only at religions who peddle highly im-
probable beliefs, but the growing number of spiritualities
that have replaced religions, and whose belief systems are
often equally dubious. Instead of being inspired by science to
appreciate the awe and wonder of the universe, Dawkins objects, people are "hoodwink'd with faery fancy." In his view,
it is the insights of science rather than religion that *ought* to
be incorporated into our notion of how we might best live
our lives. Science, not the delusions of religions and spiritualities, should be employed to promote feelings of profundity
and intuitions leading to artistic self-expression that can help
us make sense of it all:

We can get outside the universe. I mean in the sense of
putting a model of the universe *inside* our skulls. Not a
superstitious, small-minded, parochial model filled with
spirits and hobgoblins, astrology and magic, glittering
with fake crocks of gold where the rainbow ends. A big
model, worthy of the reality that regulates, updates and
tempers it; a model of stars and great distances, where
Einstein's noble spacetime curve upstages the curve of
Yahweh's covenantal bow and cuts it down to size; a
powerful model, incorporating the past, steering us
through the present, capable of running far ahead to offer

detailed constructions of alternative futures and allow us to choose.[24]

Dawkins' use of "delusion" is repeated in his block-buster, *The God Delusion* (2006), and his attack on those "hoodwink'd with faery fancy" is followed up in his 2007 TV series "Enemies of Reason" that investigates New Age spiritualities. Since much has been written about *The God Delusion*,[25] I shall not cover what may well be familiar ground. However, I invite the reader to recall my premise in this chapter and note the failure of commentators to mention that key arguments in *The God Delusion* can be found in Dawkins' earlier scientific books. Indeed, he has sustained his attack on religion for many years. He did not just appear from nowhere in 2006 and decide to attack religion.

It should have come as no surprise that he wrote such a book for, as I have already shown, religions and spiritualities are similarly decried as delusions in his earlier works. *The Blind Watchmaker, River out of Eden, Unweaving the Rainbow,* and *The Ancestor's Tale* all argue for an interpretation of existence that stands on its own without relying on a Divine Author or Creator. Dawkins has long thought God to be a delusion, as one sees in such haunting phrases as:

DNA neither cares nor knows.

Poets could better use the inspiration provided by science.

Belief that there is a god or gods, belief in heaven, belief that Mary never died, belief that prayers are answered— not one of these beliefs is backed up by good evidence.

What is different now is that Dawkins is openly hostile to religion to the degree of *not* sanctioning *its right to present its own explanation of existence with reference to God.* In many ways, the reaction to *The God Delusion* amounted to a reprise of the debate between Dawkins and Stephen Jay

Gould—a spat *within* the scientific community that soon became public. Both were evolutionary biologists but they had very different ideas as to the place of and the respect to be accorded religion.

Stephen J. Gould

Gould's position is set out in a book published only three years before his untimely death at the age of sixty. In *Rocks of Ages: science and religion in the fullness of life*, he argues that there can be no synthesis of religion of science because each operates within its own separate domain (*magisterium*). Science takes precedence in the empirical realm while religion operates in "the realm of human purposes, meaning and values" (i.e., the moral realm). Gould, an agnostic Jew, values religion and advocates a "respectful, even loving concordat between the magisteria of science and religion." Thus "science and religion do not glower at each other . . . [but] interdigitate in patterns of complex fingering, and at every fractal scale of self-similarity." However, whilst there might be meaningful dialogue, ultimately there is a separation between *magisteria* and people "must live the fullness of complete life in many mansions."[26] Indeed, there are other *magisteria*, for example art (a passion of Gould's), which can inform and even enlighten us. As I mentioned in Chapter 2 of this book, Gould's intention in promoting non-overlapping *magisteria* (NOMA) was to counter the growing threat and influence of creationism. In particular, he wanted to establish that creationism was part of the *magisterium* of religion and thus had no place in science classroom in schools. Largely on the basis of this stand, Gould came to be viewed as a moderate (and moderating) voice in the science versus religion debate.

In fact, Gould's NOMA thesis was not new: foretastes of it can be found in the writings of the eighteenth-century philosopher David Hume and the more contemporary and somewhat less original G. E. Moore, whose 1903 book, *Principia Ethica* is the most famous presentation of the NOMA hypothesis. Adopting the role of an historian of science, Gould contributed to the dialogue by presenting citations from both sides of the controversy, especially from the writings of Thomas Henry Huxley (Darwin's Bulldog) and the encyclicals of two modern and very conservative Popes (Pius XII and John Paul II). Moreover, Gould was not quite as conciliatory towards religion as it first appears. Michael Ruse offers an apposite comment:

> Despite Gould's lip service to "Magisteria," as soon as a Christian wants to make any existential claims—for instance, that God the creator sent his son to earth to save us from our sins so that we can enjoy salvation and an afterlife—Gould dismisses the claim (and by implication the person) as silly or stupid.[27]

Here is the nub of the problem: How much respect can one give to religion when it encroaches upon another *magisterium*? And when Gould distinguishes between science, a discipline that "covers the empirical universe [asking] what is it made of (fact) and why does it work this way (theory)," and religion, "which extends over questions of moral meaning and value," how watertight are his categories? Moreover there are glaring inconsistencies in the NOMA thesis. Does not religion make factual claims about the origins of the universe (i.e., that it was brought into being by a supernatural creator)? Can one pretend that science is totally unaffected by cultural values? Can ethical questions never be applied to scientific investigations or experiments?

Is Science Value Free?

Whilst the philosopher of science, Karl Popper (1902–1994), argued that science yields objective, culture-value-free knowledge in that there is a real world independent of the scientist, others have noted that any scientist offers a personal "spin" on the scientific enterprise, one that is culturally influenced and even gender-bound. Indeed, Margaret Wertheim in *Pythagoras' Trousers* argues that the origins of physics were intimately connected with religion. As such, physicists became a gender-specific priestly caste and thereby prevented women from entering the field. Moreover, she proposes, if women had been permitted to study this "sacred" subject then the results of science would have been different. In particular, there would have been less emphasis on hierarchy and unified theory, and the equitable participation of women would have fostered a more "embodied" and less abstract notion of mathematical formulas. In her view, women can become comfortable in physics only if and when certain of its basic assumptions are changed. Wertheim notes that among other positive changes, women would make science more ethically and socially accountable.[28] And after all, she insists, the scientist cannot shield him/herself from the potential effects of what might be discovered in the laboratory:

> We need a physics that is more centered on human needs and concerns, a physics whose practitioners are more ethically and socially accountable, a physics that is, in effect, more "grounded." Physicists have always claimed that their science is ethically neutral. But in recent years, philosophers of science—particularly feminist philosophers—have challenged this claim. Knowledge, they say, is not neutral, but always the fruit of some intention, whether consciously recognized or not.[29]

That ethical responsibility of scientists in their day-to-day pursuits is an issue that resurfaced in 2007 when in the United Kingdom Professor David King, the British Government's senior science advisor, proposed a seven-point *universal* ethical code for all scientists:

1. Act with skill and care, keep skills up to date
2. Prevent corrupt practice and declare conflicts of interest
3. Respect and acknowledge the work of other scientists
4. Ensure that research is justified and lawful
5. Minimize impacts on people, animals and the environment
6. Discuss issues science raises for society
7. Do not mislead; present evidence honestly[30]

This universal code was aimed at "building trust between scientists and society" and encouraging ethical integrity amongst scientists. Thus, for example, it would not be ethical for a scientist employed by a tobacco company to present scientific arguments in favor of smoking. Likewise, by adopting the code the scientist would be forced to address such thorny questions as the extent to which corporate institutions, most notably in the USA (but also elsewhere around the globe), are manipulating scientific research for commercial and political ends? How much is the scientist being influenced by the politician or led by corporate greed to manipulate outcomes that benefit multi-nationals whose only concern is financial gain? To what degree, is a scientist a pawn in a larger and ethically dubious game? Do scientists uphold ethical standards in their work situation—indeed is their "work" ethically sound? Thus, for example, should scientists be in the employ of arms' manufacturers who produce weapons of mass destruction? Knowing that harmful outcomes might arise from the results of their research, can scientists be truly objective?

The idea of the value-neutral scientist beavering away in total isolation to unearth the mysteries of the universe is a far cry from the modern scientist who requires significant corporate funding for research that aims at fulfilling specific commercial requirements.[31] Very few (if any) today can emulate Darwin by pursuing a "gentleman savant's lifestyle" while relying solely on a family inheritance to support a life dedicated to studying natural science. Scientists are no longer upper-class gentlemen pursuing independent studies; rather, scientific faculties in major universities across the world are commonly sponsored by multi-billion dollar organizations. Budding scientists who are not only recipients of research grants but also possible future employees of sponsoring companies cannot avoid dealing with ethical questions. The frontiers of such fields as microbiology and stem-cell research create new dimensions for both good and evil. An unforgettable case in point is that of geneticist Dr. Josef Mengele, the Auschwitz "Angel of Death," who sent thousands to their death in the course of experimentation performed in the name of science. As Richard Holloway astutely notes the pursuit of knowledge can lead to bad ends:

> We create convenient new methods of transportation that shrink the world, but planes, trains and automobiles kill more than distance; they kill people as well. The Internet enables me to be instantly in touch with my daughter in the US, but it also facilitates the activities of international pedophile rings. Nothing scares us quite as much at the moment as the possibilities created by the new genetic technologies. Some commentators promise us a future of wealthy clones, with the bodies of film stars and the intellects of Nobel Prize winners, who will hire women whose eggs they will harvest to clone embryos in order to farm them for spare parts. In this way, death will be endlessly postponed for a wealthy elite. An even more worrying possibility is that genetic engineering and biotechnology could transmogrify humanity's physique and mentality in the not too distant future if the technology enabling parents to "design" genetically advantaged children were exploited by the wealthy. . . . There is no doubt that the science of genetics has added a new fear to our repertoire

of anxiety. This is the very stuff of life we are meddling with. . . . We admire scientists, but we worry about the way they sometimes allow themselves to be seduced into doing terrible things. So we feel that scientists should not be left to establish the ends to which their discoveries are put.[32]

Dawkins is generally silent on the role of ethics in science; he repeatedly evades the issue by insisting that the question of what is right and wrong is a genuinely difficult one that science cannot answer. His most celebrated airing of this argument was a response to Prince Charles, who had criticized the production of genetically modified food on the grounds that corporations were conducting a "gigantic experiment with nature and the whole of humanity which has gone seriously wrong." Scientists, he believed, were overstepping their proper boundaries by "meddling with the building blocks of nature" and "playing God." Dawkins countered by saying "a wheat grain is a genetically modified grass seed, just as a Pekinese is a genetically modified wolf. Playing God? We've been playing God for centuries!" For Dawkins, all agriculture is unnatural because as a species we left behind our natural hunter-gatherer lifestyle ten thousand years ago. Scientists have been at the forefront of helping us adapt to that modification of lifestyle in its pursuit of more effective ways to feed and clothe ourselves. In Dawkins' eyes, it is not the scientist who is at fault, but nature itself:

> Nature really is red in tooth and claw. Much as we might like to believe otherwise, natural selection working within each species, does not favor long-term stewardship. It favors short-term gain. Loggers, whalers and other profiteers who squander the future for present greed, are only doing what all wild creatures have done for millions of years.[33]

He then deals his trump card by announcing that we cannot create ethics from Darwinian principles, i.e., from science. We need other strategies, and our brains are so highly developed that we can rise above natural selection to see long-term consequences that might arise from what science has been able to reveal. Does that then lead Dawkins back to religion as the source of inspiration for ethics? Most definitely not! Religion is not the sole repository for finding how best we might live. In fact, he sees religion as a potpourri of conflicting attitudes towards a whole range of issues, and he notes that even religious people tend to be very selective about which advice they adopt. Moreover, religion does not confine itself to the ethical *magisterium*.

Dawkins has criticized the NOMA principle on the grounds that religion does not, and cannot, steer clear of the scientific matters that Gould considers outside religion's scope. Dawkins argues that "a universe with a supernatural presence would be a fundamentally and qualitatively different kind of universe from one without. The difference is, inescapably, a scientific difference. Religions make existence claims, and this means scientific claims."[34] These "existence claims" include miracles such as those promulgated by most Christian churches: the virgin birth and bodily resurrection of Jesus and the soul's survival of physical death. Though properly described as "faith claims," these are set forth as factual, that is, scientific, statements to the effect that Jesus was born without the help of a man's sperm and that some element of the human person survives death. Clearly, Dawkins says, these are scientific claims and thus outside the moral *magisterium* to which NOMA would limit religion. Science must repudiate these claims because no evidence has ever been shown to substantiate human parthenogenesis, people surviving death, or the existence of souls. NOMA would work only if religions abandoned their supernatural dogmas, something they are unwilling and unlikely to do.

Thus Dawkins asserts that "there is something dishonestly self-serving in the tactic of claiming that all religious beliefs are outside the domain of science."

Conclusion

I have argued in this chapter that atheistic scientists attack religion because in their view science offers a *rival explanation* that is far more wondrous than anything religion could ever propose. The materialist, mechanistic, naturalistic worldview is far from meaningless:

> Quite the contrary, the scientific worldview is a poetic worldview, it is almost a transcendental worldview. We are amazingly privileged to be born at all and to be granted a few decades—before we die forever—in which we can understand, appreciate and enjoy the universe. And those of us fortunate enough to be living today are even more privileged than those of earlier times. We have the benefit of those earlier centuries of scientific exploration.[35]

The crux of the scientist's critique of religion is that his story is not only more wondrous, but *truer* than that of scripture or creed. Dawkins most ferocious criticism of religion is that it insists on peddling untruths. He demands that science be taught with an anti-religious agenda and with the same kind of evangelical fervor that is normally attributed to the followers of religion. Under the rubric of "science" he includes pure and unfiltered neo-Darwinism, and he uses his media skills and other means to "evangelize" for evolution to the masses, especially children, because "evolution is a fact." Yet his evangelism and self-assured dogmatism make Dawkins' appeal resemble the very thing he loathes: religion. He grants its proponents no special privilege or deference; after all, the forces of reason and religion are locked in a desperate battle for the hearts and minds of people. For Dawkins science and *only science* provides the answers to the nature of our universe and our origins. He adopts a distinction proposed by the philosopher Daniel Dennett between what he called "skyhooks" and "cranes."[36] Just as objects can be lifted by imaginary skyhooks or by real cranes, so ideas can be described as originating by supernatural or natural means. A crane is an explanation that is meaningful and can be tested. Darwinian natural selection is such a crane: it explains in an acceptable way the complexities of human origins and life. On the other hand, a skyhook is a non-explanation. It is like a great hand reaching out of the sky to describe in supernatural terms what is in reality a natural phenomenon. People use skyhooks to explain something by attributing its origins to a spirit, God or magic. However, one is always left with the questions: "Where does the God/spirit/magic come from or who is controlling the God/spirit/magic?" "Was our existence foreordained, drawn up as by a skyhook from the world of matter into the realm of angels?" "Or are we the unforeseen accumulation of chance mutations selected by interaction with the environment, matter lifting itself into ever greater domains of complexity, eventually into consciousness, as if by those cranes used by builders of skyscrapers that ratchet upward as the buildings rise?" For Dawkins, the answer is clear: Darwinian natural selection is the dominant crane because its explanation is far more satisfactory than that presented by any of the skyhooks. Science is full of cranes whereas religion peddles skyhooks. The author Philip Pullman neatly sums up Dawkins' scientific writings and the atheist scientists' case against religion:

> All these extraordinary descriptions, with every one of
> their myriad connecting links, are there to perform a task
> at which Dawkins says supernatural beliefs miserably fail:
> namely, "to do justice to the sublime grandeur of the real

world." And that's exactly what Dawkins' writing does. It's what he's been doing ever since *The Selfish Gene,* and I think that is what readers are responding to most deeply. He is a coiner of memorable phrases; he is a ferocious and implacable opponent of those who water the dark roots of superstition. But mainly he celebrates. He is a storyteller whose tale is true, and it's a tale of the inexhaustible wonder of the physical world, and of ourselves and of our origins.[37]

In short, Dawkins' attack on religion confronts the believer with a stark choice: believe the story told by *your* particular religion or believe the story told by science. It is an either/or scenario and all of us must choose which side we are on. This claim will be examined more fully in chapter 7.

The attack on religion by scientists has been a sustained one over many years and is perhaps predictable enough considering the historical antecedents. It has really only involved Christianity defending itself against the claims of godless scientists. Indeed, most of the other mainstream religions seem to have been escaped criticism from scientists largely because the debate has been most vociferous in the West. However, as Taner Edis correctly notes Islam might soon have to face the same controversy:

> Modern science will simply not give conservative
> Muslims of any stripe what they want. And a liberal
> Islam similar to a liberal Christianity which self-consciously avoids challenging modern science is barely existent. . . . It would be a mistake to see the relationship
> of science and religion in Islamic culture as following the
> West with a time lag of a few centuries. It is not certain
> that the institutional and cultural conflicts between Islam
> and science will be resolved in an accommodation like
> that of liberal Christianity. If anything the impressive

strength of the Islamic revival of the past few decades suggests otherwise. So "Science vs. Religion" debates may come to have an increasingly Islamic flavor in the coming years. [38]

Moreover, the resurgence of Islam in recent years has provoked another virulent attack on that religion. Whilst this has included some from outside its borders, the chief protagonists have been those who have experienced the religion first-hand. These are former believers who now are openly hostile to the faith seeking to liberate others from it; and those who heeding Edis' challenge now seek to establish a "liberal Islam." This is a new phase in the war against religion: progressive and ex-Muslims against Islam and it forms the basis for my next chapter.

Notes

1. Michael Brooks, "Beyond Belief," *The New Scientist*, 18 November 2006, 11.

2. Morris, *Life's Solution*, Polkinghorne, *Exploring Reality*, Collins, *The Language of God*.

3. "The Darwin Wars" is a title of a book by Andrew Brown and "the battle for science" is part of a subtitle of book by Ullica Segerstråle.

4. Brown, *The Darwin Wars*, 56.

5. Wilson, *Sociobiology*, 4.

6. Segerstråle, "An Eye on the Core," in Grafen and Ridley (eds.), *Richard Dawkins*, 80.

7. See Brown, *The Darwin Wars*, 18–19.

8. Segerstråle, "An Eye on the Core," 76.

9. Richard Dawkins, Obituary for W. D. Hamilton, *The Independent*, 3 October 2000.

10. Segerstråle, "An Eye on the Core," 77.

11. Segerstråle, "An Eye on the Core," 77. "The rule states that for altruistic behavior to come about, the benefit (b) of an act has to outweigh its cost (c) times a number that is reciprocal of the coefficient of relationship (b › i/r x c)."

12. Segerstråle, "An Eye on the Core," 85.

13. Dawkins, *The Selfish Gene*, 2.

14. Dawkins, *The Selfish Gene*, ix.

15. Dawkins, *The Selfish Gene*, xiii.

16. Dawkins, *The Selfish Gene*, 3.

17. Segerstråle, *Defenders of the Truth*, 75.

18. See Brown, *The Darwin Wars*, 83ff and Segerstråle, *Defenders of the Truth*, 74ff.

19. Dawkins, *The Selfish Gene*, 28.

20. Dawkins, *The Selfish Gene*, 200–201.

21. Dawkins, *The Selfish Gene*, vii.

22. The "cold, bleak message" was the response of a foreign publisher who reported that he had three sleepless nights after reading *The Selfish Gene* (See *Unweaving the Rainbow*, 1).

23. Dawkins, *Unweaving the Rainbow*, 6.

24. Dawkins, *Unweaving the Rainbow*, 312.

25. See http://en.wikipedia.org/wiki/The_God_Delusion for a good summary of the debate; and a list of those who either support or disagree with Dawkins.

26. Gould, *Rocks of Ages*, 4.

27. Ruse, *The Evolution-Creation Struggle*, 274.

28. Wertheim, *Pythagoras' Trousers*, chap. 10.

29. Wertheim, *Pythagoras' Trousers*, 251.

30. http://news.bbc.co.uk/2/hi/science/nature/6990868.stm.

31. For a balanced discussion of this important though overlooked issue, see Krimsky, *Science in the Private Interest*.

32. Holloway, *Looking in the Distance*, 164–65.

33. Richard Dawkins, "When religion steps on science's turf: the alleged separation between the two is not so tidy," *Free Inquiry*, vol. 18, no. 2.

34. Dawkins, "When religion steps on science's turf."

35. Richard Dawkins as quoted by Gordy Slack, in salon.com, "The Atheist," 29 April 2005. http://dir.salon.com/story/news/feature/2005/04/30/dawkins/print.html.

36. For more see Dennett, *Darwin's Dangerous Idea*.

37. Philip Pullman, "Every indication of inadvertent solicitude," in Grafen and Ridley (eds.), *Richard Dawkins*, 276.

38. Edis, "A World Designed by God," in Kurtz (ed.), *Science and Religion*, 124.

Chapter 4

Islamic Voices
of Dissent

Shari'a?

In a lecture delivered to the Royal Courts of Justice in 2008, entitled "Civil and Religious Law in England: a religious perspective," the Archbishop of Canterbury, Rowan Williams, managed to create yet another controversy by suggesting that Muslims in the United Kingdom might be justified in applying *Shari'a* (Islamic Law) in their local communities. In Arabic *Shari'a* means "the clear well-trodden path to water." In Islam it refers to the matters of religion that Allah instructed his followers to obey. Just as water is vital for life, so *Shari'a* is deemed necessary to maintain a religious life in obedience to the will of Allah. Williams' comments sparked outrage, yet beneath the surface of his dense and almost impenetrable prose was the hoary question: "What does it mean to be a religious believer (of any persuasion) and yet also a citizen of a 'secular' state?" That dilemma is often answered by Christians by reference to those celebrated words attributed to Jesus in Matthew 22:21 who on being shown Roman tribute money told his hearers, "Render therefore unto Caesar the things that are Caesar's; and unto God the things that are God's." Williams was simply revisiting an ancient quandary but including a modern-day religious phenomenon: Islam.

The Archbishop wondered aloud whether "to be a citizen is essentially and simply to be under the rule of the uniform law of a sovereign state, in such a way that any other relations, commitments or protocols of behavior belong exclusively to the realm of the private and of individual choice." In short, he challenged not only the fundamental authority of secular law, but also its provision of ultimate sanction of a citizen's identity. Secular law, he proposed, is but one part of a religious believer's identity: to be religious means that one subscribes to an additional though sometimes contradictory set of rules, usually expressed in creeds or articles of faith. Williams' lecture challenged secularism and its insistence that prescriptions and proscriptions of religious belief systems must always defer to secular law. Theo Hobson neatly summarizes the Archbishop's arguments:

> What the Archbishop wants to question is the assumption that universal secular law is the master-builder of civil society, and that religious ideas of law are a nuisance that might or might not be tolerated. Instead, religious forms of corporate life are a key part of civil society, and their particular rules are therefore worthy of respect.
> For example (my example not Williams's), a local parish church might refuse to recognize the right of a homosexual to be its youth worker. But this (small-scale) resistance of secularism is not the whole story: the church is also running soup-kitchens, protesting against the arms trade, inviting the local Member of Parliament to speak, or organizing a fair. It is helping to form civil society, or public culture—despite its partial dissent from universal secular law. Williams is warning against the tendency to

dismiss this church's contribution to public life, to say
that its partial dissent from secular liberalism makes it a
force for social bad. The stronger such secularist hostility
becomes, the more likely it is that this church will turn
inward, stop engaging with the culture around it, become
a ghetto. This is the background to Rowan Williams's
partial sympathy with *Shari'a*. The Muslim community
should not be despised as a nuisance for having, or seeking, particular legal arrangements. For the bigger picture
is that religious communities contribute to overall civil
life, and must be encouraged to strengthen their engagement.[1]

To be sure, beliefs have consequences and believers are
sometimes torn between obedience to their god and the dic-
tates of the state. This opens up a multitude of thorny questions. Is religion simply a "private" concern or are religious
beliefs permitted to remold society? Does secular law apply
to all, irrespective of religious belief, or is there room for
religious groups to apply their own legal systems? Is there
a separation between religion and government (often called
the separation between "Church" and "State") or can religions demand that certain secular laws be deemed unsuitable
for their followers? Among the questions that Williams left
hanging and indeed refused to answer were these: "What
happens when religious doctrines conflict with secular law?"
"To what extent can a person's religious beliefs oppose the
prevailing secular law?"

Accommodation to religious sensibilities is already enshrined in secular law in many ways; we have, for example,
such cases as conscientious objection to military service and
churches being exempt from laws banning denial of employment on the basis of gender or sexual orientation. Williams
was proposing that the same openhandedness be extended
to those who follow *Shari'a*. Interestingly, the Vatican has

debated this very issue *vis-a-vis* Italian Law, and that august body has begun **to disengage itself from adherence to laws promulgated by the government.** The Vatican considers that too many provisions of Italian civil and criminal codes conflict with Church doctrines. As of 1 January 2009, the Vatican no longer involuntarily approves laws passed by the Italian parliament, but vigorously examines them in the light of Catholic teaching before deciding whether to adopt or reject them. Two things should be noted.

First, this new policy is in contravention of the Lateran Treaties signed in 1929 between Italy and the Holy See, according to which Italian laws were to be applied automatically by the Vatican. Second, Williams' reasoning was based on the same line of thinking as that followed by the Vatican. Unfortunately, his turgid writing style and dense text combined to create confusion and an angry backlash—not only from fellow Anglicans and the British public, but also from feminist activists who pointed out the often dehumanizing impact of *Shari'a* on females.

Indeed, even a cursory reading of the recent history of strict enforcement of *Shari'a* shows that the result would be to eradicate hard fought anti-discrimination gains that have been made by women. Kahlida Messaoudi (née Toumi), a prominent Algerian feminist, notes:

> Among the [*Shari'a*] edicts are the following: women are never considered adults under the law; men are always heads of their households, and must be treated as such; a wife must respect the wishes of her husband *and* of his family; women cannot travel without the approval of a male family member; women cannot arrange their own marriage contracts unless a male guardian speaks for them; and women are unable to apply for divorce.[2]

Furthermore, she argues, Islamists in her native country achieved total *Shari'a* by attacking and successfully overthrowing the three pillars that defend a secular constitution: women, education and the justice system.[3] In other words, accepting the validity of *Shari'a* as a parallel legal system is the thin end of the wedge in the dismantling of democratic principles. Even though Williams qualified his proposal by claiming that did not mean the whole of *Shari'a*, but only those provisions dealing with "family matters," he was left with no other option but to offer a formal apology to the Synod of The Church of England (2008) and to promise not to involve himself again in the affairs of another religion.

The subject matter and the questions posed by Williams' foray into the field of jurisprudence form the background to this chapter. Religion has come under attack not only from those who reject its often antediluvian ideas of the origins of the world, but who see many faith-based creeds and doctrines antithetical to the nurture of a well-educated, independent, and rational citizenry. Some associate religion with feudalistic and medieval ideas that have no place in the contemporary world. In particular, Islam has been attacked as a religion that still contains an archaic moral code whose use-by date has now expired. Here is the crux of the problem: Is *Shari'a* an acceptable alternative to secular law? As Messaoudi pertinently puts it: "[If] divine law accepts polygamy . . . and cutting off the hands of thieves and killing apostates . . . [all] this can be done legally."[4] What sort of nation do we want to construct: one that is based on a divine law or one that is based upon a universal declaration of human rights?

Universal Declaration of Human Rights

At this point the debate takes an interesting turn. Article 18 of the United Nations Universal Declaration of Human Rights (1948) states:

> Everyone has the right to freedom of thought, conscience
> and religion; this right includes freedom to change his
> [sic] religion or belief, and freedom, either alone or in
> community with others and in public or private, to mani-
> fest his [sic] religion or belief in teaching, practice, wor-
> ship and observance.[5]

Several key freedoms are enshrined in this Article: the right
to adopt any religion; the right to replace one religion with
another; and the right not to profess any religion. It thus
protects theistic, non-theistic and atheistic viewpoints. Every
person is granted freedom of conscience in matters of religious belief.

Article 18 must also be read together with Article 29(2):

> In the exercise of his [sic] rights and freedoms, everyone
> shall be subject only to such limitations as are determined
> by law solely for the purpose of securing due recognition
> and respect for the rights and freedoms of others and of
> meeting the just requirements of morality, public order
> and the general welfare in a democratic society.[6]

Obviously, this modifies the "freedom of practice, worship,
and observance" clause of Article 18 by placing limitations
upon expressions of religious belief that might adversely affect or cause harm to someone. Thus, for example, religious
sanction cannot be claimed for "practices such as human sac-
rifice, self-immolation, mutilation of oneself or others, and
slavery or prostitution carried out in the service of, or under
the pretext of, promoting a religion or belief."[7] Religious
beliefs and practices can be restricted only if the state can
demonstrate that they are injurious—either to followers or
others——or that they undermine the safety and good order
of the country. Recent examples of religious groups that have
been outlawed by democratic governments in the spirit of
Article 29(2) are the Branch Davidians (Waco, Texas), The

Peoples' Temple (Jonestown, Guyana)—both of whose tenets led to the deaths of many of their followers—and the Aum Shinrikyo (Japan) whose disciples carried out sarin attacks in the Tokyo subway, killing twelve Japanese civilians and injuring many more. The Universal Declaration of Human Rights (UDHR) presumes that religions are beneficial to humankind and promote harmonious living that contributes to the overall good of society.

Apostasy

But not all religions have accepted the UDHR. In particular, many Islamic countries have rejected the clause in Article 18 that grants people the right to change their religion. The sticking-point is that according to the traditional understanding of *Shari'a*, apostasy is punishable by death. Likewise, whilst coercion to follow Islam is specifically outlawed in the Qur'an (*"to you your religion, to me my religion"*), the superiority of Islam is all but universally asserted by Muslim scholars; they assume that anyone who investigates Islam will find it better than any other religion. It is likewise inconceivable to the rulers of these nations that anyone would want to leave Islam in favor of a clearly inferior religion. Moreover, if anyone mistakenly decides to leave Islam, the isolated traditions of the Prophet (*hadiths*) are invoked to enjoin the faithful to urge such apostates to repentance and to pronounce the death penalty upon them if they refuse to see the error of their ways.[8] In short, apostasy is not a universal right because Islam does not generally sanction it.[9]

In 1999 a coalition of Islamic states led by Saudia Arabia issued an alternative "Islamic Declaration of Human Rights" insisting that one must speak within "the limits set by the *Shari'a*" and that "it is not permitted to spread falsehood and disseminate that which involves encouraging abomination or forsaking the Islamic community."[10] This was based on an earlier 1990 Cairo "Declaration on Human Rights in Islam" where nineteen Islamic Foreign ministers promoted *Shari'a* as the "only source of reference" for the protection of human rights in Islamic countries. Thus there is no such thing as a "universal" declaration of human rights unless the declaration is consistent with the teachings of *Shari'a*. Indeed, the UDHR is viewed by some Islamic countries as a "western document" and, furthermore, one that is a human construct as opposed to the "Divine Law" as revealed to Mohammed. And in the view of this coalition, of course, all human laws must conform to the Divine Law. The celebrated case of Malaysian Lina Joy who converted from Islam to Christianity underscores this issue.

Born Azlina Jailani in 1964 in Malaysia to Muslim parents of Javanese descent, she was baptized into the Roman Catholic Church in 1998 and applied to have her conversion legally recognized by the Malaysian courts. Though her change of name to Lina Joy was recognized in 1999 and noted on her identity card, her new religion was not. After eight years of legal wrangling, in a majority verdict delivered on May 30, 2007, the Federal Court rejected her appeal. The ruling stated that "a person who wanted to renounce his/her religion must do so according to existing laws or practices of the particular religion. Only after the person has complied with the requirements and the authorities are satisfied that the person has apostatized, can she embrace Christianity." In other words, a person cannot renounce Islam and then embrace another religion because Islam does not permit him/her to do so.

Here is the nub of the problem at the core of this chapter. Whilst secular countries are not opposed to people following whichever religion they choose (as long as it is peaceful and law-abiding) religious groups are very often hostile to secular states, because for many believers no law can be valid that conflicts with the commands of their god. And all too often, this leads to the conclusion that theocracy should replace democracy. To be sure, this is sometimes more moderately expressed by claiming that democratic freedoms are permitted within the limits set by religion, but I would contend that this amounts to the same thing. This can be seen in the case of the British newspaper reporter Johann Hari in 2009. Hari came under fire for questioning the new role of the Special Rapporteur on Human Rights at the United Nations. Instead of investigating governments who abuse human rights by refusing to allow free speech, the Rapporteur has now to investigate abuses of free expression including "defamation of religions and prophets." Hari suggested that this so-called "Blasphemy law" (U.N. Resolution 62/154) means that religions are exempt from criticism and anyone who dared to openly question religious beliefs of *any* religion could be prosecuted. When an Indian newspaper, *The Statesman* reprinted his article there was rioting by Islamic fundamentalists and the editor of the newspaper was arrested.[11] Moreover, whilst Christian leaders from time to time inveigh against secularism, it is Islam that has gained notoriety in its clash with the secular world. Muslim fundamentalism, as Lloyd Geering neatly puts it, "has set itself the task of eliminating all the evil influences which have come from the outside."[12]

And yet, Islam is not monochrome: it is many-faceted and polysemous. Most commentators fall into the trap of applying a broad brushstroke to what is a rich and diverse religion that lacks both a unifying voice and a centralized authority. Its three main branches—Sunni, Shi'a and Sufi—are suspicious and even hostile to each other as evidenced by the disregard in which Sunnis and Shi'as hold the more mystical Sufis; and the example of the Iran-Iraq war (1980–1988) during which more than five-hundred thousand Sunnis and Shi'as were killed by their fellow Muslims.[13] The situation becomes more confused with local mosques being autonomous and imams or mullahs offering their own different and even eclectic interpretations of Islam.

Moreover, the Archbishop of Canterbury's discussion of *Shari'a* failed to note the many voices of dissent *within Islam* that urge an Islamic reformation: one that would include the repeal of many of the outdated provisions of *Shari'a*. Equally unfortunate was his failure to take into account the many ex-Muslims for whom Islam is no longer an acceptable way of living and who therefore actively seek to curb its sphere of influence.

Why Criticise Islam?

The subtext of this chapter is that among Islam's most vociferous and active opponents are (i) those who remain loyal to the faith but are highly critical of it and (ii) those who have renounced it. The two reasons for this are inextricably linked.

First, as many scholars have argued, Islam and Western-style "liberal" democracy seem to be irreconcilable. The renowned Middle Eastern commentator Bernard Lewis noted as early as 1993 that "their creed and political program are not compatible with liberal democracy and traditional Islam has no doctrine of human rights."[14] The politicization of Islam has terrified many Western people with the prospect of an Arabic ideology being forced upon people. That is why the reaction to Williams' proposal was so ferocious. *Shari'a* was viewed as not simply a theological or religious set of rules applied *only* to its believers, but an all-encompassing doctrine that insists on absolute priority over democratic and secular rule. The specter of the United Kingdom becoming a Muslim theocracy was the unspoken fear of many of its citizens. The situation was not helped by British Muslim extremists like Anjem Choudary, who publicly declared that he would not rest until the flag of Allah was raised above Ten Downing Street. Likewise, highly sensationalist and inflammatory books like *Londonistan* with its attack on Britain's policy of multiculturalism and the denunciation of all Muslims as "sleeping terrorists" fuelled popular discontent and suspicion of an Islamic conspiracy aimed at taking over the country.[15] Thus, Islam was seen not merely as a religion, but "a fully fledged global political movement that seeks to impose its ways onto every human being on the planet."[16] I will discuss the validity of this perception later in this chapter.

Second, whilst the Archbishop of Canterbury's comments might have been an attempt to foster tolerance for another religion's moral worldview, they failed to take into account *what that ethical worldview might entail*—in particular, with regard to the rights and status of women, who find "the veil its banner and gender apartheid its pillar." Moreover, it is mainly, though not exclusively, *women* who have filed the indictments against Islam.

Women's Rights

The inequality of women has been described by feminist activist Azar Majedi (Chair of "The Organization for Women's Liberation: Iran") as "the Achilles heel of Islam." Indeed, in recent years women representing both Islamic countries and Islamic communities in Western nations have produced an outpouring of books recounting the brutality and shame inflicted upon them solely because of their gender. These horrendous but true stories of the subjugation and degradation tell of women who have been unfairly imprisoned, cruelly whipped, deprived of their liberty or sexually and emotionally abused in the name of religion. In books like *Behind the Burqa, Muslim women lift the veil of silence on the Muslim world* and *Rage Against the Veil* the harsh treatment of women is revealed by those who have experienced it first-hand; they offer the living testimonies of women grappling with the religion of their birth.[17] Of course this not only affects Islamic communities. Many Asian women belonging to other religions within the United Kingdom have suffered domestic violence and honor-based crimes, as is eloquently revealed by courageous women like Sikh, British-born, Jasvinder Sanghera in her book *Shame*. It is noteworthy how many books of protest against religion have "Shame" in their title. According to Yasmin Alibhai-Brown, "what he (the Archbishop) wishes on us is an abomination" and Majedi urged that "we do not need to establish *Shari'a* in any form or shape [but] need a secular, free society, free of racism, misogynism and inequality."[18]

Even the Archbishop's attempts to lessen the impact by saying that he was referring only to the "family matters" in *Shari'a* is highly contentious. Indeed, as an international traveler he must surely be cognizant of the dire plight of countless women in a number of repressive Islamic countries. In June 1984, for example, the Algerian National Assembly in collusion with Islamic fundamentalists adopted a Family Code that restricted the rights of women and codified social relations between men and women. Labeled by its opponents "*Le Code de l'infamie*" (The Infamy Code), it transformed women into second-class citizens and allowed men full control over wife and family—including the right to have multiple wives. How can women's emancipation be guaranteed with laws from an Arabian patriarchal culture rooted in the eighth and ninth centuries? How can any enlightened person in the twenty-first century endorse Family Codes providing that a Muslim woman cannot marry a non-Muslim man (Article 31); that a wife is obliged to obey her husband and respect him as the head of the household as well as his parents and relatives (Article 39); that a husband or father's signature is required for any number of personal liberties (even to leave the country); and that in case of divorce, the family residence goes to the husband (Article 52)?[19]

Regular news reports of women living under the threat of "honor" killings, forced marriage, female genital mutilation, rape, and mandatory obligation to wear the *hijab* or the *burqa* make the Archbishop's silence particularly puzzling. And such reports as that of the public stoning of a thirteen-year-old girl who was the victim of a rape but in accordance with *Shari'a* found guilty of adultery do nothing to justify its provisions to Western detractors. What valid reason can be given for girls as young as ten to be married? But according to *Shari'a* in Yemen it is perfectly acceptable as the true story of Nujood Ali reveals in her shocking autobiography *I am Nujood, Age 10 and Divorced* reveals. According to the book her under-age marriage is not a solitary incident, with half the marriages in that country being conducted when the girls are under the legal age. How can *Shari'a* countenance the killing of an Afghani woman whose only "crime" was to seek to dance in public? Why would one support *Shari'a* when it requires a woman in Pakistan to prove that she was raped by bringing to court four adult males of "impeccable" character who have witnessed the act of penetration? How can we take seriously a religious tradition that would treat women as cruelly as this first-hand account by an Iranian girl living under *Shari'a* testifies?

> I did not understand why divorce was a unilateral right of a man, or why women had to surrender to their father's family when their husbands divorced them or when the husband died. Why women inherited half as much as their male siblings and why a boy could do as he pleased and girls were denied all rights. Why we always had to wait for men and boys to finish eating and then we nourished from their leftovers. Why was my body everyone else's property except mine? If I stood at a doorstep and

talked to the neighbor boy, every male relative of ours made it his responsibility to force me inside the house. I felt like a prisoner. In fact, the only males I could actually talk to were the ones chosen for me. . . . When I was a teenager in Tehran, I went to a relative's wedding. This girl was only fourteen years old. Her parents were so concerned about her virginity that they were practically glued to the newly married couple's bedroom. They stood there until the groom, a thirty-year-old man, came out of the room. They then entered and removed the bloody sheet from under their raped daughter and with jubilation offered the sheet to the groom's parents as proof of their daughter's virginity.[20]

As noted earlier, major critics of Islam tend to be either reformists or revolutionaries. The reformists, while aware of the need to update many of the traditions of Islam, still wish to remain within the fold. Their catch-cry is a more progressive Islam in tune with modernity and open debate on "the trouble with Islam today."[21] The revolutionaries, especially the many former members of the faith, are opposed to Islam and dedicated to freeing others from its grip. Both tread a perilous path, for they are equally considered "apostates" and as such, a number of them have been issued with *fatwas* by Muslim leaders.

Warraq correctly notes that it is only Christianity and Islam, whose belief systems have *exclusive* claims to salvation (i.e., no one in any other religion can attain paradise), that have traditionally referred to those who leave or challenge their faith as "apostates." Buddhism and Hinduism, on the other hand, are among those faith traditions that exhibit more inclusive and universal ideas of salvation, and therefore lack the notion of "apostasy." Whilst many Christian traditions now distance themselves from the word "apostate" by labeling ex-Christians as "lapsed" or "non-practicing" and reformers as "liberals," many Muslims use the epithet "apostate" in such a way as to imply treachery and damnation. Thus to leave or actively debate the Islamic faith is a dangerous undertaking, for "apostasy [is] a crime as well as a sin, and the apostate [is] damned both in this world and the next. His crime [is] treason—desertion and betrayal of the community to which he belong[s], and to which he owe[s] loyalty; his life and property [are] forfeit. He [is] a dead limb to be excised." One can easily imagine the reaction of the faithful to those revolutionaries and reformers who write honestly about Islam. Let us now explore in greater detail the revolutionaries who are not only hostile to Islam, but seek to overthrow it.

Revolutionaries

Before beginning research on this topic I was under the impression that those actively critical of Islam were only a few embittered ex-Muslims who had rejected their faith and in a fit of pique decided to expose what they thought were the inadequacies of Islam. I naively thought that such best-selling authors as Ibn Warraq and Ayaan Hirsi Ali would constitute pretty much the sum total of ex-Muslim dissent. But the picture that emerged is very different: as with an iceberg, most of it remains below the surface. A huge number of individuals—not only well-known dissidents but also ordinary people—have abandoned their faith and are prepared to declare openly that they no longer claim allegiance to Islam. I shall first examine two of the "famous" ex-Muslims; and then shed some light on the increasing number of everyday active apostates.

According to the website, *Apostates of Islam*, the most illustrious ex-Muslims are Ibn Warraq, Taslima Nasrin, Ali Sina, Parvin Darabi, Nonie Darwish and the late Anwar

Shaikh. To this list I would add Ayaan Hirsi Ali, Nawal Al
Saadawi and Wafa Sultan.[22] It should be noted that six of
the nine people on this list are women, a striking reminder
that the majority of Islam's most strident critics are female.
Inasmuch as the status of women in Islam is at variance with
the increasingly worldwide emancipation of women and
their equality in terms of gender and human rights, this is
perhaps to be expected. Women who are denied freedom by
their religion will naturally rebel against it when they experience first-hand the freedom of living in a Western democratic
country. Still, one is surprised to find women leading the
cry of injustice against the very Islam that demands of them
total obedience and submission. Having been assigned a pre-
ordained subordinate position and role in society, they are
not supposed to challenge it. In an oppressively patriarchal
environment where gender roles have been divinely revealed
in a holy book, how can women not comply?

This is powerfully expressed in the opening scene of the
best-selling film, *Brick Lane*.[23] The heroine, Nazneen, a
Muslim who is living in the United Kingdom after being
forced into an arranged marriage, recounts the tragic suicide
of her mother in Bangladesh, but stops herself from examining the possible reasons for so drastic an action. Her disqui-
eting words echo her faith:

> If Allah had wanted us to ask questions he would have
> made us men. We are women, what can we do?

This clash of gender identity is a recurrent theme of the
film: her quarrelling with the neighborhood representative
of the ideal Muslim wife (fittingly called "Mrs. Islam"), her
sexual awakening in an adulterous affair, her defiance of her
husband by taking on paid employment and finally refusing
to return to her religious homeland despite her husband's
protestations.

It is this impassioned plea for the rights of women and how Islam is abusive to the female sex that is at the core of the writings of Hirsi Ali and Taslima Nasrin. All of their criticisms arise from their own experiences of being female and Muslim. Their writings reveal the pain and injustice they feel at having to live as a woman under such an oppressive religion. In particular, Hirsi Ali and Taslima Nasrin's autobiographies recount what it means to be a girl growing up as a Muslim. Although they were born in differing countries—Somalia and Bangladesh—their stories echo the same complaints against their religion.

Ayaan Hirsi Ali

The reasons for discontent against Islam are set out most cogently by Hirsi Ali in *The Caged Virgin*. She identifies three shortcomings in Islamic societies: "insufficient individual freedom," "inadequate knowledge," and a "lack of women's rights." She argues that women are locked in "virgins' cages," because of male obsession with controlling women's sexuality. Whilst this fixation is also found in other religions, it has begun to disappear from Western cultures in the face of new secular, sociological, and biological understandings of gender and sexuality. However, many Islamic societies have remained committed to seventh and eighth century Arabic traditions that defined gender roles before these modern scientific understandings. Islam is locked into tribal customs that are simply inappropriate for most of the world's people today. For example, Muslim girls are told "that a girl with a ruptured hymen is like a used object" and defending the "honor" of their daughters becomes a family's compulsive responsibility that borders on the neurotic. The result is that not only women's bodies, but their lifestyle is closely regulated. They are permitted at most a rudimentary education because their society has assigned them the restrictive roles of mother and perfect wife. They are imprisoned not only in body but also in mind; and they unfortunately perpetuate this system by forcing it on their own offspring. Hirsi Ali sums it up this way:

> This "virgin's cage" is in fact, a double cage. Women and girls are locked up in the inner cage, but surrounding this is a larger cage in which the entire Islamic culture has been imprisoned. Caging women in order to guard their virginity leads not only to frustration and violence for the individuals directly involved, but also to socioeconomic backwardness for the entire community. These caged women actually exert a harmful influence on children, especially young boys. Since most women in the Islamic world are excluded from education, and are purposely kept ignorant, when these women bear and raise children, they can pass on only their limited knowledge, and so perpetrate a vicious cycle of ignorance from generation to generation.[24]

The "virgin's cage" thus entraps both the individual and the society. The individual woman cannot free herself from an oppressive way of life, and because of lack of education passes this life on to the next generation. In a caged society there is no escape from outdated ways of thinking and behaving.

Hirsi Ali outlines three Muslim responses to such a crisis. The first is that of the silent minority who free themselves from the harsher prescriptions of Islam and ignore discussion of its more controversial issues. They might flee to the West or find ways of living loosely attached to their faith in their own country; but ultimately they are more interested in gaining better opportunities for themselves and their families. The second response is to be offended by criticism of their faith, to take it personally, and project the source of their outrage on others. All blame for the atrocities committed by members of their faith is due to outside influences—usually crystallized as the West (or more specifically the United States of America). The third response is the most radical. Those who choose this path want to open the cage and allow others the opportunity to escape from it. In their view only sustained criticism will modify the tenets of Islam and do away with its outmoded practices and ideas.

Hirsi Ali says that when she arrived in the West (the Netherlands) she adopted the first response. She ignored the plight of other Muslim women, and for five years feverishly tried to improve her own lot. Then she realized that she could not turn a blind eye to her fellow-prisoners who were constantly subjected to physical and psychological abuse. And she knew her efforts could not be restricted to helping in women's refuges, but required opposing the unenlightened religion that was the root cause of oppression. Hirsi Ali's objection to Islam is that it refuses to critically examine how its beliefs are at variance with the common understanding of human freedom in the twenty-first century. In her autobiography she recounts how shocked she was to hear an imam condemn homosexuality:

> One evening we were watching TV when an item came
> on about gay schoolteachers being harassed by Moroccan
> kids. . . . So when an imam came on, wearing traditional
> clothes and with the imam manner about him, speaking
> Arabic, I turned up the volume. He looked at the camera
> with great authority and explained that homosexuality
> was a contagious disease that could infect schoolchildren.
> It was, he said, a threat to humanity. I remember standing
> up and saying, "This is so backward. He is so stupid."
> To the Somali in me, this attitude was familiar; but the
> Dutch person in me was shocked. The interview caused a
> commotion, and I sat down and wrote an article and sent

it to the *NRC Handelslad*. I wrote that this attitude was much larger than just one imam: it was systemic in Islam, because this was a religion that had never gone through a process of Enlightenment that would lead people to question its rigid approach to individual freedom. Moreover, I wrote, Islam didn't oppose only the right of homosexuals to live undisturbed. Anyone who had been to an abortion clinic or a women's center could readily see that the sexual morals of Islam can only lead to suffering.[25]

Hirsi Ali credits her "political coming out" to this incident; she could no longer remain silent about a religion that refuses to be self-critical.

Submission: An Islamic Story of Job

It is in this spirit of how religion must be self-critical that we must view her collaboration with Theo Van Gogh on the short film (a mere eleven minutes), *Submission*. I wish to propose that far from being the controversial Muslim-bashing film that its detractors promote, it is an Islamic retelling of the Old Testament book of Job.

In that story the hero questions why he has been beset with suffering when he has lived a righteous and God-fearing life. Job cannot understand why marauding enemies and natural disasters have stripped him of his possessions and his family. Instead of silent acquiescence, Job demands a reason for his misfortune and assails God for permitting such injustice. The story seeks to forge a new understanding of the relationship between an individual and God by means of a dialogue in which the individual dares to question and even criticize God's management of things, his authority, and his wisdom. Job interrogates God in ways previously unimaginable in Hebrew thought: he will not remain silent but plumbs the depths of his anguish. Moreover, he insists that God respond. He defies the accepted wisdom (religious dogma) represented by four friends who insist that humans cannot question God's will and that the Almighty does not deign to answer humans directly—especially about his absolute power, immutable laws, and the fate of individuals. In an astonishing outburst Job declares, "I would speak to the Almighty, and I desire to argue my case with God" (Job 13:3). Significantly, by the end of the story, God does listen to Job and even answers him—though the answer is little more than rebuff of Job's bumptiousness.

Hirsi Ali asks those same questions in *Submission*. (Here it should be pointed out that the title is the English translation of the Arabic word *Islam*.) Her dramatic depictions of women with quotes from the Qur'an written on their bodies is designed to "introduce a shift in the relationship between the individual and God." Just as Job cannot passively accept what befalls him, so in *Submission* Hirsi Ali wants to "move us from a relationship of total submission to one of dialogue."[26]

She tells the story of five women who, like Job, cannot understand why injustice has befallen them and who wonder where God (Allah) is and why God remains silent. Each is praying to God and, like Job, desires to argue her case. Aisha has been sentenced to one hundred strokes of the cane for being in love with a man she chose herself: her crime was "fornication." At the age of sixteen Safiya was married off by her family to a man she had never met, and does not love nor respect. Every time he forces her to make love she considers that she has been raped. Zainab's body is covered in bruises from repeated beatings by her tyrannical husband. Fatima is a dutiful girl who conforms to Islamic customs of dress and decency, but she is systematically raped by her uncle and has become pregnant. Her uncle having disappeared, she faces shame for not having remained a virgin, and fears that her family will kill her for having betrayed their honor. When she questions the justice of this, she is told to remain silent and not question her uncle's actions. The use of Qur'anic texts written on the women's bodies dramatizes the use of scriptural texts to justify injustice. The film challenges the notion that these faithful women should be expected to remain passive in the face of such brutal treatment. Do these texts represent God's intentions, or must they be amended or even deleted? Like Job these women cry out in pain, "Look, God, I've submitted completely to you, but now everything has gone wrong and yet you remain silent."[27]

Unfortunately, the subsequent brouhaha resulting from the film and the horrific murder of director Van Gogh has prevented any serious discussion of the film's meaning, which Hirsi Ali summarized thus: "*Submission* is about God and the individual." Is it possible to enter into a relationship with God and find appropriate ways of living *religiously* in the twenty-first century? Is it acceptable to treat women in this way in the name of God? May people question the dogmas of their religion or are those formulas fixed for all time? Does belief in God mean that a woman cannot choose her lover or her husband and must remain silent if physically abused? In short, how does this religion define the place of women and what is the status of the religious texts that are used to justify these acts?

Submission simply raises these urgent concerns without supplying the answers. It is a consciousness-raising film that probes Islamic society's view of women and scripture. Instead of a reasoned response from Islamic scholars and leaders came a brutal murder that raised yet further questions: Is the film an accurate portrayal of Muslim attitudes toward women? Are there versions of Islam that would not treat women this way? Hirsi Ali was challenging Muslim communities to be self-critical and respond to these challenges. The chilling irony is that as Theo Van Gogh lay dying, he asked his killer, Mohammed Bouyeri, "Can't we *talk* about this?"

Taslima Nasrin

The Bangladeshi writer, Taslima Nasrin, continues the attack on Islam on two fronts: first, by recounting her own harrowing experience of growing up a girl in a Muslim family and second, by examining the history of her country and its culpability in not preventing the Muslim-led genocide of Hindus in Bangladesh in 1992. The censure of Islam is both personal and political and has resulted in several *fatwas* issued against her by religious leaders, the banning of her books, and forced exile. As with Hirsi Ali, the reaction to her writings is out of all proportion to the criticisms that she puts forward. Most disturbing of all, Islamic leaders and scholars have offered no response to her charges.

In another stunningly frank and intimate autobiography, *Meyebela*, Nasrin reveals the torment of growing up female in a Muslim world. The very title of the book is a challenge to gender-based oppression. The word *meyebela* cannot be found in a Bengali lexicon, but Bengalis do have the word *chelebela* (literally *boyhood*) that refers to the childhood of both girls and boys. Nasrin's coinage thus directs a sharp protest against the prevalent male bias in her language, and highlights the inhumane treatment of countless girls in societies that treat females as nonentities or second-class citizens. Her main attack, however, is on the way that her religion treats women. Nasrin's story of her girlhood reveals the nature of life in a Muslim household. Her father, a medical doctor, is outwardly pious yet eagerly engages in extra-marital affairs. A strict authoritarian, he regularly beats his children and is obsessed with the value of education. His wife takes refuge in religion and tries to impose her traditionalist beliefs upon her daughter, and these excesses of religious fanaticism become the focus of Nasrin's attack on Islam. Three major criticisms of Islam comprise the core of *Meyebela*.

First, like Hirsi Ali, she blames religion for gender stereotyping and, in particular, for sanctioning the sexual abuse inflicted on her by her uncles. Her frank descriptions of sexual assaults by these family members and molestation by strangers whilst on a riverside walk speak volumes about the cruelty that Muslim women endure because of socio-religious taboos against discussing such matters lest the family suffer shame and dishonor. Moreover, any fault lies not with the man but with the girl who, once "defiled," is degraded and considered worthless. After menstruation Nasrin is confined to the inner courtyard of the house, told how to dress appropriately, and presented with the names of suitable future husbands. On the other hand, in telling how easy it was for men in their village to divorce their wives, she opines that "they had not broken a single rule set by Allah."[28] In the face of such powerful brainwashing, it is clear that such a religious climate must change if women are to be treated with simple humanity.

Second, religion produces psychological abuse. This is strikingly displayed in Nasrin's portrait of her mother. The local religious leader, Pir Amirullah, casts his spell over her and generally exploits female followers emotionally and financially. Nasrin's mother becomes a fanatical follower of Islam and, dividing the world into believers and unbelievers, tries to impose her extreme religious views on everyone:

> Those who did not follow the Koran and the hadiths
> were not Muslims; Ma was very clear about that. They
> would burn in hell: no one would be spared. It was as
> simple as that. The basic rules were all very simple: the
> fire in hell would roast you alive if you did not do your
> namaz or observe roja; if you went out without draping
> on a burkha; if you talked to a man who was not your

relative; if you laughed too loudly or cried noisily. No matter what you did, there could be no escape from that fire. Fire, fire and fire.[29]

Such criticism cannot, of course, be confined to Islam; for when reading this passage one is reminded of the infamous sermon by Father Arnall in James Joyce's *A Portrait of the Artist as a Young Man*—a Roman Catholic priest's ranting about judgment and hellfire that similarly frightens Stephen Dedalus. The length of the sermon (twenty-three pages) reflects the severity of the warning to would-be sinners and its psychological effect on a young boy.[30] Psychological abuse knows no religious boundaries.

And closely allied to this malpractice is one that draws Nasrin's third criticism: the false belief that religion "belongs to another time and place." This issue is highlighted when Nasrin's grandfather travels to Mecca in obedience to the fifth pillar of Islam, performing the sacred pilgrimage (*hajj*). Her sarcastically terse comment is that "the year he sailed for his *hajj* was the same year that Neil Armstrong went to the moon. The *hajj* drew Grandpa, the moon pulled Armstrong."[31] Religion is locked into customs and practices that are inconsistent with modernity and all-but-universally accepted scientific knowledge.

Nasrin's political writings have, of course, incurred the outrage of the Islamic world. In her provocative book *Lajja* (*Shame*) she describes through the lives of a fictitious family (the Duttas) the horrors of being Hindu in Muslim Bangladesh. After the 450-year-old Babri mosque in Ayodha in India is destroyed by Hindus, Muslims inflict harsh reprisals on Hindus living in Bangladesh. The novel centers on the suffering of the patriotic anti-Indian but Hindu Dutta family: their daughter is raped and killed and they are financially ruined. Their nightmare is representative of the violent persecution of Hindus by Islamic extremists. It is estimated that 5000 Hindu families were victims of genocide in the Bhola

District where the novel is set. Many women and girls were raped and over 200 women were abducted. Likewise, 2500 houses, 3600 places of worship, and 2500 commercial establishments were destroyed in Bangladesh. It is religious and ethnic cleansing on a massive scale and unopposed.

> I felt ashamed to see such human degradation. I felt
> ashamed for the government of my country who could
> not come out to protect the minorities. . . . I feel ashamed
> of my fellow writers and intellectuals who, despite their
> efforts, could do little to save their fellow citizens. Is not
> this shame a failure for us?[32]

Lajja was banned in 1993 on charges that it "disturbed religious feelings creating religious and cultural disharmony." In 1994 a newspaper in Calcutta published an interview with Nasrin in which she said that *Shari'a* must be abolished. Unfortunately, the newspaper misquoted her as having said that "the Qur'an should be revised thoroughly." Her actual belief, although it was for obvious reasons not stated during this interview, is that like all religious scriptures, the Qur'an is "out of place and out of time, totally irrelevant for our era." In her view, nothing will be gained by reforming the Qur'an; what is needed is a uniform civil code of laws that is divorced from religious dogma and equally applicable to men and women.

Muslim fundamentalists responded by issuing new *fatwas* against her in 1994, declaring her an apostate and demanding her execution by hanging and the banning of all her books. They were able to mobilize over 300,000 people in just one demonstration in Dhaka, and as with Salman Rushdie, offered a bounty (in this case a mere 500,000 rupees) for her beheading. For weeks, much of the country was crippled by a general strike, demanding her death, and Islamists killed some who refused to strike. The Bangladesh government responded by banning the book in June 1993 and filed a criminal case against her in July 1994, charging her with offending the religious feelings of the people. Forced into hiding, she later fled Bangladesh, and thence to a life of exile in various European countries. Although she returned briefly to India and Bangladesh, she was recently forced to flee again and now lives in France.

What, then, are we to take away from *Lajja*? Apart from its obvious denunciation of ethnic cleansing—which recalls recent events in Croatia/Serbia pitting Orthodox Christians against their Muslim neighbors—the book is a plea for an end to religion. The central plea of the book is "let humanism be the other name of religion." This is expressed eloquently in the words of Maya's brother, the atheist, Suranjan:

> Let the pavilions of religion be ground to bits. Let the
> bricks of temples, mosques, *gurudawaras*, churches be
> burned in blind fire, and upon those heaps of destruction
> let lovely gardens grow, spreading their fragrance. Let
> children's schools and study halls grow. For the welfare
> of humanity, let prayer halls be now turned into hospi-
> tals, orphanages, schools, universities. Let prayer halls
> now become academies of art, fine arts centers, scientific
> research institutes. Let prayer halls now be turned into
> golden rice fields in radiant dawn, open fields, rivers,
> restless seas. From now on let religion's other name be
> humanity.[33]

For Nasrin, religion must be replaced by secularism and religious laws superseded by secular laws that promote justice and equality for women. This is the irreducible demand that has produced outrage in countries ruled by Islamic law, for her writings are a threat to theocratic governments everywhere that refuse to accord full status and equal rights to women. Simply put, women should no longer accept the archaic strictures of Muslim family laws. It is no accident that when Nasrin's ever-devout mother died, no imam would conduct her funeral: she was "the mother of an infidel."

Ordinary Apostates

Hirsi Ali and Nasrin are but two examples of a number of writers who have gained notoriety for their criticism of Islam. The prolific Ibn Warraq (a pseudonym) is both the Bertrand Russell and Albert Schweitzer of the Muslim world, for he has undermined Islam (*Why I Am Not a Muslim*) and applied historical and literary criticism to the Qur'an and the historical person of Mohammed (*The Quest for the Historical Mohammed*). In these ground-breaking volumes the founder of Islam, like the founder of Christianity, becomes more human rather than divine; and the sacred texts are fallible human documents that reflect the outlooks of special interest groups who wrote them many years after the events they purport to describe. In another of his books he tells of the many ordinary folk who have taken leave of Islam: the disaffection he records comes not only from the educated.

In *Leaving Islam* Warraq has assembled a compelling list of writings from individuals of Muslim birth who have renounced their faith. It is a companion volume to his personal statement, *Why I Am Not a Muslim*, in which he sets out his reasons for rejecting the faith in which he was raised. The problem he personifies, that of dissent within Islam, has been a troubling issue from the earliest days of Muslim history. Although the Qur'an famously declares that "there is no compulsion in religion" (2:256), we have already seen that apostasy is commonly considered a capital offence. Moreover, the fear that dissent might be viewed as, or even promote, apostasy serves as an insidious yet useful weapon for religious and political leaders who wish to control the masses. Despite the crucial importance of apostasy, it has not been systematically documented or investigated until recently, and Ibn Warraq's collection of essays was something of a watershed. *Leaving Islam* offers an insight into the minds of those individuals who have struggled with and eventually rejected the faith tradition into which they were born. As noted previously, the phenomenon of defection is as old as Islam itself.

Warraq begins by summarizing some of the most notable cases of apostasy from the early centuries of Islam. These include such eminent freethinkers as Ar-Rawandi (c. 820–830) and Ar-Razi (865–925), skeptical poets such as Omar Khayyam (c. 1048–1131) and Hafiz (c. 1320–1389), Sufi practitioners among whom the most notable victims of orthodoxy were Mansur ibn Hallaj (executed in 922) and As-Suhrawardi (executed in 1191). However, it is contemporary testimonies that Ibn Warraq has collected from across the Muslim world that make the most fascinating reading. These documents were submitted, sometimes anonymously, to the widely-known website, "Institute for the Secularization of Islamic Societies" (ISIS). They offer insight into the lives and thoughts of modern-day Muslims who struggle with a faith that they find irreconcilable with modernity. The voices are those of men and women from Bangladesh, Pakistan, India, Iran, Tunisia, Turkey, Malaysia and Morocco. They are those who reject the obscurantism, dogmatism, and intolerance within Muslim societies; as Taner Edis marvelously puts it, they "have opted out." For Edis, a scientific rationalist, Islam was simply meaningless.[34] The overwhelming consensus derived from these testimonies is that religion is not only irrelevant, but often destructive of both the self and society.

In a similar ground-breaking book, *Why We Left Islam*, former Muslims explain their rejection of Islam. This is another compilation of accounts by former Muslims who have decided to tell why they no longer belong to Islam. Their depositions echo those found in *Leaving Islam,* and although their reasons for leaving are extremely diverse, they can readily be categorized:

> These former Muslims walk away for various reasons: some to join other religions, some to leave behind religion altogether. However, for the most part, these so-called "apostates" depart because they feel that Islam allows little space for individual freedom; nor does it suitably value human life. Many concluded that Islam does not promote tolerance or individual rights but instead offers suppression and intolerance.[35]

This trend toward expressing displeasure at Islamic teachings and finding solace in networks that provide forums for the disaffected is becoming increasingly common. In Europe this has resulted in the formation of the "Central Council for ex-Muslims." This organization was founded in January 2007 by thirty ex-Muslims, including Iranian women's rights activist Mina Ahadi (chair), who was sentenced to death in 1981 in her home country; the Turkish born publicist Arzu Toker (vice chair); and Nur Gabbari, the son of an Iraqi clergyman. They claim that Islam cannot be modernized and that many secular Muslim immigrants want to leave their religion but are intimidated by the hostility of officially sanctioned Muslim organizations like the Central Council of Muslims that actively condemn apostasy. The aim of the ex-Muslim group, then, is to act as a counterweight to Muslim organizations that fail to represent the silent minority (or is it a majority?) of secular Muslim immigrants. This has spawned British, Scandinavian and Dutch branches of the organization with the manifesto of the Council of ex-Muslims in Britain encapsulating their grievances:

1. Universal rights and equal citizenship for all. We are opposed to cultural relativism and the tolerance of

inhuman beliefs, discrimination and abuse in the name of respecting religion or culture.

2. Freedom to criticize religion. Prohibition of restrictions on unconditional freedom of criticism and expression using so-called religious "sanctities."
3. Freedom of religion and atheism.
4. Separation of religion from the state and legal and educational system.
5. Prohibition of religious customs, rules, ceremonies or activities that are incompatible with or infringe people's rights and freedoms.
6. Abolition of all restrictive and repressive cultural and religious customs which hinder and contradict woman's independence, free will and equality. Prohibition of segregation of sexes.
7. Prohibition of interference by any authority, family members or relatives, or official authorities in the private lives of women and men and their personal, emotional and sexual relationships and sexuality.
8. Protection of children from manipulation and abuse by religion and religious institutions.
9. Prohibition of any kind of financial, material or moral support by the state or state institutions to religion and religious activities and institutions.
10. Prohibition of all forms of religious intimidation and threats.[36]

At the heart of this manifesto is the plea for religion to remain a **private concern**. According to members of the Council it is the politicization of Islam and its "increasing intervention in and devastation of contemporary society [that] has necessitated our public renunciation and declaration." People are no longer willing to remain silent when they see the hard-earned reforms of the Enlightenment being swept away by religion. Once more, it is *Shari'a*, women's rights, and discrimination on the basis on gender ("sexual apartheid") or sexuality that are most often condemned. It is a familiar cry, and as might be expected female and feminist voices form a large proportion of the chorus.

Silent Apostasy

Although commentators do not usually acknowledge it, a large percentage of Muslims belong to Islam simply as a part of their cultural identity. Similarly, when I was growing up in the United Kingdom, most of its populace, without reflecting on the matter, considered themselves to be "Christian" and that they belonged to a "Christian nation" because that religion formed part of their cultural heritage; They used the local (Church of England) church for their family's rites of passage: birth, baptism (normally referred to as "christening"), marriage (weddings) and death (funerals). The local minister performed these ceremonies for them because it "was what was expected" and an integral part of local culture. Sociologists have labeled this phenomenon "folk religion." It is difficult to be certain whether people actually believed in the Christian God or gave much thought to any of the Church's doctrines, but the Church was so ingrained in the fabric of society that people regarded themselves as belonging to it. Until a couple of decades ago, most ordinary Britons called themselves Christians, and more specifically, members of "the Church of England." Today that popular allegiance to Christianity has seriously waned in Britain. Similarly, we might question how strong does Islam remain in Islamic countries? How often do scholars ask: what percentage of Muslims are really believers or how many people have little inward commitment to Islam yet outwardly conform because of cultural necessity? Saeed and Saeed have coined the phrase "silent apostasy" to describe a phenomenon that is rarely discussed by students of religion.

Of course, silent apostasy is not confined to nominal or non-practicing Muslims, not least because it is extremely difficult to determine what people actually believe.

> Practicing Muslims themselves vary in their commitment to Islamic rituals, commandments and prohibitions. Some may be totally committed and devoted both to the fundamentals and non-fundamentals of the religion; others may adhere only to the fundamentals such as the five daily prayers, fasting, *zakat*, and pilgrimage. Some believers may practice many fundamentals but ignore others and be irregular in their practice. Besides those practicing Islam at varying levels there are the merely nominal or "cultural" Muslims; that is those who have only a minimal affiliation with Islam. Nominal Muslims may carry a name of Muslim origin, live in a Muslim community and identify themselves with Islam when asked about religious affiliation. They may have a superficial, distorted or vague familiarity with what Muslims "do." Nominal Muslims are not usually interested in observing religious practices apart from occasional attendance at *'Id* prayer or participation in community religio-cultural activities. They have little commitment to Islam, and do not abide by its commandments or prohibitions.[37]

Saeed and Saeed estimate that there may be as many as **three hundred million Muslims** who fall into this last category and therefore have little interest in the tenets and practices of Islam. This represents an obvious threat to the unity of Islam. Indeed, some data suggested that Islam is not on the increase, but rather the skewing effects of cultural factors mask a different trend. Consider this description of a Muslim family in Singapore:

> I was born a Muslim but rejected Islam when I came to university. I studied it extensively and found that it made fanciful claims about the existence of a supernatural

Being. My parents are Moslems. But my dad and mom are not fanatics. Dad only prays on Hari Raya days. I'm Singaporean. There are many Malay Singaporeans who do not believe, let alone practice the teachings of Islam. Nobody seriously prays five times [a day] here. And Friday mosques are rarely filled up as people are busy working. If all Moslems prayed there weren't [sic] be enough mosques to go around. People are socially engineered to maintain their pseudo identities but these days nobody cares whether you fast, pray or eat non-100% halal food.[38]

The most potent attack on Islam might indeed come from within its own ranks, led by those who outwardly profess Islam but really have no commitment to Allah or its practices except out of cultural loyalty. These silent apostates might ultimately be the undoing of Islam.

Islam: A Private Religion?

Besides raising the issue of silent apostasy, Saeed and Saeed make the intriguing assertion that many in the Muslim world now regard Islam as "a covenant between an individual and God."[39] This echoes the movement in the last few hundred years of Christianity away from belief in the truth of doctrinal propositions and toward the idea of religion being an individual's response from the heart to an encounter with the Almighty. To the degree that Islam becomes a private matter such notions as apostasy become irrelevant. When people embrace Islam voluntarily, they do not need to be coerced into believing: they are Muslims because of a conviction that they have had a "personal experience" of Allah and are committed to following his ways. Fears of the politicization of Islam melt away with Islam relegated to one of many religious options (or none) that an individual can choose in the religious supermarket.

Saeed and Saeed claim that "a large number of Muslims throughout the Muslim world" consider Islam to be a private concern between an individual and Allah and believe that anti-apostasy laws can be rescinded. Research support for this assertion is scant, but if it proves to be correct the way is open for a reformed, more tolerant Islam. Unfortunately, would-be reformers have met with *fatwas* or suspicion within Islamic communities. We will next examine two writers who lead the effort to revise Islam: Irshad Manji and Reza Aslan.

Reforming Islam

The most vociferous and courageous attack on her own faith tradition has come from the Irshad Manji. She was born in Uganda but her family fled to Canada in 1972 during the violent and oppressive regime of President Idi Amin. She is currently Director of the Moral Courage Project in New York University. As a feminist, lesbian, and Muslim she has been dubbed "Bin Laden's nightmare."[40] She describes her best-selling book, *The Trouble with Islam Today*, as an "open letter" to her fellow Muslims in which she details the problems afflicting her faith: oppression of women in the Arab and Muslim world, unwavering intolerance for other religions, and rampant worldwide anti-Semitism.

Manji argues that Islam has been captured by religious zealots who espouse a malignant, narrow interpretation of the Qur'an and promote an anachronistic Islam rooted in the glories of the seventh and eighth centuries rather than a peaceful vehicle for moving into an ever-changing world. Manji calls this rigid adherence to the past "fundamentalism," or "desert Islam," and suggests that the Muslim world is being colonized not by America, but by Saudi Arabia. Indeed, she says, the majority of Muslims—who are non-Arabs—have been hijacked by "desert Islam" and have come to imitate the tribal rites of the Arabian Peninsula. However, this narrow, intolerant and paternalistic system isn't the only representation of Islam. She urges the silent majority of moderate Muslims, beginning with those in the West who are free to speak their minds, to join in a rejection of "fundamentalism." In particular, she proposes that they revive the Islamic tradition of *ijtihad*—independent thinking and questioning. Far from a new idea, this concept goes back to the philosopher Ibn Rushd and Islam's Golden Age (750–1250 CE). Only in the thirteenth century was disputation in Islam stifled by scholars in Baghdad, and Muslims have lived with the consequences ever since.

In contrast to the Islamic revolutionaries we examined earlier, she describes Islam as "in theory a beautiful and tolerant religion." Following the example of the alleged words of Mohammed she defines religion as "the way we conduct ourselves towards others." Of her religion, she says, "how Muslims behave, not in theory but in actuality, *is* Islam."[41] Orthopraxis takes precedence over orthodoxy: right behavior is more honorable than right belief. For Manji right behavior is synonymous with individuality and human rights, but Islam remains shackled by Arabian cultural imperialism and the oppression of women.[42] Still, with only a few small shifts in thinking, the present fundamentalist Islam could become a reasonable faith that would end female oppression, dialogue with other faiths, and make the world a more harmonious place.

The tradition of *ijtihad* is about giving Muslims permission to think and to ask critical questions: Does God really permit the beating of women? Why must women be veiled? Since when does a merciful God outlaw joy—or fun? How can we be so sure that homosexuals deserve ostracism or death when the Qur'an states that everything God made is "excellent"? What if the Qur'an isn't infallible? What if it is not verbatim divine inspiration, but is riddled with human biases?[43] Manji pins her hopes on Western Muslims who will have the courage to "discover for [them]selves how ambiguous and contradictory the Qur'an is, and to discuss [their] findings freely." This is the core of her plea: for Muslims to think for themselves and make Islam a very different religion. Her mantra is a verse from the Qur'an: "God does not change the conditions of a people until they change what is in themselves."

However, it remains unclear exactly what sort of belief system would result from what she labels "operation *ijtihad*." If *itjihad* is the application of reason to the message of the Qur'an, and every Muslim reconsiders its meaning in the changed context of the twenty-first century, what elements of Islam will remain? Is it simply belief in God—and if so, why Allah and not some other deity? Or is she advocating a form of pluralism—the belief that God is greater than all local deities? That would make her a theist, but what about her critique of the position of Mohammed? Manji dismisses a literal reading of the Qur'an, but does she view it as simply a resource or guide-book?

Furthermore, she vigorously denounces all those who use Islam to further their own political ends and she stands up for the rights of Muslim women, passionately urging their empowerment so that "God-conscious, female-fueled capitalism might be the way to start Islam's liberal reformation."[44] And indeed, women will be at the center of operation *ijtihad*, for liberating women will undermine Islamic ideas of gender and change the religion. Moreover, she calls for the end of Islamic tribalism and uncritical acceptance of mullahs at Friday prayers. But in sharp contrast to Taslima Nasrin she insists that secularization is not the only way to end religious strife, for Islamic reform is possible. Likewise, she proposes interfaith dialogue and peaceful co-existence of all faiths, and even contemplates an "Abrahamic *hajj*" to Mecca that would include Christians, Jews and Muslims! One is left wondering how her version of Islam would actually work in Muslim communities.

Although one must both applaud Manji for her courage in tackling Islam head-on and decry those who have issued yet another *fatwa* against her dissenting voice, further steps need to be taken. In short, what is needed is a follow-up book that addresses the theological and religious implications of *ijtihad*. Perhaps, either herself, or a liberal Muslim scholar such as Omar Safi, needs to write an Islamic version of John Shelby Spong's *A New Christianity for a New World* in order to flesh out the implications of Manji's proposal.[45]

Of particular note is that Manji's "coming out" as a lesbian and Muslim has been echoed by quite a few Muslim scholars and writers. The once strictly "taboo" subject of being Muslim and homosexual is now being challenged. There is slowly emerging a corpus of literature that explores how it is acceptable to be both Muslim and gay. Scott Siraj al-Haqq Kugle's ground-breaking *Homosexuality in Islam*, an academic engagement with Islamic scripture, law and tradition is matched by more popular writings that confirm what has been recognized for some time that homosexuality transcends religions and cultures. Religions cannot erase Gay, Lesbian and Transgender sexual relationships; and of particular note is the fact that some of these sexual minorities are actually devout Muslim believers![46]

REZA ASLAN

The other notable Islamic revisionist is Reza Aslan. Like Irshad Manji he moved to the West (from Iran) at an early age and writes out of the same liberal cultural context. Unlike Manji he has a background in academia and as a professor of comparative religions offers a much more detailed and nuanced book. In *No god but God: the origins, evolution and future of Islam*, he effectively makes the case that Islam itself is not uniform, but consists of many differing voices.

Currently unfolding in Islam, he says, is a struggle over what kind of Islam will triumph—conservative or liberal. Far from envisioning Samuel Huntingdon's "clash of civilizations," Aslan proposes that the current dispute is a working out of suppressed internal conflicts *within* Islam. Moreover, the puritanical sect that is most vocal and supported financially by Saudi Arabia—Wahhabism—represents a very small minority of the Muslim world. Indeed, he insists—and documents his case thoroughly—Islam has always existed in many different manifestations.

In particular, Aslan highlights that Islam is beset by three major competing traditions. The first tradition seeks to keep the vision of Islam pure and in keeping with what it believes to be the original teachings of Muhammad. This is usually seen in Sunni Islam. A second tradition is that Muhammad was not pure enough, and so Islam must become more rigorous (a modern example is the Taliban). The third tradition, Aslan's choice, is that Islam must adapt to the modern world by shedding the chains of ignorance and poverty. Above all, Aslan insists on distinguishing between the Islam revealed to the prophet in the Qur'an and Islam as it was redefined by Islamic scriptural and legal scholars in the centuries that followed. He emphasizes the distinction between "faith" and "religion": the former defines that which is of ultimate importance and is described in terms of a search for the transcendent; the latter seeks to provide the appropriate language for that search. Unfortunately, he says, most religions decide that "the language is not a means to achieving transcendence but the end in itself." In other words religion commonly misappropriates faith: something Aslan argues has happened in Islam.

The cultural and social biases have resulted in a reshaping and distortion of Islam that was "in direct defiance of Mohammed's example and the teachings of the Qur'an."[47] For Aslan, the key challenge confronting modern Muslims is to return to the basics of the original Islam (faith), since its fundamental principles—egalitarianism, inclusivity, progressive thinking and the search for God—are all essentially good. By carefully examining the social and political setting from which the tradition emerged, he presents a persuasive case for viewing Islam as very much a product of its age. He notes that during the Prophet's youth the region around Mecca gave rise to such religious fashions as iconoclasm and the fusing of faiths into one embracing doctrine, ideas that were to become central to Muhammad's message. Not only outsiders but Muslims themselves need reminding that during Islam's first centuries the Torah was often read alongside the Qur'an. Both Muslims and their detractors also conveniently forget that the Qur'an calls specifically on Jews, Christians and Muslims to "come to an agreement on the things we hold in common."

Aslan reflects the thinking of a liberalized version of Shi'a Islam.[48] He believes in theological pluralism (many religions lead to God), but also holds that the Qur'an is divinely inspired by God, and Muhammad is a true prophet. He comes across as fervently partisan but far from fanatical. He also endorses feminism by arguing that the basis for the subordination of women in Islam comes not from the Qur'an itself, but from oral anecdotes about the prophet and the scriptural commentaries on the Qur'an. He sees the prophet as a revolutionary social reformer who worked to enhance the status of women, and yet acknowledges apparent ambiguities on this point, observing that the Qur'an itself contains an equivocal passage: shall a man beat a potentially rebellious woman or make love to her?[49] Using such anomalies to support his argument that the Qur'an should be interpreted in its historical and social context, he calls for Islamic pluralism, Islamic peace and Islamic tolerance; and he insists that revisionist Islam cannot be created by the West, but must be built by Muslims themselves. The West, he says, is "merely a bystander—an unwary yet complicit casualty of a rivalry that is raging in Islam over who will write the next chapter in its story."[50]

For Aslan, the crux of the problem is the lack of Islamic unity: since no central authority; no "papal" figure represents the faith, it is driven by the diverse and competing understandings of the faith. This was first and most forcefully expressed by the prominent Muslim scholar Edward Said in his controversial book, *Orientalism*. Said argued on nominalist and historicist grounds that there was really no such thing as "Islam." He denied that "Islam" could possibly breed theocracy, terrorism, anti-Semitism or misogyny because "Islam" doesn't exist. Because no normative version of Islam existed, "Islam" was a creation of the Western mind. Said's thesis was that "any talk about Islam was radically flawed because an unwarranted assumption was being made that a large ideologically freighted generalization could cover all the rich and diverse particularity of Islamic life."[51] Said in particular targeted orientalist writers such as Bernard Lewis whom he accused of treating Islam as "a monolithic entity without the nuance of its plurality, internal dynamics, and historical complexities" and accused him of "demagogy and downright ignorance."[52]

Aslan likewise insists that Muslims have developed many differing strategies to reconcile their version of the faith with the social and political realities of the modern world. After freeing themselves from colonialism, the emergent Islamic states have been torn between retaining their tribal and Islamic pasts and establishing a modern future. They have unsuccessfully addressed the fundamental question of what it means to be Muslim living in the twenty-first century. This is the debate raging *within* Islam. It has resulted in a passionate, sometimes violent confrontation between those who seek to enforce a rigid and archaic legal code on society and those who struggle to harmonize the teachings of the Prophet with contemporary ideals of democracy and human rights. This is the reason why Aslan asserts that we are now living in the era of "the Islamic Reformation," which will be every bit as terrifying as that experienced in the Christian world. What is more interesting, he believes that we are living in the twilight of the Reformation and not at its beginning.

And this reformist tradition should include liberal scholars like Patricia Crone, who is skeptical about the historicity of much of the Qur'an, and Mohammed Sven Kalisch, who goes so far as to deny Mohammed's existence. The genie is being released from the bottle, and just as the search for the historical Jesus has roiled Christianity, so Islam is in for turbulent times.

Conclusion

This sweeping overview of Islam shows that it is not as monolithic, nor its religious traditions as homogeneous as the popular media portray. There is no such entity as "the Muslim world" but many "Muslim worlds." Likewise, no one Islam but many Islams. Many concerned practicing and ex-Muslims either seek to reform Islam or have left it.

For those who have departed, the answer to the increasing politicization of Islam is active confrontation. They enter the public debate ready to risk even their personal safety to free those they view "imprisoned in the fear of hell and [who fear] the very natural pursuit of life, liberty and happiness."[53]

On the other wing of the movement are liberal and conciliatory religious voices that also deserve to be heard; indeed, their names should be trumpeted in the very cause that they so strenuously promote—reasonable faith. They seek reformation of the world's religions from *within*. It has been correctly observed that the religion that never hears the cry of "Heresy!" from within its own walls is dead. As Manji admits:

> For too long, we Muslims have been sticking fingers in
> our ears and chanting "Islam means peace" to drown out
> the negative noise from our holy book. Far better to own
> up to it. Not erase or revise, just recognize it and thereby
> join moderate Jews and Christians in confessing "sins of
> Scripture," as an American bishop says about the Bible.
> In doing so, Muslims would show a thoughtful side that
> builds trust with the wider communities of the West.[54]

It is unclear what will be the most effective strategy for the reformation of Islam—the revolutionary or the liberal. It is certain, though, that the public debate stirred up by these malcontents will at last require Islamic scholars and believers to explain to an increasingly skeptical audience what *exactly* their faith entails. What does it mean to be "a Muslim" in the twenty-first century?

So far, I have concentrated on the most vociferous of opponents of religion—scientists, atheists and those opposed to the increasing fundamentalism of religion. However, there are quieter, more peaceful groups of people who have rejected organized religion and invented (or discovered) other ways of coping with the vicissitudes of life without recourse to Christianity, Islam or mainstream religions. They have discarded the label "religious" in favor of a more inclusive, less dogmatic epithet: "spiritual." It was a word that I never heard when I was growing up, but today it is all pervasive and part of the landscape of postmodernity. Indeed, many now claim that a "spirituality revolution" is upon us, so much so, that the numbers of those in spiritual groups will overtake those in religious denominations within a decade or two.

In the next chapter I shall focus on those who claim not to be religious, but spiritual.

Notes

1. Theo Hobson, "Rowan Williams: *Shari'a* Furore, Anglican future." http://www.opendemocracy.net/article/rowan_williams_sharia_furore_anglican_future.

2. Messaoudi, *Unbowed*, xii.

3. Messaoudi, *Unbowed*, 48.

4. Messaoudi, *Unbowed*, 139.

5. Saeed and Saeed, *Freedom of Religion*, 10.

6. Saeed and Saeed, *Freedom of Religion*, 11.

7. Saeed and Saeed, *Freedom of Religion*, 11.

8. Apostates are either "voluntary" or "innate"—for a detailed discussion see Warraq, *Leaving Islam*, 16ff. Apostasy is considered an extremely serious offence by most Muslim communities.

9. For a liberal Muslim approach that argues against apostasy laws see Saeed and Saeed, *Freedom of Religion*, chap. 13.

10. Jonann Hari, *The Independent*, 27 January 2009.

11. See Hari, *The Independent*, 13 February 2009: "Despite these riots, I stand by what I wrote."

12. Geering, *Fundamentalism*, 29.

13. No one is certain of the total casualties of the Iran-Iraq war with estimates ranging from 500,000 to one million dead and one to two million wounded.

14. Bernard Lewis, "Islam and Liberal Democracy," *The Atlantic Monthly*, February 1993. http://www.theatlantic.com/issues/93feb/lewis.html.

15. Phillips, *Londonistan*.

16. Crimp and Richardson, *Why we left Islam*, xvi.

17. See also for example Goodwin, *Price of Honor*; Brooks, *Nine Parts of Desire*; Latifa, *My Forbidden Face*, Sulima and Hala, *Behind the Burqa*, Darabi, *Rage Against the Veil*.

18. Yasmia Alibhai-Brown, "What he wishes on us is an abomination," *The Independent*, February 10, 2008. Azar Majedi, Archbishop's 8 March centennial message: "Let Sharia Law govern women's lives, Amen," http://www.azarmajedi.com.

19. Mihalache, "The Algerian Family Code," 15–16. See also Messaoudi, 54. In February 2005 President Abdelaziz Bouteflika amended the Family Code, although not all changes totally eliminate discrimination against women. The duty of a wife to obey her husband has been removed. Divorced women now have guardianship rights and the right to custody of their children. The law on divorce is still not egalitarian and favors men. Importantly, the taboo on even discussing the Family Code has been removed, thus opening up the possibility of further amendments.

20. Crimp and Richardson, *Why We Left Islam*, 10–11.

21. Manji, *The Trouble with Islam Today*.

22. In this chapter I have concentrated on Hirsi Ali and Taslima Nasrin; other apostates are discussed elsewhere in this book.

23. Adaptation of the novel of same name by Monica Ali.

24. Hirsi Ali, *Caged Virgin*, 26.

25. Hirsi Ali, *Infidel*, 267.

26. Hirsi Ali, *Caged Virgin*, 141.

27. Hirsi Ali, *Caged Virgin*, 141.

28. Nasrin, *Meyebela*, 155.

29. Nasrin, *Meyebela*, 288.

30. Joyce, *Portrait of an Artist as a Young Man*, 100–123. This was written in 1916 and shows that the doctrines of Christianity have changed dramatically within the last century, although there are some denominations and sects that still preach "hellfire and damnation."

31. Nasrin, *Meyebela*, 127.

32. Nasrin, *Meyebela*, 288.

33. Nasrin, *Meyebela*, 288.

34. Warraq, *Leaving Islam*, 275. Edis rejects the Islamic theism of his birth together with all other theistic belief systems and proposes a thoroughgoing naturalism in *The Ghost in the Universe*.

35. Crimp and Richardson, *Why We Left Islam*, xvi.

36. http://www.ex-muslim.org.uk.

37. Saeed and Saeed, *Freedom of Religion*, 171.

38. http://www.ex-muslim.org.uk. The writer identifies him/herself as "Yeem, Singapore."

39. Saeed and Saeed, *Freedom of Religion*, 172.

40. Hirsi Ali, *The Caged Virgin*, 93.

41. Manji, *The Trouble with Islam Today*, 4.

42. Manji, *The Trouble with Islam Today*, 201.

43. Manji, *The Trouble with Islam Today*, 1–4. I have changed some of her statements into questions.

44. Manji, *The Trouble with Islam Today*, 159.

45. Omid Safi is Professor of Religious Studies at the University of North Carolina. He is author of *Progressive Muslims*. He writes that he "doesn't want the kind of Islam that's just opposed to extremism; I want to show how religion can be a force for love, justice and transformation." Safi writes out of Sufism, a mystical tradition of Islam that acknowledges God in everyone and everything; the divine pervades the cosmos.

46. See: Habib, *Islam and Homosexuality*, Murray and Roscoe, *Islamic Homosexualities*; and Whitaker, *Unspeakable Love*. More populist writings include Jama, *Illegal Citizens*, Luongo, *Gay Travels*

in the Muslim World and the wonderfully haunting *Cleopatra's Wedding Present* by the late Robert Moss.

47. Aslan, *No god but God*, 103.

48. Shi'a means "party" and is a shortened form of Shi'at Ali or "party of Ali." Shi'as believe that Mohammed's cousin Ali was the first caliph and accept only his descendants as true caliphs. The Shi'a tradition has many manifestations, but is usually regarded more liberal than the dominant Sunni tradition—with the exception of the late Iranian Ayatollah Khomeini who is considered something of a maverick Shi'ite. 15 per cent of the world's Muslims are Shi'ites. For a good recent exploration of Shi'a see Nasr, *The Shi'a Revival*.

49. Aslan, *No god but God*, 70.

50. Interestingly, Father Robert McCulloch, an Australian Columban priest who has been working in Pakistan for nearly thirty years, has predicted that the next major conflict will be between Sunnis and Shi'ites. See ABC Radio National, "The looming conflict between Shi'ites and Sunnis," *The Religion Report*, 23 August 2006. http://www.abc.net.au/rn/religionreport/stories/2006/1721813.html.

51. Edward W. Said, "Islam Through Western Eyes," *The Nation*, 1 January 1998.

52. Said famously clashed with Bernard Lewis accusing him of orientalism in *New York Review of Books*, 1982. See also, Edward Said. "The Clash of Ignorance, *The Nation*, 22 October 2001. http://www.thenation.com/doc/20011022/said

53. Hirsi Ali, *The Caged Virgin*, 176.

54. Irshad Manji, "When denial can kill; why we Muslims must admit that our religion might be motivating the bombers," *Time* Magazine, 17 July 2005. A new organization called *Musawah* (Arabic for "Equality") was formed in 2009 after an international conference of Muslim women in Malaysia. They tackled the "untenable" treatment of women including issues such as polygamy, consent to marry, inheritance rights, and custody of children after divorce. It is a small step towards Muslim reform.

Chapter 5

I'm Not Religious, *But I Am Spiritual*

If I had $1000 for every time I have heard that phrase, I would be a wealthy man. People are particularly inclined to say it at social functions when they discover, either to their horror or amusement, that they are seated next to a "minister of religion." Unwilling to accept or deal with some traditional religious label, they claim the much more flexible and therefore superior status of being part of a broader spiritual search. They equate religion with hard-nosed dogmas and authoritarianism. They prefer rituals that are highly adaptable and beliefs that will never become calcified into creeds. The implication is that established religion is unsuitably disciplinarian for modern-day people, while spirituality is appropriately in tune with an eclectic search for comforting beliefs from many and varied sources. Since everyone knows traditional religion is in decline, spirituality is where sophisticated people now find the necessary resources to cope with what life throws at them. In short, "the spirituality revolution" threatens to erode the customer-base of traditional religious groups.

This sea-change is nowhere better documented than in *The Spiritual Revolution,* an insightful analysis by Linda

Woodhead and Paul Heelas. They argue that within two or three decades Christianity in the United Kingdom will be eclipsed by spirituality, and that this movement will prove more significant than the Protestant Reformation of the sixteenth century. Their findings are based on research conducted in Kendal, a typically traditional British town ("self-contained and regional center") of 28,000 inhabitants, in which they measured the growth of the "holistic milieu" (alternative spiritualities) and the decline of Christian congregational worship. And not only does the explosive growth of alternative spiritualities affect all age groups in this particular town, but this study also found that Kendal mirrors the national statistics with eerie precision: at the time of the study 2,207 people in the town (7.9 percent of the local population) attended church on Sunday, while 600 (1.6 percent) took part in some kind of holistic activity. During the 1990s, when the town's population grew by 11.4 percent, participation in some form of "new spirituality" grew by 300 percent.

Woodhead and Heelas contend that "mini revolutions" have already taken place, and point out that in Kendal the holistic milieu now outnumbers every major denomination except for the Church of England. They estimate that if the holistic milieu continues the linear growth it has shown since 1970 and the congregational domain continues to decline at the same rate over the same period, then the spiritual revolution will take place during the third decade of the third millennium. A striking example of this ongoing social transformation can be seen in the recent history of one of the local churches:

> If you were searching for a symbol of this revolution,
> you need look no further than the United Reformed
> Church in Dent. This building was once the nucleus
> of the Christian community of Dent, a quintessentially
> English village a few miles outside Kendal. But over the
> years apathy crept in and the congregation declined until

it was down to one. To raise money, the church hired out
its old schoolroom as a spiritual meditation centre. Local
interest in meditation ballooned. When the church was
forced to sell the building the meditation group bought
it and refurbished it. Now it is flourishing where the old
church failed. One of its trustees is a Church of England
warden.[1]

As I have noted elsewhere,[2] the rise of the spirituality revolution is so far advanced that we must acknowledge the arrival of a new stage in the spiritual development of the Western world. The resulting challenge to traditional religious practices is uncomfortably real.

The aim of this chapter is to analyze the spiritual community's main objections to religion and to examine how traditional religion is being affected by this assault. Our attention will focus on five criticisms that derive from the insights of the Australian researcher of religion, David Tacey.[3] While this list is clearly not exhaustive, the five criticisms are central to *why* spirituality is a serious contender for the hearts and minds of people and a major threat to religion. Moreover, I will show that some Christian leaders have taken these objections to heart and have begun to incorporate the beliefs and practices of spirituality into Christian worship and practice in such a way as to create a new blend of faith that I shall term "religious spirituality."

Five Objections to Religion from Spirituality

1. **Religion is patriarchal.** *It is designed by men to further their own power; it oppresses women and undermines their authority; it represses the feminine element in men; and it excludes the feminine dimension of the divine.*

In recent years the feminist movement has had an enormous impact upon Western societies, with women gaining considerable political, economic, and social status. People are careful to use inclusive and non-sexist language in everyday speech. Women are treated as equals and afforded positions of authority to a degree unthinkable decades earlier. In contrast, religions have failed to achieve similar progress towards establishing gender equality.

It is still true to say that with the exception of Hinduism *most* of the major religions are dominated by male images and male authority figures. The stubborn resistance in several Christian denominations to the ordination of women as priests and bishops is symptomatic of this patriarchal nexus. It should be acknowledged that some denominations have recently accorded ordination and even leadership roles to women, but it remains the norm that clergy are male, while women are assigned roles with little or no authority.

Even though most religious communities declare God to be beyond sexist and sexual categories (again with the possible exception of Hinduism), the divine is universally designated by the use of masculine imagery; and the founders of the major religions were all males. Moreover, the feminist critique of Christianity—led since the 1960s by notable radical women theologians such as Daphne Hampson, Mary Daly, Monica Furlong, Rosemary Reuther and Carol Christ—has met stiff resistance. The proposed renaming of theology as **thealogy** to represent the feminine within the godhead has not been widely embraced. Calls to redefine the doctrine of the Trinity—replacing "**Father, Son, and Holy Spirit**" with "inclusive" categories such as: "Creator, Redeemer and Sanctifier"—have for the most part fallen on deaf ears. Indeed, many feminist theologians have become so frustrated with the Church's lack of support for their ideas that they have declared it "irredeemably sexist" and have left. The most dramatic departure was that of Mary Daly, who announced as long ago as 1971 to the congregation at the Harvard Memorial Chapel that the only possible route for women was "to affirm our faith in ourselves and our will to transcendence by rising and walking out together."[4] It is hardly an eye-opening revelation that most churches show negligible change in the status of women since Daly's pronouncement more than forty years ago.

Popular spirituality, on the other hand, readily incorporates the feminine. Female images and designations abound with much populist spirituality affirming one or more of various goddesses either by accepting them as objects of worship or by imploring followers to find "the goddess within." It is perhaps no coincidence that women are thought to comprise two-thirds of those who have joined the spirituality revolution. Moreover, the resurgence of neo-paganism, and in particular Wicca, may be attributed in part to the fact that in this spiritual tradition women have a goddess to worship.

Wicca has a ditheistic understanding of the Divine as a single goddess and a single god. The goddess is accorded primacy over her consort the horned god, but her precise status is equivocal. For some, the goddess is simply a local or tribal deity, whereas for others, the goddess is considered a universal divinity similar to the ancient Egyptian Isis, the "Queen of Heaven" or even Gaia the Creator. Some Wiccans believe in a number of goddesses, while for others only the one goddess is worshipped and her consort is of little or no consequence.

Rachael Kohn in *The New Believers* is extremely scathing about Wicca. She argues that Wiccan feminists are simply replacing the tyrant patriarchal God with an intolerant and power-hungry Goddess. The Goddess reflects "woman's vanity back to themselves" and "the Wiccan movement has learned from the Church's mistakes and repeated them exactly." I am inclined to be more sympathetic to Wicca in that I consider it to be a legitimate expression of the recovery of the feminine. Perhaps this judicious understanding of Wicca explains its appeal to women:

> In Wicca, although the Divine is seen as ultimately One, within the Divine we see a duality. The Divine is energy: energy is movement and change. Where there is movement and change, there is active and receptive, ebb and flow. The Divine therefore is seen as male and female, Goddess and God. With different covens and traditions the emphasis on the Goddess and God may vary, but all traditions believe that for wholeness an image of the divine must comprise both male and female. To worship either aspect alone will produce imbalance.[5]

The recovery of the goddess and the discovery of God in feminine form, whether in Wicca or in other forms of spirituality, are starting to have an impact upon people's understanding of God. Moreover, spirituality today liberally and freely raids the treasure-chests of all religious traditions as in the following popular devotional poem by Ethan Walker. Addressed to the "Divine Mother, the Goddess" it imitates the style of the Hindu poet Ramprasad and Islamic Sufi writers Rumi and Hafiz:

> My beloved Divine Mother
> Dance with me
> under the soft moon shining
> in the wide open fields
> far beyond the toil and trouble
> of my busy mind
>
> Dance with me
> before the night grows old
> while the winds of love
> still bow the grasses
> and the coyotes cry for you
> to step their way

> Dance with me my beloved
> while the Mystery's Edge
> still flirts in the shadow
> of your radiant light[6]

Such forms of spirituality are especially appealing to women, to many of whom traditional religions appear archaic and sexist, imprisoned and imprisoning by their masculine rhetoric, concepts and leadership. Women who feel excluded by traditional religions may well look elsewhere for wholeness; and the spirituality revolution is eager to accommodate their needs.

2. Religion is otherworldly (supernatural), fixated upon
life in another place—in heaven. It is not ecologically friendly, but reinforces the idea of us having "dominion" over the earth and everything in it. Why bother to care for the planet when the Rapture is coming?

Religions often promote dualistic thinking by contrasting this "flawed" or "sinful" world to a "better place," a "heavenly realm" to be enjoyed in the afterlife. Followers of such religions are considered to be pilgrims or sojourners whose earthly life is a mere prelude, a testing-ground for the more permanent and real world beyond death. Don Cupitt neatly expresses this sense of despair about the world:

> A great deal of received traditional religious ideology begins by telling us that we feel ill-at-ease in this world. We are alienated; something's gone badly wrong; the world and we are "fallen" and disordered; we don't fit happily into life as it is now. We are not at home in this world, and will never be able to make much of it.[7]

This negative and pessimistic attitude towards the world is expressed in the Biblical myth of the Fall, which was distorted to create the doctrine of Original Sin and the concept of a soul that will survive death. We are merely temporary residents of this planet, and our true home is elsewhere—in that special resting-place called heaven. As the Victorian hymn expresses it:

> Lead us on our journey
> Be thyself the Way
> Through terrestrial darkness
> To celestial day.[8]

Of course, such sentiments affect our relationship to the world we inhabit and how we approach contemporary concerns. For instance, a dualistic worldview is likely to consider such potentially fateful ecological threats as global warming and saving the planet as secondary to believing in a system of supernatural doctrines, including God's imminent arrival to judge humanity.[9] This anachronistic prioritization is all too well attested by the popularity of the *Left Behind* series, which glamorizes the Rapture and reinforces ideas of the imminent End Times and the Second Coming.[10] None of the protagonists in those books can alter the course of events in any way because everything that happens has been pre-ordained by Biblical prophecy. And if all is predestined and the final consummation of God's plan is upon us, then why bother trying to preserve the planet?

In contrast, the spirituality revolution is deeply committed to care and respect for the planet. Most alternative spiritualities are eco-friendly; they deplore consumerism and promote "green" consciousness and practices. In all these matters the goddess plays a vital role. She is often equated with "mother earth" and is to be cherished and properly nourished, not raped or despoiled. And since animals are part of the same created order that we are part of, they are to be treated with respect, not viewed as dispensable items or human foodstuff. Champions of animal liberation, saving the whale, care for the oceans, and the like are naturally in tune with vegetarianism, free-range products, and organic farming; they are just as naturally opposed to destroying the rain forests, drilling for oil in national parks, and genetically modified foods. The spirituality revolution promotes holistic health programs that emphasize *natural* therapies and *organic* foodstuffs. It offers an alternative to religions that ignore the growing plight of the planet and its creatures while fixated on a world to come elsewhere.

3. Religion is hierarchical and elitist. It rules from above, and excludes the voice of the people and democratic understanding. Religion belongs to a former era in which spiritual authority was invested in authority figures—priests, bishops and male clergy. In those days people freely gave authority to such figures. Now we want to own such authority for ourselves, and for two reasons: the inner authority of conscience and spirit is compelling; and people no longer trust old authority figures.

In short, religion is hierarchical and authoritarian whereas spirituality is democratic, as befits its spontaneous and disorganized development generated at the grassroots level, and not imposed from above. It reflects no specific religious authority, no Pope or Chief Imam to whom one must defer. It is amorphous, its borders are highly permeable, and it can subsume a wide range of beliefs. There is no "orthodox" teaching, for its adherents often create eclectic belief systems or even combine truth claims that in former times might have been considered mutually inconsistent. The key people in these groups tend to be known as "facilitators," "spiritual mentors" or "spiritual friends," and one often hears the mantra, "We are all on a path, we are all on a journey, and we are all learning together." And because followers frame the human dilemma in spiritual terms, they apply their practices to everything from eating disorders to depth psychology. Generally shunning denominational or other religious labels, they often identify themselves simply as practitioners of a particular spiritual path.

Of particular importance is that such people choose their own spiritual path *for themselves*. Everything centers on the choice that *I* make and the spiritual path that *I* choose. *I* and *I alone* am responsible for *my* spirituality. It is interesting to note that people in the spirituality revolution advocate following the technique that is best suited for oneself. Particularly challenged is the idea that a person born into a particular religious tradition should remain in it until death. Central to the dynamic of spirituality is that it allows one to be different from one's parents, peers or even partner. Rather than relying on the inculcations or views of others for an appropriate faith, people are responsible to themselves for what they become.

Accordingly, spirituality is promoted as being much more tolerant than religion. In contrast to the common religious pretensions to provide the best or the only way, spirituality is characterized by its respect for other belief systems. It is henotheistic in that it affirms its own version of the infinite to be ultimate without denying the ultimacy of other systems. This makes it highly attractive to many postmoderns, who claim the right to pick and choose their lifestyle—a vital part of which is the spiritual path they find most meaningful. Instead of insisting on obedience to an existing religious system, contemporary spirituality sanctions the kind of self-direction gleaned from introspection, meditation, and sharing with like-minded seekers.

4. Religion imposes the "big story" of theology upon our lives without exploring the "little stories" of our individual lives.

This important issue arises from the question of how life in postmodernity is to be understood. The publication in 1979 of *The Modern Condition,* Jean-Francois Lyotard's ground-breaking work, marked the beginning of a debate as to whether it is still possible to promote a "meta-narrative" or "basic plot"—the all-encompassing "big story." Lyotard expressed "incredulity towards meta-narratives," arguing that both the value and validity of grand narratives came to an end with the dawn of postmodernity. The postmodern condition opposes the universal claims of the Enlightenment: no longer relevant are such grand theories and philosophies as "the progress of history," "the claim by science that it will one day understand everything" and "the possibility of Utopia." These and other sweeping generalizations have been replaced by an abundance of micro-narratives, for postmodern thinkers have become conscious of the diversity and dissimilarity of worldviews constructed by multiple social experiences. Exclusive, Universal Truths have given way to local "truths" that are constantly under revision. In the postmodern world we can no longer hope to impose our meta-narrative, but must share and assimilate numerous micro-narratives.

When a religion proposes that its Story is The Only Truth, postmodern people who lives are made up of "little stories" see that as arrogant and anachronistic. The complexities of twenty-first-century lives do not readily fit into the straight-jackets too often provided by religion:

> [People] are likely to dabble in a wide variety of spiritual activities and not be bothered by what in an earlier time would have been seen as inconsistent or conflicting involvements. I know of Anglicans who consult their horoscopes, Catholics who do Tai Chi, Atheists who wear crosses, Baptists who meditate, Vietnamese immigrants who see no conflict in being Catholic and Buddhist at the same time, and Jews who seriously practice witchcraft.[11]

Spirituality is much more in tune with the fragmented lives of people who prefer to sample what I have referred to it elsewhere as a "smorgasbord of therapeutic spiritualities." They choose spiritual options (note the plural!) according to what serves their personal sense of well-being, much as one selects from the wide variety of dishes at a smorgasbord. If it tastes good and promotes health and happiness, people will buy it and use it. If it doesn't work, they will discard it or try another brand. And because this consumer approach to spirituality does not limit the buyer to a single product, the search is not limited to traditional religions or alternative spiritualities or any particular combination of both. The former spiritual myopia that presented faith as an either/ or scenario and resulted in restriction of choice no longer works, for if told that "this is the only way," seekers simply jump in their car and go elsewhere. And the choice is nearly endless: walking labyrinths, meditating, yoga, color therapy, the Enneagram, Neuro-Linguistic Programming, the Myers-Briggs Type Indicator, spiritual healing, creation, and eco-centered spirituality. Because it is commonplace for people to "pick and mix" from such a wide selection, people create new spiritual pathways from different sources that might once have been thought contradictory. Moreover, as the next section of this chapter will show, many Christians who seem to be "doctrinally orthodox" have joined this new wave of spiritual enquiry.

5. Religion is based on a pre-modern understanding of God and an archaic vision of reality that can no longer be believed. Its God is externalist and interventionist:

> [T]he major factor in the waning of Christian faith is its continuing insistence on a supernatural God—the Almighty, the lawgiver and judge who "convicts the world of sin." A significant number of people find no longer find propositional Christianity attractive. Many are creating new ways of understanding and relating to

"God" in an attempt to make sense of their lives, the world, and the nagging notion of something that has created and sustains it all.[12]

This summary of the fifth objection to religion in effect decries an understanding of God that is too narrow, too tribal, too sectarian, and wedded to an obsolete worldview. The "God" of most traditional religions has become problematic for many because the inflexibility of that concept of Deity renders it unable to speak to the entire global community. Rather, such a Deity becomes the God of a particular ethnic group or culture that attempts to force itself on others—and this critique can apply equally to Western Christianity or Islamic jihad. Moreover, most religions at least implicitly presuppose a supernatural "Mr. Fix-it" who intervenes in world events only *on behalf of His worshippers.* One of the more extreme examples of this can be seen in the Christian evangelist Pat Robertson, who has assigned the destruction of Haiti by an earthquake to God's anger at a supposed Haitian pact with the Devil in 1804 to obtain freedom from French colonial rule! To be sure, mainline Christian leaders have distanced themselves from Robertson's abhorrent nonsense, but the fact remains that most Christian, Jewish, and Islamic believers systems continue to envision God as "a Being supernatural in power, dwelling above the sky and prepared to invade human history periodically to enforce the divine will."[13] This makes God an unknowable figure situated in another dimension who intervenes in historical events—often in an incomprehensible manner.

Spirituality, by contrast, tends to offer a far less transcendent Ultimate Power. Robert Forman describes it as a "vaguely panentheist ultimate" that is "indwelling, sometimes bodily, as the deepest self and accessed through not strictly rational means of self-transformation and group processes that becomes the holistic organization for all life."[14]

What this means is that everyone and everything is part of a single principle or essence, but the One (God) is not limited to those worldly phenomena. In other words, God is radically involved in the Universe, yet not totally defined by it, and is thus enlarged to include anything from "universal energy" to "spirit." God's presence becomes all-embracing and is reflected in the language of popular spirituality: "divine energy flows in and through us"; "god-consciousness is relational"; "there is unity in all things." The supernatural, transcendent deity is replaced by a divine principle that interconnects us all, or by Gaia, viewed as a symbol of our interconnectedness with the planet or the cosmos.

Many traditional religionists have objected that spirituality simply reprises the mystical tradition that was once found in Jewish Kabbalah, Christian writers such as Teresa of Avila, and in Islam's Sufi tradition. The spirituality revolution, they would have it, is simply recycling ancient traditions of religion that involve less transcendent notions of God. After all, they protest, religions have always taught that the "God presence" is everywhere and that God "is one in whom we move, live and have our being." The spirituality revolution is nothing more than a popularized counterfeit of the genuine mystical tradition in religion.

But of course this rejoinder begs important questions: "Why have religions promoted dogmas over the spiritual search?" Why is religion so insistent on subordinating the personal search for the Divine to creedal affirmations? Can religions reinvent themselves by tapping into their mystical past?

It is precisely as a response to such questions as these that many Christian communities now offer what I shall label "religious spirituality"—a form of Christianity that reclaims much of the mystical and spiritual tradition from the past and appropriates it for a contemporary faith.

Religious Spirituality

Some ninety beautiful polished stones sit in a clear glass bowl of water on an equally stunning purple cloth covering a small altar in the middle aisle of The Garden Church in Lansdowne, Pennsylvania. A woman in her forties is just finishing reading a poem by Maya Angelou. As the recorded music of whale sounds and saxophonist Paul Winter play in the background, one by one worshippers rise from their pews and approach the polished stones. Most of them seem to pause briefly as each reaches for a stone, grasps it closely to them, and returns to the pews. As the last dozen or so are around the table, the recorded music fades and the organ leads the congregation in singing a hymn. "God of the sparrow, God of the whale," they sing as they return to their seats, occasionally reaching out to one another for a hug or an extended hand.

Part of a regular Sunday morning service, this ritual belongs to the United Methodist Garden Church's ecologically orientated re-affirmation of their baptism. An eclectic mix of what looks like New Age practice, contemporary hymnody, a good dose of Christian scripture, and creative use of the arts, this congregation's worship regularly has expressiveness and participation its predecessors even fifteen years ago would not have dreamed of.[15]

Hal Taussig's description of a contemporary worship setting that combines traditional religious practices with new spirituality ingredients is indicative of how some churches have responded to the five objections listed above by adopting "religious spirituality." Some also offer "soul carte" programs (meditation or quiet days); pepper their worship with nature music (soundtracks of birds, dolphins or the forest);

creatively use candles, icons, pebbles, bowls of water, multi-colored fabrics, and incense sticks; encourage their congregations to walk labyrinths; and emphasize such ecological concerns as "care of the planet." Likewise, many allegedly "orthodox" Christians routinely participate in spiritual courses that a few decades ago would have been rejected as unchristian, if not downright profane. For many years I was a member of a priestly formation team that trained future ministers for the Anglican Church. Each year we began not with Bible-study, but a mélange of popular psychological programs that contained a spirituality component. These "team-building" exercises could be labeled "religious spirituality" inasmuch as they were not entirely Christian in content but contained material more accurately described as "a religious-spiritual cocktail." It is significant that no one, not even the most conservative of Christian students, ever objected to participating in this preparatory program. Religious spirituality and openness to its practices was well ingrained in Church culture.

In his ground-breaking research of one thousand progressive faith communities in North America, Taussig identifies five crucial characteristics of those churches: spiritual vitality, intellectual integrity, transgressing gender boundaries, vitality without superiority, and justice and ecology. Now, do not these five characteristics neatly answer spirituality's five objections to religion? Do they not describe the emergence within Christianity of a new movement that could aptly be termed "religious spirituality"? Significantly, Taussig argues that these churches are "a grassroots movement" that has arisen and developed not from the initiative of a religious bureaucracy, but from an "unorganized but broad-ranging Christian response" at the local level. It is also pertinent to mention that Taussig describes churches that exhibit these five characteristics as "progressive" as distinct from "liberal." The latter appellation signifies a church that despite being intellectually open and having a regard for social justice lacks "spiritual renewal/experimentation" and creativity. It is significant that he uses the word "spiritual" to describe these "progressive churches" and asserts that people have found "a new spiritual home" in them.

What, then, are the salient features of each of these five characteristics?

1. **Spiritual vitality**
    -   Participatory worship
    -   Expressive and arts-infused worship and programming
    -   Reclaiming ancient Christian rituals
    -   Claiming non-Christian rituals
    -   Development of small groups for spiritual development and nurture

Each of these indicators of spiritual vitality in a progressive church reveals a spiritual awakening that is in tune with people's deepest needs. Formal religion freed from its emphasis on hierarchy and regulation becomes participatory, emotionally expressive, and creatively artistic; its traditions are enriched with new and ancient rituals that speak to the spiritual needs of people today.

2. **Intellectual integrity**
    -   God language (including Christology)
    -   Science and religion
    -   Postmodern consciousness

Taussig notes that progressive churches freely use the words "spirit" and "energy" to describe God. They have thus transformed traditional theistic God-language to accommodate both scientific thought and the postmodern condition described earlier in this chapter.

3. Transgressing gender boundaries
- Rejection of homophobia
- Affirmation of equal rights with regard to gender and sexual orientation

Progressive churches distinguish themselves from "the family values of evangelicalism" by being totally inclusive in matters of sexuality and gender. They have adopted "feminist consciousness" and combated "homophobic practices of most denominations" by accepting openly gay or lesbian clergy.

4. Vitality without superiority
- Celebrating Christianity without claiming superiority
- Integrating non-Christian elements into Christian practice

Progressive churches are respectful of other faiths and spiritualities. Their outlook is henotheistic and they actively promote spiritual dialogue.

5. Justice and ecology
- Ecological consciousness
- Social justice programs

Progressive churches are committed to confronting social and systemic injustice. This goes beyond the traditional "soup kitchen" or "parish pantry" to actively pursuing programs that challenge political policies on social welfare etc. They also promote "green issues" as well as ecological equity and preservation to create a better planetary environment for all.

The Way Forward?

These five characteristics of progressive churches provide new hope for the future of religion. They allow people to make the necessary connection between their present spiritual search and welcoming and nurturing communities that can help them grow spiritually. To realize that promise, however, traditional religious communities must become less wedded to creedal formulas and more open to exploration. As Taussig explains,

> Now I am relatively used to a number of questions that these spiritual seekers pose as they begin to think about their own spiritual journeys in active relationship to a Christian tradition. Some of the questions are:
>
> 1. Do you have to believe that Jesus is the son of God (or rose from the dead or was born of a virgin or walked on water)?
> 2. Isn't the church really against me being GLBT? (Or, even, are you sure that I am not a sinner because I am gay?)
> 3. Do you think I can let go of the pain I experienced from the church because I am a woman (or GBLT or was divorced or living with someone out of wedlock or not dressed like the rest)?
> 4. Is meditation the same as prayer? Which part of the worship service is real prayer?
>
> And finally:
>
> 5. So what would it mean for me to associate long term with this church? What does it mean to be a church member?
>
> I have learned to honor all these questions, rather than give answers that may promise too much. . . .
>
> After having honored their questions about their own spiritual search or their own former trauma at the hands of a church, or both, I say that formal membership in a church has only relative value. **The important question to me, I say, is whether they have found a spiritual home**

in this church? Can they claim this community and this
spiritual place as a place to be comforted, be challenged,
and grow?[16]

Taussig's analysis of progressive churches is of crucial importance for those who wish to defend and promote religion
in the twenty-first century. If religion is to survive it must
respond to this groundswell of religious spirituality that has
shown itself able to serve millions of seekers. But facing this
challenge seriously means that churches must be willing to
change—not only in specifics of ritual and liturgy, but also
in fundamental doctrinal beliefs. Naturally, this aspect of the
challenge has made many in the religious hierarchy uneasy
and even hostile towards religious spirituality. In resolving
this tension, it will be crucial to examine whether beliefs
are propositional (mediated through a particular religion/
church) or exploratory (highly individual and self-serving
that responds to the perceived truth of the human condition).
In short, the key question facing religion is this: To what
degree can it let go of the known past and reach out to the
unknown future?

I shall address these important issues in chapter 7 of this
book as I attempt to delineate a faith tradition that will fulfill
the future spiritual needs of Western culture. Interestingly,
many religious writers are uncompromising in their attacks
on popular spirituality's beliefs and practices, often dismissing it all as "fairy floss." But, that is to commit two blatant
errors.

First, it is to reject a universal spiritual search that transcends all cultures and has been well documented by an-
thropologists and sociologists throughout history; and is
spelled out in such classic texts as *The Varieties of Religious
Experience* (William James); *The Long Search* (Ninian
Smart) and *A History of God* (Karen Armstrong). Second,
it is to privilege religion over spirituality, as if the former's

beliefs are superior to what might be found in the latter. As a corrective to this often unreflective attitude, when teaching theological students, I often pose the question: "Which is more credible: belief in the physical resurrection of Jesus or understanding the Universe as energy?" The class normally goes silent at this point. As we have seen in this chapter the spirituality revolution is far from being the "jumbled mess" that some have claimed, and although Richard Dawkins' documentary series *The Enemies of Reason* has spectacularly unmasked a lunatic fringe, I am persuaded that the spiritual search is more honest, sincere, and universal than most people imagine. For that reason, if for no other, practitioners of religion must respond positively towards it.

And for that same reason, it is equally important not to be lulled into complacency by the increasing numbers of those who contend that religion need not be actively opposed, but simply ignored as an irrelevancy we can live quite well without. This new breed of "non-believers" will be examined in the next chapter.

Notes

1. Carol Midgley, "Spirited away: why the end is nigh for religion," *The Times*, 4 November 2004.

2. See Leaves, *The God Problem*, chap. 4.

3. See Tacey's analysis in *The Spirituality Revolution*, 36–37. Instead of listing all ten criticisms, I have conflated some that seem to me to overlap.

4. See Leaves, *Surfing on the Sea of Faith*, 92.

5. Crowley, *Wicca*, 1. Compare, Kohn, *The New Believers*, 58–59. For a good overview of Wicca see Hume, *Witchcraft and Paganism in Australia*.

6. Walker, *Soft Moon Shining*, 12. Walker is also the author of *The Mystic Christ* in which he argues that Jesus' message was 'non-dualistic' emphasizing the mystical union of a follower of Christ with God can be achieved here on earth. He contends that this is the central message of Buddhism, Islam and Hinduism. Indeed, the idea of a universal mystical union with the Godhead transcends all religions.

Walker's thesis stretches the bounds of credibility about the historical Jesus, but it illustrates the way that many people want to unify the religions of the world in a universal message of peace and love.

7. Cupitt, *The Old Creed and the New*, 98.

8. G. R Prynne (d. 1903), "Jesu, meek and gentle" (*Hymns Ancient and Modern Revised* No. 194).

9. It is pertinent to note that it was not until 1978 that the Anglican Church in Australia included official prayers for "sharing with justice the resources of the earth" (*An Australian Prayer Book*, 141).

10. See LaHaye and Jenkins, *Left Behind*.

11. Ballis and Bouma (eds.), *Religion in an Age of Change*, 8.

12. Leaves, *The God Problem*, ix.

13. Spong, *Here I Stand*, 468.

14. Forman, *Grassroots Spirituality*, 51.

15. Taussig, *A New Spiritual Home*, 7.

16. Taussig, *A New Spiritual Home*, 174–75 (my bold). GLBT = Gay, Lesbian, Bisexual and Transgender.

Chapter 6

Losing My Religion?[1]

Do We Need Religion?

Whilst preparing initial drafts for this book, I discussed with some of my ministerial and academic colleagues the proposition that people might be better off *without* religion. I usually received one of two rejoinders.

The majority of my respondents countered: "But religion is how we have always made sense of the world we live in." Because humankind seeks to understand and interact effectively with realities that are often both invisible and vital to survival, people are by nature religious and will remain so *for ever*. Therefore, my compeers either implicitly or explicitly proposed, religious belief is an innate mechanism. Many of my fellow academics accepted the thesis proposed by Rudolph Otto (1869–1937) and developed by Mircea Eliade (1907–1986) that we are all *homo religiosus* who have in some extraordinary way encountered the divine or "Holy Other." Otto famously described this experience as encountering "the numinous"—a mystery (Latin: *mysterium*) that is at once terrifying (*tremendum*) and fascinating (*fascinans*).[2] Religions, in his view, furnish us with forms and places of worship that enable us to join with "the faithful" in sacred

167

rites and ceremonies to explore more deeply this divine encounter.

A minority, however, admitted that for some people mainstream religions might no longer be an option; these folk, they insisted, had simply replaced belief in a transcendent God with devotion to contemporary "secular gods." They thus echoed a theme anticipated more than a century ago by Friedrich Nietzsche, the atheist philosopher who wondered how we would proceed after ridding the world of the Christian God:

> How shall we, the murderers of all murderers, comfort
> ourselves? What festivals of atonement, what *sacred*
> *games shall we have to invent?*[3]

Today the secular marketplace has invented and offers up many new "sacred games." A few of my ministerial friends opined that such things as "materialism" (usually translated "hedonism"); "sex," "travel" and "sport" now constituted popular religion. Their proposals were usually tinged with disdain, and one could be certain that they did not consider these alternatives to be *real* religions. True religion necessitated belief in a supernatural god, and people should worship something beyond or greater than themselves. To be sure, religion might have become too dogmatic of late, and sometimes even fanatical, but it was a fundamental reflection of that which is good (or holy); and if its doctrines were repackaged in a more appropriate way, then the sanctuary doors could be flung wide and people would return. It was surely only a matter of time before many wandering souls would embrace religion once again. Indeed, a worldwide spiritual yearning was just waiting to be fulfilled by a more compassionate and user-friendly religion, and thereupon the tide of faith would rise once again.

What nearly all my colleagues failed to consider was a challenge voiced by a few contrary types: "Why must people replace religion with anything?" It is a startlingly simple but thoroughly unsettling question, and one that religious people need to confront. Can people live their "three score years and ten" (Psalm 90:10) without any recourse to religion? Can they live meaningful and purposeful lives without religious support? For that matter, are not many doing so *already*? Have not twenty-first century humans evolved to such an extent that they are capable of living satisfactory lives without God? Are there not entire societies in which non-religious people live prosperous and contented lives? And are not these societies among the happiest and most loving earth, and blessed with the highest living standards? Perhaps religion has proved to be so divisive that people would be better off without it. Societies that dispense with deities may in the long run be more life-enriching than those devoted to invisible beings; and far from realizing the dire predictions of some religious leaders (moral decay, suffering, and despair), they might actually create healthier and more *civil* societies.

In this chapter I will examine the increasingly significant number of people across the world who find living without religion the new norm. The reasons for this phenomenon are varied but fall under two headings. For what may well be a majority of these, it represents a further step in the development of the human race that speculative beliefs have become redundant. They have grown up in societies where "being religious" is a minority concern and hearing the word "God" is not an everyday occurrence. The others have made a conscious decision to abandon the faith of their birth and to go it alone, "finding value and virtue in a godless universe."[4] To deny the existence of any god makes more sense than believing in one:

> No myths need to be embraced for us to commune with
> the profundity of our circumstances. No personal God
> need be worshipped for us to live in awe at the beauty
> and immensity of creation. No tribal fictions need to

be rehearsed for us to realize, one fine day, that we do, in fact, love our neighbors, that our happiness is inextricable from their own, and that our interdependence demands that people everywhere be given the opportunity to flourish. The days of our religious identities are clearly numbered.[5]

In what follows, I will focus on these two categories of non-believers: those who live at ease in non-religious societies, and those who actively assert new meaning and value in life without God.

To begin with, where will we find societies in which God or gods are not worshipped, and religious beliefs receive no more than lip service?

The Least Religious
Societies on Earth?

In *Society without God* the American sociologist Phil Zuckerman presents an engaging and insightful account of how he spent fourteen months in Denmark and Sweden examining the *lack* of religious beliefs in these countries. Prior to his sojourn in Scandinavia he had been confronted by the assertion that "without religion, society is doomed"—a mantra issuing not only from such "right-wing" conservatives in the United States as Pat Robertson and the Christian Coalition, but even liberal theologians like ex-Oxford University Professor Keith Ward, whose pronouncements can seem equally procrustean:

> Societies that lack strong religious beliefs are essentially immoral, un-free and irrational (and) . . . any nonreligious society without a strong belief in God is a society "beyond morality and freedom" and ultimately predicated upon "the denial of human dignity."[6]

Zuckerman's experience of non-religious society in Denmark and Sweden reveals just how wide of the mark this claim is. Indeed, he notes that far from imposing lack of belief on their citizens (as, for example, in avowedly atheistic countries like North Korea), these countries are free democracies that permit a wide variety of religious observances. Zuckerman's research revealed that most people "stopped being religious **of their own volition.**"[7] Able and content to find meaning in life without supernatural sanctions, people simply abandoned traditional religious paths. This lack of religious belief did not lead to moral decay, anarchy, hedonism, or the dissolution of society. Indeed, the opposite seems to be the case, with Denmark and Sweden scoring exceptionally well on indicators of societal health. Predictably enough, their citizens are among the most contented on the planet: they enjoy excellent health care, high life-expectancy, exceptionally low infant mortality rates, good gender equality, extremely little political corruption, and low crime and suicide rates.

> In sum, when it comes to the *overall quality of life*, according to *The Economist's* Quality of Life Index, which measures 111 nations as to which are the "best" places to live in the world, taking into consideration multiple factors, such as income, health, freedom, unemployment, family life, climate, political stability, life satisfaction, gender equality, etc., Sweden ranked fifth in the world, and Denmark ranked ninth.[8]

Zuckerman's research led him to a conclusion quite the opposite of what theologians had assumed. In short, empirical support for the impending decay of non-religious societies was not to be found, and the evidence suggests that the less religious a nation is the healthier and more successful it becomes. Indeed, the top twenty nations show a high correlation between quality of life and secularity.

Zuckerman's analysis of non-religious Sweden and Denmark also highlighted two important issues that have been overlooked by most religious commentators. First, the recent resurgence of Islam has persuaded many that religious affiliation is once again on the increase, but Zuckerman astutely notes that worldwide the greatest growth is in those who are nonbelievers. He estimates that their some 500 to 750 million makes them the fourth largest grouping, exceeding by far Buddhism, Sikhism, and Judaism.[9] This perhaps counterintuitive but important attestation once again reveals the extent to which non-belief is far more common than is usually acknowledged. Second, and surely germane to these statistics, is Zuckerman's observation that both Sweden and Denmark are still classed as "Christian" countries. Both embraced Christianity in the 800s, and in the 1500s the Lutheran Church. This is still the national church of Denmark, to which nearly all of its citizens unhesitatingly pay the church tax each year and avail themselves of the Church's rites of baptism, confirmation and marriage. And yet, most believe neither in its creeds nor in the existence of its God. Zuckerman muses that this is similar to his own experience of growing up as a Jew:

> While living among Scandinavians, I was struck by the fact that Danes and Swedes were also, like many Jews, taught about the biblical stories as children, they learned religious songs and hymns, celebrated various religious holidays with their families, and they nearly all had Christian socialization experiences, most commonly in the form of confirmation classes. And yet, while the vast majority of Danes and Swedes that I interviewed had generally fond feelings about these ostensibly religious experiences, like the Jews I grew up with, hardly any of them believed in the basic theological content.[10]

So what went awry? Why has belief in God almost died out in the former heartland of the Reformation? How might

we explain that the majority of Scandinavians nominally belong to the Church but have abjured Christianity?

Jesus: A Utopian Teacher of Ethical Wisdom

At this point, it is interesting to note how the insights of
theologians Don Cupitt and Lloyd Geering can be seen to
correlate with Zuckerman's sociological analysis. For a long
time now, Geering and Cupitt have argued that Christianity
can survive without being wedded to a traditional doctrine
of God.[11] Christianity, which comprises much more than a
set of beliefs in a supernatural God, contains a number of
humanistic ideals. To be sure, these flowered most notice-
ably during the Renaissance and the Enlightenment when the
focus of western culture shifted from an otherworldly realm
to establishing a just kingdom here on earth; but Geering
and Cupitt go a major step further to argue that the seeds
of humanism lie *within Christianity itself*, especially in the
life and teaching of its founder. For them and for an increasing number of Christians, Jesus is not the divine figure promulgated by the Church, but a radical, humanistic, secular
figure. In particular, they have accepted the groundbreaking
research and conclusions of the Jesus Seminar concerning the
historical Jesus.

In its search for the historical Jesus this convocation of
New Testament scholars, founded in 1985 by the late Robert
W. Funk and now based in Oregon,[12] abandoned the prevailing paradigm famously proposed by Albert Schweitzer in
1905 in *The Quest of the Historical Jesus*. Building on the
work of Johannes Weiss (1863–1914), Schweitzer concluded
that Jesus was an apocalyptic extremist who preached the
imminent end of the world (Mark 9:1; Matt. 16:28; Luke
9:27; Mark 13:30; Luke 21:32, Matt. 24:34). He sent out
his twelve disciples to disseminate this message convinced
that they would not return before the end of history (Matt.

10:23). When the twelve did return Jesus modified his ideas seeing himself as the suffering servant proclaimed by the Old Testament prophet Isaiah. According to Schweitzer, Jesus willingly went to the cross in order to force God to vindicate him by ushering in the end times and sending him back as "the Son of Man" to immediately judge the world.

Schweitzer's Jesus was obviously mistaken: the end of the world did not follow upon his death or even soon thereafter—and this despite Saint Paul's claim that he would see "the Lord descend from heaven"; and that together with the faithful he would be taken up to "meet the Lord in the air" (1 Thess. 4:16–17). Conservative Christian theologians have remolded Schweitzer's portrait of Jesus in an attempt to argue that the New Testament's eschatological prophecies of "the end times" were fulfilled in the generation who were alive when Jesus preached. Thus the scholar N. T. Wright argues that Schweitzer misread the judgment that Jesus threatened. He agrees with Schweitzer that Jesus warned of imminent destruction, but contends that the destruction threatened was not the impending desolation of the planet or the entire cosmos, but an event in Jewish history that would be visited on that generation. In Wright's view, Jesus was employing apocalyptic imagery from the Old Testament to warn the Jews of a shake-up of their symbolic worldview—a paradigm shift involving the destruction of the Temple, the chastisement of the Jewish people, and the vindication of Jesus and his followers.[13] He proposes that when Christ warned in his parables and in the Olivet discourse (Matthew 24, Mark 13, and Luke 21) about approaching doom within a generation, he was not announcing the end of the world as we know it, but anticipating the desolation of Jerusalem and the razing of the Jewish Temple, events that occurred in 70 CE.[14]

This viewpoint that places *either* some *or* all eschatological events in the past, especially during the destruction of Jerusalem in 70 CE, is known as *preterism*.[15] The situation

becomes complicated with the distinction commonly made
by theologians between partial and full (hyper) *preterism*.
Partial *preterism*, the more orthodox Christian viewpoint,
states that *some* eschatological prophecy was fulfilled in the
generation following Jesus' crucifixion. Full *preterism*, on the
other hand, assigns to that period the fulfillment of *all* eschatological prophecy, and thus proposes that three of the main
tenets found in mainstream Christianity—the return of Jesus
(the Second Coming), the resurrection of believers, and the
day of judgment for the wicked (the Rapture)—**all occurred
in 70 CE**. Partial *preterism*, which takes into account the
creedal affirmation that "Christ will come again," holds that
judgment came with the destruction of the Jewish Temple in
Jerusalem in 70 CE, but that it was *a* day of the Lord not *the*
day of the Lord. In this view, no one knows when *the* day of
Lord might be, but Christians are to remain expectant for the
return of Jesus (the Son of Man) at the Second Coming and
await his advent with great anticipation.[16]

The Fellows of the Jesus Seminar unequivocally refused
to accept any portrait of an apocalyptic Jesus, whether it
entail partial or full *preterism*. On the contrary, for them the
key to discovering the historical Jesus lay not in apocalyptic
literature but in the parables, aphorisms, and wisdom sayings found throughout the New Testament and in the Gospel
of Thomas.[17] Jesus was not an eschatological prophet but a
utopian teacher of ethical wisdom:

> We (the Jesus Seminar) found very few examples of
> genuine parables in contemporary literature, and we
> observed that they are very difficult to imitate. That is
> not a residue of the Christian assertion that Jesus was a
> god/man; it is no more than the recognition of Jesus as a
> wisdom teacher of considerable rhetorical power. . . . He
> seems to have looked beyond tribalism, ethnic privilege,
> and nationalism. His concern for the birds and flowers
> may even have foreseen that God's domain was trans-

human. He certainly thought the kingdom was trans-
religious. . . . The importance of these discoveries can
scarcely be exaggerated. It enabled us to finally divorce
Jesus from his mentor, John the Baptist, and from the
early Jesus movement fueled by former followers of John.
Jesus was free at last.[18]

The portrait of Jesus presented by the Jesus Seminar was
that of a wandering oral Jewish sage who proclaimed a
message of universal love and a kingdom that had already
dawned. The time to celebrate was *now*, not in some hypothetical future kingdom after death. In his creation of
a fully inclusive community that welcomed the outsider
and outcast, Jesus showed himself a humanitarian. A new
kingdom was to be established here on earth in which "the
hungry will be fed," "the last shall be first," and we are all
to "love our enemies." In short, Jesus was seen as a visionary
prophet who preached good news about the transformation
of people and this world.[19] It was revolutionary teaching
that according to one of the co-chairs in the Jesus Seminar,
John Dominic Crossan, offers "glimpses of an inspirational
but unattainable alternative world."[20] Indeed, in Crossan's
view, Jesus was:

> a Mediterranean Jewish peasant. He revolted, not in
> violence but in offering a vision of a different way of liv-
> ing, where there would be no elite and no underclass, no
> master and no servant, no conqueror and no conquered,
> no clean and no unclean; a way of living where all
> would be shared among equals. He drew on a tradition
> of prophetic language to call this new way of living the
> "kingdom of God" or "kingdom of heaven," a kingdom
> of peace which he boldly offered as an alternative to
> the empire of Rome and its peace by force. He not only
> preached and practiced this way of life, he offered a so-
> cial program for its realization. So he was executed. But

you can nail a body to a wooden post: you cannot so easily extinguish an ecstatic vision and the program to which it gives concrete expression.[21]

Western Secular Society = Post-Christianity = Humanism

In *Jesus and Philosophy* (dedicated to the memory of Bob Funk) and *The Meaning of the West*, Cupitt adumbrates the full implications of the findings of the Jesus Seminar. If Jesus was a "secular moral teacher, an Eastern sage, a teacher of wisdom," whose central message of a new "kingdom" (sometimes translated: "realm" or "reign of God") aimed at the creation of a more just society and better relationships between people, then he would have been disturbed by Christianity's emergence as a religion focused primarily on creedal orthodoxy and the establishment of an institutional church.[22] Yet despite the historical events that early on distorted Jesus' original message and fashioned a "Church-Christianity" staffed by a self-perpetuating professional clergy (among whom Cupitt once counted himself), Jesus' message could not be forever obscured. After many centuries the prevailing Western culture to which Christianity gave rise discarded the supernatural doctrines and immersed itself in the "secular message" of Jesus. As Cupitt sees it, this culture owes everything to Jesus; indeed it is "Christianity objectified and secularized" and represents Christianity's final form as it shakes off supernaturalism and returns to what Jesus originally proclaimed—humanitarian ethics. In fact, he argues, the secular West is more Christian than Church Christianity, for it follows Jesus' teachings more faithfully than the Church, which remains fixated on its own survival.

Cupitt's thesis is that we should abandon Church Christianity and embrace secular (Western) culture. Cupitt admits that for many years he had tried to reconcile the

traditional Church with the modern world, but at last concluded the effort was futile because the Church is committed
to supernatural beliefs that cannot be squared with life in
the postmodern world. For those who have "eyes to see,"
the radical utopian message of the Jesus of Nazareth is in the
ethical humanitarianism and religious humanism of the secular West. Having discarded Church-Christianity, therefore,
we can still remain Christian (followers of Jesus) by fighting
for the core values of Western culture:

> Western culture today depends most of all upon the free
> critical style of thinking that continuously criticizes and
> seeks to reform everything including itself; and also upon
> a powerful tradition of thoroughgoing humanism which
> insistently reminds us that everything that we are and
> that we produce is "only human." This "humanism of
> weakness" makes our knowledge strong by insisting that
> it is always corrigible, and it makes our morality compas-
> sionate and humanitarian. Both in epistemology and in
> ethics, it brings strength out of weakness. Aesthetically,
> it leads us to love everything that is mutable, transient,
> "weak" and shimmering. We learn to live without eter-
> nity, without foundations, and without any kind of
> absolute knowledge or realty. Instead we are content to
> love life and to try to live it to the fullest, so that each of
> us may make our own small contribution to the human
> world as we pass away.[23]

Far from being the antithesis of faith, secularism has come
to be committed to an ethical humanitarianism that cares
for those in need solely on the basis of our co-humanity, and
regardless of race, color, gender, sexual orientation, doctrine,
or moral deserving. Not only organizations like the United
Nations and songs like John Lennon's *Imagine*, but all the
hard-won improvements in the physical and social well-being
of people everywhere point to the slow but gradual realiza-

tion of the kingdom *on earth*. And now we see the rest of the world calling on the West to live up to the high ethical standards it has long but imperfectly espoused.

The secular West is now post-Christian—or as Lloyd Geering expresses it, "the humanistic and secular world is to be seen as the legitimate product of the ever-evolving Christian culture of the West."[24] Church Christianity was never intended to be more than a temporary phenomenon, and with the advent of secular humanism it can give way to the Kingdom and let Christianity fulfill its original promise. Geering, whose position on these matters is much the same as that of Cupitt, puts the case this way: "out of the chrysalis of Christendom there is currently emerging a new kind of society—a global, humanistic and secular society." He too sees that the Church has become increasingly irrelevant as global, humanist, and tolerant secularism reframes the Christian message in the process of establishing a Kingdom of peace and justice irrespective of creed, ethnicity, and sexuality:

> Instead of continuing to walk the ever-changing path of faith from Abraham onwards, the churches have put their trust in idols that they have accumulated on the way and have become blind to the cultural situation that they have now entered. **This prevents them from seeing that the modern secular world, far from being the enemy of Christianity, is the legitimate continuation of the Judeo-Christian path of faith in the modern era.** The modern global and secular world has emerged out of Western Christendom; moreover, in doing so it has increasingly though yet incompletely manifested Christianity's central doctrine—the Incarnation, the enfleshment of "God" in the human condition. God has indeed come down to earth![25]

For Cupitt and Geering Jesus dies as a god and returns as a human teacher with a revolutionary Kingdom message that has already been adopted by the West. To echo another of Cupitt's books, "theology strangely returns" in secularism as "radical humanism" through the appropriation of Jesus' teachings:

> It is true that some kind of secular humanist outlook is inescapable today. My version of the doctrine is "Empty Radical humanism." But remember that according to both the Hebrew Bible *and* the New Testament human beings were created just for life on this earth, and the final consummation of religion will *also* be realized on this earth. To put it crudely, "secular" means "of this present world, or this present era," and secular humanism is a human-centered and purely this-worldly outlook. But according to the Bible Adam and Eve in paradise were secular humanists, God becoming man in Christ accepts secular humanity and its fate as his own, and the Kingdom of God on earth is a blessed future state of human *secular* existence. . . . *Even within a secular-humanist worldview*, Christianity may still be able to function as a religion of redemption.[26]

However unsettling this might be, this bold thesis makes sense of Zuckerman's observations in Europe. Cupitt and Geering would argue that what he experienced in Denmark and Sweden was non-realist Christianity. Its creeds were not to be taken literally but metaphorically; its spiritual ideals promoted an ethical, generous, and even sacrificial way of life. Religion was reduced to morality, and belief in God was replaced by humanitarianism. Godless morality was taking hold in Europe with remarkable results.[27]

Had Zuckerman been acquainted with Cupitt and Geering, his Chapter 8 ("Cultural Religion") might have expressed less bewilderment. As it is, he cannot account for what his evidence indicates: people living ostensibly religious lives without believing in God. And he discovers a similar phenomenon upon interviewing a number of Muslims, with three out of four of them "identifying as Muslims" but "rejecting supernatural beliefs of Islam." His recourse is to label these people "culturally religious," yet surely that masks a much more complex phenomenon that sociologists and theologians have barely begun to understand. Like all too many, he is excessively narrow in his insistence that for something to be deemed "religious," "there must be an element of supernatural, otherworldly or spiritual belief."[28] People and religious communities have moved on; many have come to agree with Cupitt that:

> Religion is primarily not about supernatural belief,
> but about hope. It is our communal way of generating
> dreams of how we and our life and our world might be
> made better. We prepare ourselves for the dream, and we
> start to think about how might actually start to make it
> all come true. . . . The so-called "decline of religion" is
> people's abandonment en masse of the kind of ecclesiasti-
> cal religion that promised comfort and reassurance in the
> face of death. Instead we should see religious thought and
> practice as imaginative and utopian. Religion is a com-
> munal way of reimagining and remaking the self and the
> world. It is what we are to live *by* and what we are to
> live *for*. [29]

Zuckerman's research shows that Cupitt and Geering's theological non-realism has found a home in Sweden and Denmark. People have discarded God and use the church sparingly. *However, many of them live in accordance with a non-supernatural, non-creedal humanism that has its origins in Christianity.* They have appropriated those teachings of Jesus that hold out the hope of new utopian realm where everyone is valued and humanitarian concerns are paramount; they have given up their old religion but gained a new one. And as for the actual number of "non-believers," Zuckerman concludes, "there are probably more than most people think" and "they are nearly always overlooked."[30] Indeed, it would be highly informative to find out exactly how many Westerners live in accordance with the ethics of Jesus but do not acknowledge his supernatural status. Are they in the majority, or have most of them moved beyond non-realism to be our second category of non-believers?

Individuals Who Have Lost Their Religion

At the same time as certain societies have become less religious, there has been a corresponding increase in *individuals* who have declared that they have "lost their religion" or "given up on religion." Moreover, they have not remained silent about this, but have put pen to paper boldly proclaiming that they can live comfortably without god and without any need for organized religion. Some have even established networks or institutes where others who have had similar experiences can find support.[31] In the following section I shall identify two "types" of individuals who have rejected religion: ex-believers (often former full-time ministers of religion) and "atheists making meaning." The first I would label polemical, in as much as their main line of attack is to provide devastating critiques of faith, evidence for debunking holy texts, and scholarly arguments against the existence of god. The second "type" takes the debate to a new level by elevating the aims of atheism from mere denial of the supernatural to ways for the non-religious to discover greater meaning in life.

Ex-Christian Believers

The most virulent attacks of religion have come from ex-Christians, and in particular those who were once its main protagonists: preachers and ministers of religion. Today a considerable body of literature is being produced by former Christians of every conceivable denomination who are now atheists. For the sake of brevity, I shall confine myself to two of the most outspoken and prolific writers who were both once Christian ministers of the most extreme persuasion—Dan Barker and John Loftus. Since both previously thundered their apology for Christianity from evangelical pulpits, and Loftus boasts academic credentials from one of the most conservative theological institutions, they aptly reflect the change that is taking place within Western culture as people renounce their religion.

Barker and Loftus spent a combined total of thirty-one years as ministers of the Christian Gospel in fundamentalist churches. They both acknowledge that it was a long, tortuous and painful struggle that led them from certainty in church doctrines and biblical inerrancy to the moment when they denied the Christian faith. It ruined both their marriages and caused family rifts. In both cases it was primarily a rational decision not to continue in Christian ministry. For Loftus it "required too much intellectual gerrymandering to believe"; for Barker it was the realization that he was "a biological organism in a natural environment, and that is all there is."[32] In short, it was the clash of faith with reason that led to their rejection of faith.[33] They concluded that Christianity was intellectually bankrupt; or, as Baker puts it, he "lost faith in faith":

> Beliefs that used to be so precious were melting away one by one. It was like peeling back the layers of an onion, eliminating the nonessential doctrines to see what was at the core, and I just kept peeling and peeling until there was nothing left. The line that I was drawing under essential doctrines kept rising until it popped right off the top of the list. I threw out all the bath water and discovered that there was no baby there.[34]

What, then, are the main reasons for this loss of faith by Christians? What makes those who were once "on fire for the Lord" strive with equal zeal to convert others to their newfound disbelief and to promote freedom from religion?

In the writings of Loftus and Barker we find five clear reasons.

1. Loss of faith in the Bible

This is perhaps the most personally distressing yet most crucial reason for loss of faith. One of the linchpins of fundamentalist Christianity is the inerrancy of Holy Scripture. When belief that the Bible is the inspired Word of God is undermined by the recognition that it contains numerous discrepancies, then the fundamentalist house of cards comes crashing down. Barker relates that as a fundamentalist minister he was astonished to learn that a Baptist pastor at whose church he was going to speak admitted that some of his congregation did not believe in the historicity of Adam and Eve. Barker considered this liberal attitude to be the first step on the slippery slope to perdition. Admitting the existence of metaphor or myth in the Bible must inevitably lead to unbelief.[35]

Loftus, who spent years at the conservative Trinity Evangelical Divinity School, Illinois, immersing himself in the Bible, concurs. He confesses that once familiar stories came to appear "strange" and "superstitious":

> We find a world where a snake and a donkey talked,
> where giants lived in the land, where people could live
> to be nine-hundred-plus years old, where a woman was
> turned into a pillar of salt, where a pillar of fire could
> lead people by night, where the sun stopped moving
> across the sky or could even back up, where an axe head
> could float on water, where a star could point down to a
> specific home, where people could instantly speak in un-
> learned foreign languages, and where someone's shadow

or handkerchief could heal people. It is a world where
a flood could cover the whole earth, and where a man
could walk on water, calm a stormy sea, change water
into wine, or be swallowed by a "great fish" and live to
tell about it.[36]

This discord between the ancient and modern worlds at
last required Barker and Loftus to reject the literalist understanding of the Bible, and when it thereby lost its presup-
posed authority and integrity, they saw it for what it clearly
is: a human-made anthology written by dozens of authors
with diverse agendas. Whilst the liberal Christian has some
critical thinking "tools" to cope with these inconsistencies,
the conservative fundamentalist is not prepared to deal with
the realization that the Bible contains facts and assumptions that are incomprehensible to a person with a modern
worldview. The resulting cognitive dissonance often leads to
unbelief. And this nexus leads to the second reason for loss
of faith—the modern scientific worldview.

2. Scientific evidence

Since I outlined the rise of the modern scientific worldview
earlier in this book, this section will be very brief. Suffice it
to say that the scientific establishment has now taken the
fight to the creationists and the Genesis account of creation
cannot be squared with modern knowledge of the universe.
Besides, creationists themselves are split between a "young
earth" wing who believe that the world was created less than
ten thousand years ago and those who admit to a much longer time-frame. The *only* honest road left for theologians is
that expressed by Christian scientists such as Francis Collins
who argues that the Universe was created through the Big
Bang; that life on earth was created through evolution, and
that the Genesis account is an ancient myth that points to supernatural activity at the Big Bang.[37] For Barker and Loftus

the addition of "God" to the Big Bang Bang Theory was an exercise in redundancy and they moved into non-belief.

3. Historical considerations

The historical argument against Christianity has recently taken a new direction, with some scholars now proposing that Jesus was not an historical figure. This notion was especially championed by the members of now defunct *The Jesus Project* who have reprised earlier works by John Allegro and G. A. Wells to argue that Jesus was a literary creation based on the figure of the Teacher of Righteousness found in the now famous Essene writings known as the Dead Sea Scrolls.[38] *The Jesus Project* should **not** be confused with *The Jesus Seminar*. The latter's members consider Jesus an historical figure and I have shown earlier sought to separate the mythical Christ from the Jesus of history. On the other hand, *The Jesus Project* regarded Jesus as pure myth and fiction with no basis in history.

Labeled "mythicists," these *Jesus Project* scholars asserted that the Jesus of the earliest Christians, far from being based on an historical person, was rather a purely mythical character derived from mystical elements of the Jewish Wisdom tradition. They viewed the Gospels as a later stage of the development of the Jesus myth, in which a concrete historical setting was embellished with more and more details. And predictably enough they pointed to the paucity of corroboration that the Gospels find in non-polemical historical sources.

Barker following the lead of the mythicists asserts that "the Jesus story is a combination of myth and legend, mixed with a little bit of real history *unrelated* to Jesus."[39] In like manner, the resurrection and other reported miracles are taken to be not historical events, but literary devices to give the story credibility and thus perpetuate it. In short, Christianity is a Jesus myth with no historical basis that evolved into a cult.

4. Our multi-religious world

One of the most common explanations of the loss of faith is the impact of the plurality of world religions and spiritualities. With such a smorgasbord of religious options in our world, why should one suppose *any* of them to be true? Nor can those who cling to the churches explain why Christianity is more appealing than other religions. Indeed, as Barker reflects while on a visit to Brazil, people might just be better off without religion:

> Although 90 percent of the population claims to be Catholic, in reality most of the people practice a syncretism of Afro-Brazilian religions mixed with Christianity, plus Pentecostalism, Islam, Buddhism, Hare Krishna and dozens of other faiths. They don't need any more missionaries. They need freethought. They need fair economic opportunities. I noticed that although many Brazilians struggle to put milk on the table, they all seemed to have enough money for Carnival, the lottery, beer and church. . . . Getting rid of the church would give everyone a 10 percent raise, for starters.[40]

The prevalence of religions and spiritualities—to say nothing of the constant increase in new manifestations—reveals that religion is a human creation. Throughout the ages societies have created their gods using the thought forms of their particular times and cultures—from ancient animist gods and spirits to the likes of Thor and Apollo and on to the ineffable abstraction of the Trinity. Once we recognize that religion is humanly created, it is but a small step to admit that God too might be an invention of the human imagination. Having conceded that one born in Iran would likely be a follower of Islam and a Midwestern American a Christian, one is obliged to recognize the regionalization of gods, and "God" becomes both a human and a *local* construction.

5. "Life" is the new religious object.

This thesis was first proposed in 1999 by Don Cupitt in his ground-breaking book, *The New Religion of Life in Everyday Speech.* Following the philosopher Ludwig Wittgenstein, Cupitt proposes a novel, empirical method that has far-reaching implications for both the study of academic theology and the religious thought of the future. Instead of looking back to the "classic" texts and authoritative figures, he argues that the theologian must attend closely to the way language is changing, and the direction in which the Zeitgeist (spirit of the times) is moving. This necessity has been forced on theologians because religious language is nowadays scattered throughout reports of ordinary experience. To find out what people believe we should take note of the way changes in language reflect their primary concerns.

Cupitt collects more than one hundred and fifty phrases ("ordinary English idioms") that contain the word "life," and that capture the philosophy of life encoded into common speech during the last few years of the twentieth century. These life-idioms connect with his radical doctrine that the objective God is now dead, having been replaced with a new religious object—"life." Democratic philosophy, following Wittgenstein's later emphasis on ordinary language, turns out to be the best evidence available to the radical theologian.

Rather than adopt the oft-quoted view that there has been a steady secularization of religion, Cupitt offers a different interpretation: what has happened is the *sacralization* of Life. Despite frantic and often violent efforts by religious fundamentalists, our religious vocabulary—the words we use to express our ultimate concerns—has shifted from God-centered to Life-centered.

This is clear, for example, in the subtle changes that have taken place in Western Christian funeral services. The new emphasis on *this life* has transformed the way that many

Christian clergy conduct funerals, as evidenced by the common practice of replacing "funeral" with "memorial service," retitling the celebration "Thanksgiving for the life of, . . ." and replacing the sermon with a eulogy by a friend or relative that focuses on the "life" of the deceased rather than a hypothetical future. No longer does the clergyperson preach to the bereaved family concerning the "miseries of this sinful world" and commend the soul of the deceased to God's everlasting arms, but his/her role is that of an "officiant" or "celebrant." In Western countries the distinction between religious and non-religious funerals has become increasingly blurred, with many families choosing civil or other non-religious celebrants to conduct funerals services for their loved ones. The long and short of it, Cupitt contends, is that for most people "life" has taken on most if not all the attributes of the "lost God," and is revered or even worshipped in much the same way.

This insight comports with the position of Barker and Loftus, both of whom admit that without religion "the value of life is enhanced." The knowledge that we are going to die one day will then lead not to anarchy, but to responsible living. In fact, belief in an afterlife often keeps people from a full enjoyment of life in the here and now. It is beyond doubt that many in the Western world now agree that life is the new religious object, and equally clear that they wish "to get the most out of life while they can." That does not mean that life should be a thoughtless or reckless pursuit of selfish and hedonistic goals, but rather a committed attempt to find meaning in who and what we become:

> There is no purpose of life. Life is its own reward. But as long as there are problems to solve, there will be purpose *in* life. When there is hunger to lessen, illness to cure, pain to minimize, inequality to eradicate, oppression to resist, knowledge to gain and beauty to create, there is

meaning in life. A college student once asked Carl Sagan; "What meaning is left, if everything I have been taught since I was a child turns out to be untrue?" Carl looked at him and said, "Do something meaningful."[41]

Conclusion

In this chapter I have argued that many people today have rejected religion and are extremely comfortable spending their lives without belonging to a religious organization or identifying themselves by using a religious label. Sociological evidence from Scandinavia has pointed towards a new model; no longer can humankind be glibly described as *homo religiosus*.

More and more, people of the West are voluntarily discarding religion, preferring to be known as "non-religious," and openly declaring it on their census forms. Some still cling to religious practices for cultural or aesthetic reasons, but they may well reject all supernatural claims. Such nominal or cultural Christians have much in common with the non-realist ideas expressed by Geering and Cupitt. They have translated ancient beliefs into ethical living, and live religiously but godlessly. They practice a non-creedal humanism that has its origins in Christianity. That is one of the reasons why, for example, Christmas carol services are still popular and remain a feature of postmodern festivals in highly secularized countries. The sentiments are highly humanistic and universal— "good will to all" with central themes of love, joy, and peace. Traditional Christianity is no more than the historic-cultural tradition from which these ideals have emerged.

On the other hand, a growing number have abandoned any pretence of religious belief and judge it to be redundant. They consider that "life" rather than God is their major concern. For them life has replaced God as the locus of the holy. Most noteworthy of all is that far from collapsing or falling into moral decay, non-religious societies score the highest on socio-economic indicators that place them among the most contented people on the planet.

Furthermore, the demographic showing the greatest increase is that of non-religious people, who now comprise roughly 20 percent of Western populations. This staggering statistic points to a rapidly disappearing Christian populace. Some of these were formerly strident believers (including full-time ministers) who have swapped sides and are openly hostile to religion and campaign against it. They argue that atheism more than religion enhances life and that the former doctrines can be reworked to fit in with prevailing scientific theories:

> As an atheist, I actually think that there is an afterlife, and it lasts exactly as long as my own life, and I am living it right now. During my "previous life," beginning on that deserted beach in Santa Monica just before my mother's egg was fertilized, I was merely one of many sperm, all striving to reach the goal. Millions of my potential brothers and sisters were swimming and fighting, directed by an inner drive to survive that was no less eager than mine, with no less potential for a future existence. But out of those countless throngs of little bodies who strove for the prize, I am the one that made it. I reached the goal, the "afterlife" of the egg. My body, the sperm, died and disappeared, and only the information in the little packet of DNA "passed on" to "the other side" and was united with my maker. I got to live on, and the others did not. I got to develop and be born and to walk and go to school and take piano lessons and taste chocolate. I get to die. Many are called but few are chosen.[42]

If it is accepted that the non-religious option is now deeply embedded in Western countries, what is the future for religion? Religion has not given up on people, but maybe people are giving up on religion. As I have often noted in this book, religion is under attack from many different quarters, and in the last few decades a seismic shift can be seen in people's attitude towards religions, their clergies, and even their followers. No longer is automatic deference accorded to religious leaders and other people's creeds and practices; many are now prepared to question their validity and value.

We have now reached the point in this book when some hard questions must be addressed: How can one defend religion from sustained attacks on a broad front? What continuing importance—if any—can religion claim? Even more important, perhaps, what kind of religion can be expected to survive? In the next chapter, I will attempt to show that it is still possible to be religious without reverting to fundamentalism, and that a coherent faith can stand up to the criticisms that have been aired in the previous chapters.

Notes

1. Title of two different books by American, William Lobdell and Australian, Tom Frame. These are discussed in chapter 7. "Losing my religion" is also the title of a popular song by the American rock group R.E.M. in which the title phrase is a southern expression that means "losing one's temper or civility" or "being at the end of one's rope." The song explores romantic expressions and tells about "someone who pines for someone else."

2. Otto, *The Idea of the Holy*; Eliade, *The Sacred and the Profane*. Karen Armstrong makes the same point in chapter 1 of *The Case for God* which is called: "Homo Religiosus."

3. Nietzsche, *The Joyous Science* (my italics).

4. Book title by Erik Wielenberg.

5. Harris, *The End of Faith*, 227.

6. Zuckerman, *Society without God*, 20.

7. Zuckerman, *Society without God*, 23 (my bold).

8. Zuckerman, *Society without God*, 29.

9. According to Zuckerman (p. 96), Christianity has 2 billion followers, Islam 1.2 billion and Hinduism 900 million. Of course this does not take into account those who might say they belong to

a particular faith but do not practice it or who are only nominally Christians, Muslims, Hindus, etc.

10. Zuckerman, *Society without God*, 152.

11. See, Geering, *God in the New World* (1968) and *Faith's New Age* (1980) and Cupitt, *The World to Come* (1982). Cupitt's *Taking Leave of God* (1980) does **not**, despite the title of the book, adopt a non-realist position: see Leaves, *Odyssey on the Sea of Faith*, 27–33.

12. In 2009 The Jesus Seminar relocated from Santa Rosa, California to Willamette University in Salem, Oregon.

13. Unfortunately, Wright's argument leads him to endorsing the traditional Christian view that the Jews were guilty of Jesus' death and as such deserved the punishment that came in 70 CE with the destruction of Jerusalem and the Temple by the Romans (Matthew 27:25). This raises two intriguing points. First, Titus and the Roman army would appear to be the Christian God's agents sent to eliminate the Jews. Second, anti-Semitic viewpoints are extremely dangerous, since they can lead to such abominations as Adolf Hitler's infamous 1938 declaration: "I believe I am acting in the service of the Almighty creator. By warding off the Jews I am fighting for the Lord's work." (Shirer, *The Rise and Fall of the Third Reich*, 153.)

14. Much depends on what one considers the length of a generation. If Jesus died circa 30 CE and a generation is accepted as twenty years then to claim that the judgment took place in 70 CE is problematic. However, if dating begins with the ministry of Paul (40–45 CE), then 70 CE might just fit. Christian theologians using proof-texts like Numbers 14:34 and Psalm 95:10 argue that a "Biblical generation" is forty years and this time-scale is what Jesus would have meant. However dubious this presupposition is, it neatly renders his predictions extremely accurate! But still the question remains: "Why would God want to punish the Jews?"(See, note 13 above.)

15. Sproul, *The Last Days According to Jesus*, 228.

16. Partial *preterism* is defended by R.C Sproul and N.T. Wright. Full (or hyper) *preterism* (also known as covenant eschatology) was begun in the 1970s by Max King, a Church of Christ minister—see *The Spirit of Prophecy* (1971). In the 1990s Virgil Vaduva popularized it by aligning it with the postmodern Emergent Church movement emphasizing universalism ("comprehensive grace"), for if the final judgment had occurred in 70 CE, then all were not condemned, but saved. For more on Virgil Vaduva see www.unfinishedchristianity.com. *Hyperpreterism* groups have split in recent years and exhibit a wide variety of teachings.

17. The Jesus Seminar rejected the 'fixed' canon of the New Testament, widening their terms of reference to include the sayings

source 'Q' and the Gospel of Thomas.

18. Funk, "A Faith for the Future," in *The Once and Future Faith*, 7–8 (my bold). For a detailed discussion of whether Jesus was an apocalyptic or wisdom teacher see Miller (ed.), *The Apocalyptic Jesus*.

19. See Funk, *A Credible Jesus*.

20. Boulton, *Who on Earth was Jesus?*, 210.

21. Boulton, *Who on Earth was Jesus?*, 220.

22. Cupitt, *Jesus and Philosophy*, xiii.

23. Cupitt, *The Meaning of the West*, 148–49.

24. Geering, *Fundamentalism*, 27.

25. Geering, *Coming Back to Earth*, vii (my bold).

26. Cupitt, *Theology's Strange Return*, 79–80. See also chaps. 10 and 15.

27. Richard Holloway also predicts this shift of emphasis in his aptly named book, *Godless Morality*.

28. Zuckerman, *Society without God,* 154.

29. Don Cupitt, "Christianity after the Church," 11. Unpublished paper presented at UK SOF Conference 2000.

30. Zuckerman, *Society without God,* 166.

31. See Barker, *Godless*, chap. 18. Websites that are committed to helping people recover from their religious past include losingmyreligion.com; the secular web at http://www.infidels.org/ and freedom from religion: http://www.ffrf.org. See also Loftus' blogspot: http://debunkingchristianity.blogspot.com.

32. Loftus, *Why I became an Atheist*, 27. Barker, *Godless*, 42.

33. For a more positive reconciliation of personal belief with scholarship see Hedrick (ed.), *When Faith Meets Reason*. Thirteen scholars write candidly about how they negotiate the conflicting claims of faith and reason.

34. Barker, *Godless*, 40.

35. Barker, *Godless*, 33–34.

36. Loftus, *Why I became an Atheist*, 124.

37. See Collins, *The Language of God*.

38. Allegro was vilified for his views, especially after his most controversial book, *The Sacred Mushroom and the Cross*, in which he argued that the Jesus myth was created by a secret Jewish mushroom cult. Wells has written a series of books disputing Jesus' existence, although his latest writing concedes that the community responsible for the hypothetical document known as 'Q' *might* point towards an historical itinerant preacher called Jesus. However, there is little that can be accurately known about him. For an excellent summary of Wells' work see Boulton, *Who on Earth was Jesus?*, 347–50. *The*

Jesus Project disbanded in 2009 after disagreement amongst its scholars and withdrawal of funding. For more information see R. Joseph Hoffmann, "Quodlibet: The Jesus Project," April 25, 2009. http://rjosephhoffmann.wordpress.com.

39. Barker, *Godless*, 251.
40. Barker, *Godless*, 320.
41. Barker, *Godless*, 345.
42. Barker, *Godless*, 344.

Chapter 7

Saving Religion
from Itself:
Theology!

Religion Must Change or Die

After reading my earlier book, *The God Problem*, a high-ranking Anglican cleric opined that surely I had forgotten to include a final chapter. He urged me to explain how the understandings of God outlined in my book would be consistent with the faith received and transmitted by Christianity (or in this case through the historic formularies of the Anglican Church). I came closest to satisfying his request by arguing in *When Faith Meets Reason* that Anglicanism as a faith was evolving and continually responding to the countless different contexts and cultural situations in which it found itself:

> I choose to . . . pursue the . . . Anglican vision that first
> inspired me all those years ago and nourished me through
> university studies and along the path to ordination. I look
> to the time when the church becomes a beacon leading
> to a fully inclusive and transformed humanity in which
> "the creed and the color and the name won't matter." I

am happy to play in my writing the role of theological gadfly, to be the one who challenges the church to make the necessary changes in its thinking to the disputations thrown up by the latest scientific and intellectual discourse. Indeed, my own Anglican theological training was one that urged us relentlessly to plumb the depths of not only ourselves but also our scriptures and traditions. I am in so many ways a true product of the Anglican system and its theological methodology. Theological investigation *is* expected to be a life-long passion. Faith *is* an ever-evolving process that shall never end for as T. S. Eliot put it in his poem "Little Gidding," "we shall not cease from exploration." It is only by so doing that the church will become the fully inclusive kingdom that Jesus preached.[1]

My words were a heartfelt plea to my fellow Anglicans to view their religion as dynamic and open to change. For me, it is a vibrant faith, evolutionary in content, and continually changing as it proclaims afresh to each succeeding generation its encounter with the deepest of mysteries—God—and the historical person of Jesus of Nazareth. Thus I would contend that today "it is (still) possible to be Christian and post-modern, to be a member of a church and a supporter of feminism and the rights of sexual minorities, in spite of the witness of Christian tradition."[2] I position myself in the line of seminal Anglicans like John A. T. Robinson, Marcus Borg, John Shelby Spong, Desmond Tutu, Gene Robinson, Richard Holloway et al. for whom "Christianity must change or die." The key to Christianity's future lies in its adaptability and its response to the questions raised by the preceding chapters. But mine is obviously not the sole interpretation of Anglicanism: other competing strands of the tradition continue to jostle for control of the hearts and minds of the faithful. And what is true about Anglicanism is true of all religions: there are many versions of the faiths that jostle to be heard. So, how do we discriminate between them?

Theology—The Key
to a New Religious Attitude

In this chapter I propose a novel approach to the defense of *any* religion. It is startlingly simple and yet it goes to the heart of the crisis that I have diagnosed in this book. Simply put: we must make a *theological* response to the attacks on religion. Indeed, like Scott Cowdell, I want to assert that "all our failings in the church are theological."[3] My mantra is: **your theology will determine your response.**

In short, I return once again to the God problem! Your characterization of the Deity, what you mean by the word "God," will in large measure determine how conservative, liberal, or radical is your religion. Your understanding of God will dictate how far along the exclusivist—inclusivist continuum you will go. If your understanding of God is similar to the categories that I outlined in *The God Problem* then your religion will tend towards the inclusivist. Indeed, you will probably use the words spirituality and religion interchangeably, welcoming everyone, as in Taussig's *A New Spiritual Home*, to explore a common spiritual journey with like-minded fellow sojourners in an "open" community of faith. If your idea of God is more conservative, your religion will tend towards the exclusivist end of the continuum, regulated by dogmas and creeds that are fixed for all time, eternal verities that are not subject to the vagaries of the historical process. Such a religion is marked by belief *in* immoveable "fundamentals of faith."[4]

The Emerging/Emergent Church

This theological division between conservative and progressive can be neatly illustrated by reference to the new movements within Christianity called the "emerging" and "emergent" church. The term "emergent church" was popularized in the 1980s by the Roman Catholic theologian, Johann

Baptist Metz. He adopted the idea inherent in liberation theology that the next type of church would not emerge from its traditional middle-class base, but would grow from the "grassroots." The new church would be based on the principles of "right practice" (orthopraxis) rather than "right belief" (orthodoxy). The emergent church would be committed to social and political justice and to the founding of a new world order based on the gospel imperative to establish the reign (kingdom) of God and equity for all.

At the same time as the growing call for an "emergent church" was being heard in some quarters, others were proposing the idea of "the emerging church." To describe it briefly, this was a response to the challenge that the churches faced as they came to grips with what it meant "to be the Church in postmodernity." When the prevailing Western culture no longer acknowledged the primacy of the Christian religion and had moved from Christendom to post-Christendom, how should the churches react? How could you create Christian community in postmodern cultures where church attendance was in decline and the newer generations, known as "X" (born between 1965–1977) and "Y" (born between 1978–1994), no longer subscribed to the same beliefs as their parents?

The churches were now in a new phase of mission, trying to attract converts not as previously on "the mission-fields" abroad, but on their very doorstep and in Western lands. Books with intriguing titles such as *ChurchNext*, *The Post-Evangelical* and *The Missionary Congregation* began to appear together with the announcement of new creative liturgies and worship-services with unorthodox names like "Nine O'Clock" and "Warehouse." Church communities were renamed with designations such as "Sublime," "Cutting Edge," "Revelation," "Visions," "ReIMAGINE," "Graceland," "ikon," and "Resonance." The emerging church was one that urged the faithful to find new ways of "being/doing church" and innovations such as "house church," "café/messy church," "Gen-X services," "Taizé-style worship" emerged. This was complemented with "out-reach" community projects that ranged from dance to popular music to befriending goths, punks, and those in marginal sub-cultures. The buzz-words were "conversation," "fresh expressions," and "transforming secular space" to emphasize the decentralized and evolving nature of the church. The title of an emerging church-book, *They like Jesus but not the church* (2007), reflected the disillusionment felt by many for the institutional church and emphasized how they wished to deconstruct traditional liturgical formulations to accommodate more contemporary styles of worship. At the heart of the emerging church was developing new worship-services that would be more suitable for people in the late twentieth and early twenty-first centuries.

While it must be acknowledged that the emerging church exhibits many variations, it is best characterized by a desire to tinker with ecclesiastical structures but not with theology. For most within the emerging church the theologian *par excellence* is conservative N. T. Wright. In his book *Jesus and the Victory of God*, Wright proposed that Jesus announced that the longed-for kingdom of God was arriving. Despite the inferior situation of the Jews in the first-century Roman Empire, God had returned in Jesus the Jew, who had reinterpreted the Torah with a message that the Kingdom of God was here. The Messianic Age had dawned and everyone was to be involved with Jesus in bringing the good news of the kingdom to the world. To oppose this message was to be working against the will of God. Jesus had prayed to bring heaven to earth and this was now the task of the church:

> Rooted in the work of N. T. Wright emerging churches
> embrace the gospel of the kingdom as revealed in Mark
> 1:15–16. At the outset of the Gospel narrative, the good
> news was not that Jesus was to die on the cross to forgive

sins but that God had returned and all were invited to participate with him in this new way of life, in this re- demption of the world. It is this gospel that the emerging church seeks to recover. As one leader confided privately, "We have totally reprogrammed ourselves to recognize the good news as a means to an end—that the kingdom of God is here. We try to live into that reality and hope. We don't dismiss the cross: it is still a central part. But the good news is not that he has died but that the king- dom has come."[5]

This is clearly a move in the direction of what is known in theology as "realized eschatology"—that the anticipated last days ("the Day of the Lord") have become realized in the person and work of Jesus.[6] The task of the Christian is to make God's kingdom begun in the incarnation become a reality today. Emerging churches emphasize God's redemp- tion in Christ who inaugurated the kingdom of God; and the continuing salvation of the world by those who help establish that kingdom. The focus is Christ and there is no doubting their exclusivity in their devotion to Jesus. As one emerging minister succinctly puts it:

A group of people who are merely reading Jesus together as one among a range of possible sources of inspiration for a shared life (or a slice of it) [is] different **from a group of people trying to follow him as the Lord of their journey.**[7]

It is obvious that emerging churches are in this latter category. The God they worship is to be found *only* in the Christian tradition. In Jesus and in him alone, people can dis- cover an *invitation* to participate with God in the redemption of the world by building the kingdom that he founded. But God's purpose in sending Jesus was to save and transform the world; and therefore the church is not an immutable or sacred institution, but a means by which people might hear that message and act upon it. The new note that is sounded is that the structure of the church can change, new ways of "being the Church" can emerge, and novel Christian communities are being created.

On the other hand, the **emergent** church has no such qualms about radical theological reformulation. The key figure is Brian McLaren who was the founding pastor of Cedar Ridge Community church in Maryland. In his books McLaren rejects propositional theology based on creedal affirmations in favor of postmodern theology. This includes the postmodern notion of the "generous" encounter with the "Other," which is both God and "the stranger." This means, among other things, that evangelism becomes a conversation in which people explore together their respective faiths:

> To help Buddhists, Muslims, Christians and everyone else experience life to the full in the way of Jesus (while learning it better myself), I would gladly become one of them (whoever they are) to whatever degree I can, to embrace them, to join them, to enter into their world without judgment but with saving love as mine has been entered by the Lord.[8]

McLaren appropriates postmodern literary theory to Biblical hermeneutics. This leads him to a generosity towards sexual minorities and an outspoken advocacy in matters of social justice. He rejects the political conservatism of much of American (evangelical) Christianity and notes that much interpretation of the Biblical texts reveals more about the reader than the text itself. Thus, he rejects literalist readings of Christian doctrines such as hell:

> The language of hell, in my view like the language of Biblical prophecy in general, is not intended to provide literal or detailed fortune-telling or prognostication about the hereafter, nor is it intended to satisfy intellectual curi-

osity, but rather it is intended to motivate us in the here and now and to realize our ultimate accountability to a god of mercy and justice and in that light to rethink everything and seek first the kingdom and justice of God.[9]

For McLaren, the emergent church is both deeply committed to, and deeply critical of religion. After all, Jesus did not come to found the church, but to transform the earth and its people. Marcus Borg expresses the new theological paradigm being used in emergent theology this way:

> Being Christian is not about meeting requirements for a future belief in an afterlife, and not very much about believing. Rather the Christian life is about a relationship with God that transforms life in the present. To be Christian does not mean believing in Christianity, but a relationship with God lived within the Christian tradition as a metaphor and sacrament of the sacred.[10]

It is not surprising to learn that McLaren's emergent church has been attacked by the followers of the emerging church. It is highly significant that the major criticism has been *theological*. Especially problematic for the more conservative theologians of the emerging church, is the fact that McLaren replaces dogma with generosity and conversation. The most strident attack has come from the controversial Calvinist Mark Driscoll, pastor of a large emerging church in Seattle and also the "Acts 29 Network" that considers itself "emerging but not emergent." In an oft-quoted passage Driscoll uses flowery language to describe their differences:

> I eventually had to distance myself from the emergent stream of the network because friends like Brian McLaren and Doug Pagitt began pushing a **theological agenda** that greatly troubled me. Examples include referring to God as a chick, questioning God's sovereignty over and knowledge of the future, denial of the substitu-

tionary atonement of the cross, a low view of Scripture, and denial of hell.[11]

For Driscoll (and many others) McLaren has strayed too far towards the "inclusive" end of the continuum and has watered down the real Gospel to accommodate secularism and postmodern philosophy. Ironically, Driscoll himself is frequently attacked by conservative evangelicals for his own attachment to such trappings of the prevailing culture as rock music and alcohol, as well as his mocking portrait of their "feminine" Jesus to whom they sing prom songs: "a wuss who took a beating and spent a lot of time putting product in his long hair." Again the debate is theological: what kind of God does your religion promote?

That's Not My God!

This brief excursus into a recent trend in Christianity brings into stark relief the continuing debate raised by this book and the contemporary phenomenon of attacks on religion. Those who condemn religion usually do on theological grounds: "How can your God allow such suffering?" "How can your God permit you to undertake holy war?" "Where was your God when such a terrible atrocity occurred?" Richard Dawkins has waded into this debate mockingly supporting the American evangelist Pat Robertson labeling him "the true Christian" because of his assertion that the Haitian earthquake was the result of God's displeasure over a pact the Haitians made with Satan many years ago:

> We know what caused the catastrophe in Haiti. It was the bumping and grinding of the Caribbean Plate rubbing up against the North American Plate: a force of nature, sin-free and indifferent to sin, un-premeditated, unmotivated, supremely unconcerned with human affairs or human misery. The religious mind, however,

restlessly seeks human meaning in the blind happenings of nature. As with the Indonesian tsunami, which was blamed on loose sexual morals in tourist bars; as with Hurricane Katrina, which was attributed to divine revenge on the entire city of New Orleans for harboring a lesbian comedian, and as with other disasters going back to the famous Lisbon earthquake and beyond, so Haiti's tragedy must be payback for human sin. The Rev. Pat Robertson sees the hand of God in the earthquake, wreaking terrible retribution for a pact that the long-dead ancestors of today's Haitians made with the devil, to help rid them of their French masters. Needless to say, milder-mannered faith-heads are falling over themselves to disown Pat Robertson, just as they disowned those other pastors, evangelists, missionaries and mullahs at the time of the earlier disasters. What hypocrisy. Loathsome as Robertson's views undoubtedly are, he is the Christian who stands squarely in the Christian tradition. The agonized theodiceans who see suffering as an intractable "mystery," or who "see God" in the help, money and goodwill that is now flooding into Haiti, or (most nauseating of all) who claim to see God "suffering on the cross" in the ruins of Port-au-Prince, those faux-anguished hypocrites are denying the centerpiece of their own theology. It is the obnoxious Pat Robertson who is the true Christian here.[12]

Dawkins' attack on liberal Christians who repudiate Robertson's views point to the fact that **religion has an identity crisis**. The crux of the problem is that people who exclaim, "That's not my God!" are forensically obliged to provide an alternative theological perspective. But where is that alternative understanding of God to be heard? How often are new ideas of God promoted and debated—as, for example, in *The God Problem*? Dawkins is partly correct in caricaturing Robertson's view as that of "the true Christian" because unfortunately that particular God is very often the only one promulgated.

In an interesting twist in her thinking Ayaan Hirsi Ali argues in *Nomad* that liberal Christians might be an effective corrective to Muslim fundamentalism. Her reasoning is *theological*. In a stimulating chapter entitled: *Seeking God but finding Allah* she contends that most Muslims are seeking a redemptive God who is peaceful and compassionate. Unfortunately, they are presented with a vengeful, all-conquering, intemperate God. Simply put: "they do not know about *other concepts of God*, or *the concepts they do have are wrong.*"[13] She then takes up an idea I canvassed in *The God Problem* that there should be a coalition of liberal Christians, agnostics, critical thinkers and atheists to counter the rise of religious fundamentalism. Surprisingly, she also considers that liberal Christianity might be what Muslims are really looking for!

My caveats to Ali are twofold. First, she paints a rather rosy and over-generous picture of Christianity. It has been my argument in this book that Christianity too must address its own intolerant fundamentalist wing and propose a different image of God. Second, does not Islam have within its manifold traditions a more reasoned idea of God? Moreover, there are liberal Islamic scholars who would eagerly embrace the opportunity for reasoned debate on the nature and mystery of God. These need to be part of the coalition against fundamentalism. Thus, I would want to broaden Ali's horizons to include people of reasonable faith of *every* religious tradition. Fundamentalism is not restricted to Islam. Moreover, the persistence of "religion" in its various forms down through the ages suggests not only that it will survive in one form or another as long as humankind exists, but also that our continued existence may depend on getting it right. The major component of "getting it right" is theological.

Religion has become an easy target, for it has too often been hijacked by fundamentalist voices who dominate the media and heap abuse on fellow religionists and secularists alike. Moreover, even ostensibly liberal groups often root out or suppress the creative thinkers and writers *within* their own circles. The list of those who have been so denounced, for example, within Christianity because they dared to say "That's not my God!" is depressingly long and discouraging: it stretches from early church writers like the author of the Gospel of Thomas to New Testament scholars like David Strauss to latter-day prophets like John Shelby Spong and Robert Funk to troublesome modern-day priests like Peter Kennedy. At the root of this opposition, as Karen Armstrong explains, is fear:

> It is important to recognize that these theologies and ideologies are rooted in fear. The desire to define doctrines, erect barriers, establish borders, and separate the faithful in a sacred enclave where the law is stringently observed springs from that terror of extinction.[14]

That fear is no better exemplified than by an incident recounted by Richard Holloway during the Lambeth Conference, a meeting of Anglican Bishops every ten years. The issue was the status of homosexuals within the Church. The debate became polarized theologically:

> Anticipating the debate, a group of Christians mounted a demonstration, holding up banners of the sort that gay and lesbian people are familiar with: *No sodomite can enter the kingdom of heaven, Abandon your evil practices or God will smite you. . . .* A few of us at the conference, not many, had worn a rainbow ribbon to signify our commitment to the cause. After the debate the ribbons suddenly sprouted—on the breasts of the young people who served us food in the dining hall. They wore the ribbons as quiet badges of protest against a culture

that had trampled on one of their most fundamental ethical values, which is not simply tolerance for, but celebration of, the wonderful variety of humanity. . . . It is tragic
that religion that grew round the remembrance of Jesus
of Nazareth should become the vehicle of such hatred
and intolerance.[15]

The battle for God is being fought on every level—from the
ethical to the political. For those of us who still need to use
the word, we must use it correctly and educate others in its
use. If "That's not my God," we must declare it loudly, for
the alternative message is being heard unequivocally.

Who Is My/Our God?

This central question has arisen from my exploration of the
sustained attacks on religion that have come from many
sources. It is the cry of the ordinary person as she witnesses
indecencies and even insanities committed in the name of a
divine being. Indeed, it has led some to reject their faith. In
particular the American journalist, William Lobdell, "lost"
his Christian faith after investigating the sexual abuse scan-
dal within the Roman Catholic Church on behalf of the *Los
Angeles Times*. His faith was shattered when he could not
reconcile the beliefs and the practices of a Christian organization, especially in view of the lack of change after he
confronted it, with abusive practices perpetrated in the name
of religion. As I write these words, the crisis in the Roman
Catholic Church deepens as protesters call for the resigna-
tion of Pope Benedict XVI for his failure to protect children
from priestly sexual abuse during his tenure as Archbishop
of Munich and later as Head of the Congregation for the
Doctrine of the Faith during the pontificate of John Paul II.
The furor over the alleged cover-up of pedophile priests, and
the yet more reprehensible practice of "moving them on"

to other parishes or schools(!) when offenses have come to light, has precipitated a loss of credibility in that Church. Revelations of large-scale pedophile activities by priests and Cardinals in the U.S., Ireland, and Germany have seriously undermined the reverence that Christians have traditionally shown for their clergy, and the Church's failure to face up to its responsibilities has only provided further ammunition for those who wish to destroy it. Indeed, one can but wonder what kind of God is being defined by those who willfully refuse to acknowledge systemic abuse on such a grand scale. For when ecclesiastical survival has replaced theological integrity, the institutional church has been deified and God has been demoted.

It is into this void created by the inability of religions to promote a credible God that those I have identified in the preceding chapters—"the new atheists," scientists, the spiritual revolution and non-theists—have stepped in to claim the space for themselves. Karen Armstrong aptly describes the situation as "the Dawkins phenomenon":

> The fact that these intemperate anti-religious tracts have
> won such wide readership not only in secular Europe
> but also in religious America **suggests that many people**
> **who have little theological training have problems with**
> **the modern God.** Some believers are still able to work
> creatively with this symbol but others are obviously not.
> They get little help from their clergy, who may not have
> had an advanced theological education and whose world-
> view may still be bounded by the modern God. Modern
> theology is not always easy reading. It would be helpful
> if theologians tried to present it in an attractive, acces-
> sible way to enable congregants to keep up with the latest
> discussions and the new insights of biblical scholarship,
> which rarely reaches the pews.[16]

Armstrong's plea for the dissemination of new scholarship and theological literacy into the life of the Church has been echoed by such organizations as The Westar Institute, Common Dreams, The Center for Progressive Christianity, and the Progressive Christian Network in addition to individual churches and a few progressive denominations like those outlined by Taussig and noted earlier in this book. It must nonetheless be acknowledged that in many churches the laity are deliberately starved of new theology and fed by "the old Church (that) takes no notice but simply chugs on, *semper eadem*, always the same. In the end it tends to win, for the Church is an anvil that has worn out many hammers."[17] **It is my claim that in the absence of a major theological revolution, traditional religions will continue their further decline into either obscurity or fossilized fundamentalism.**

The Apophatic Tradition

So, what notion of God can best save a religion from itself and its self-proclamation as "the only way"? In *The Case for God* Armstrong has argued for recovering "the apophatic" tradition within religion because "it speaks strongly to our current religious perplexity."[18] She contends that much of our present God-talk is fixated on definitions of God that deny mystery and unknowing, whereas the human search for God throughout history has emphasized that God is beyond words and concepts. It is only with the rise of Modernity and the Enlightenment that people have tried to demystify God. The Modern God has overturned the traditional presuppositions of most religious traditions, for they stressed God's transcendence and unknowability. Modernity has domesticated God with infantile theologies that pit one God against another or against those who would deny God's existence:

> Paul Tillich pointed out that it is difficult to speak about
> God these days, because people immediately ask you if

a God exists. This means that the symbol of God is no longer working. Instead of pointing beyond itself to an ineffable reality, the humanly conceived construct that we call "God" has become the end of the story. . . . During the early modern period the idea of God was reduced to a scientific hypothesis and God became the ultimate explanation of the universe. Instead of symbolizing the ineffable, God was in effect reduced to a mere *deva*, a lowercase god that was a member of the cosmos with a precise function and location. . . . Above all, many of us forgot that religious teaching was what the rabbis call *miqra*. It was essentially and crucially a program for action. You had to *engage* with the symbol imaginatively, become ritually and ethically *involved* with it, and allow it to effect a profound change in you. That was the original meaning of the words "faith" and "belief."[19]

Reduced to its simplest terms, Armstrong's thesis is that the fundamental concern of religion has long been and should still be not to provide proofs of God's existence, but to help people "discover new capacities of heart and mind." The result will be to foster "spirituality" that "is expressed in practical compassion" and "the ability to *feel with* the other."[20] By recovering such pre-modern thinking about religion, by recognizing its ultimate function as that of helping us "to live creatively, peacefully and even joyously with realities for which there are no easy explanations," people will once again honor the "ineffable mystery they sense in each human being and create societies that protect and welcome the stranger, the alien, the poor and the oppressed."[21]

She recommends that religions engage in true Socratic dialogue with an acknowledgment that another viewpoint might have merit and that such dialogue can help people refine their beliefs. This goes beyond the empty rhetoric of many inter-faith meetings that refuse to take seriously the voice of "the other" and thereby leave most participants outwardly friendly but unchanged by the encounter. How effective, for example, is something like the five-yearly Parliament of the World's Religions in seriously examining what each faith really believes and fostering true dialogue where people have to defend their faith and answer how it creates a more peaceful/ better world? Or, does it simply "showcase" each religion without any critical evaluation? This echoes an earlier appeal from John Shelby Spong that each religion begin the process of critically examining its own understanding of God in the course of open dialogue with those of other belief systems who similarly search for an ineffable mystery:

> My hope is that my brothers and sisters who find
> Judaism, Islam, or Buddhism as their point of entry,
> based upon their time and place in history, will also ex-
> plore their pathway into God in a similar manner, until
> they too can escape the limits of their tradition at its
> depths and, grasping the essence of their system's reli-
> gious insights, move on to share that essence with me
> and the world. **Then each of us, clinging to the truth, the
> pearl of great price if you will, that we found in the spiri-
> tual wells from which we have drunk, can reach across
> the once insuperable barriers to share as both givers and
> receivers in riches present in all sacred traditions.**[22]

This quest presupposes, of course, that God is beyond all language, all religions and human knowledge. Spong expresses it as "walking beyond theism, but not God": for Armstrong it is a meditation on the ineffable that helps us to live well in the here and now.

Will Religions Change?

Armstrong and Spong's proposals provide religions with a way forward by making them more inclusive and less susceptible to the failings I have outlined in this book. Three major benefits can result from such an approach.

First, if instead of proclaiming Certainty and Truth, religions emphasized the unknowability of God and the *necessarily endless* search for meaning, then those devoted to empirical thinking might no longer view them as a competing *magisterium* to be vanquished, but instead accept theirs as another legitimate form of discourse. I thus depart from Stephen Jay Gould's celebrated view of religion and science (see chapter 2) as two totally separate, non-overlapping *magisteria* ("empirical/facts" and "ultimate meaning/morality"), but view science and religion as two discourses that are complementary inasmuch as they share a single *episteme*: an endless interrogation of the nature of existence. Such a definition of religion will of course prove controversial, but if God is the Creator of the cosmos, then science is also a theological enterprise! This is not to advocate a return to "intelligent-design" or "scientific creationism," but rather to suggest that religion and science should be equally committed to open, intellectual rigor *in and across* their respective discourses.

I am thus advocating an approach like that outlined by Robert John Russell and *The Center for Theology and the Natural Sciences* at Berkeley with its model of science and religion as "creative mutual interaction":

> Religion once again needs the rigors of science to rid it
> of superstition, for religion inevitably makes truth claims
> about this world that "God so loves," claims which must
> be weighed against the grueling tribunal of evidence.
> More surprisingly, science needs religion to expose its
> pretensions to absolute authority and unique and un-
> equivocal truth. The universe is more mysterious and
> more infinite that either science or religion can ever fully
> disclose, and the urgencies of humankind and the natural

environment demand an honest interaction between the discoveries of nature, the empowerment afforded us by appropriate technology, the inherent value of the environment, and the demand that we commit ourselves to a future in which all species can flourish. We can no longer afford the stalemate of past centuries between theology and science, for this leaves nature Godless and religion worldless.

When this happens, our culture, hungering after science for something to fill the void of its lost spiritual resources, is easy prey to New Age illusions wrapped in science-sounding language—the "cosmic self-realization movement" and the "wow of physics"—while our "denatured" religion, attempting to correct social wrong and to provide meaning and support for life's journey, is incapable of making its moral claims persuasive or its spiritual comfort effective because its cognitive claims are not credible. Nor can we allow science and religion to be seen as adversaries, for they will either be locked in a conflict of mutual conquest, such as "creation science" which costs religion its credibility or "scientific materialism" which costs science its innocence.

Instead it is time to begin a new and creative interaction between theology and science—an interaction which honors and respects the integrity of each partner, an interaction in which convictions are held self-critically and honest engagement is prized, an interaction which focuses specifically on the most rigorous theories of mainstream natural science and the most central positions of mainline theology, an interaction which aims at serving the broader concerns of the global human and ecological communities.[23]

Religion and Science need to interrogate not only their own assumptions and conclusions more, but also be critical of each other. Otherwise, they will retreat into two distinct camps—one focused exclusively on "facts" and the other on "morals." Indeed, it seems clear that if most religious communities had long ago taken on board some empirical thinking, they might not be in quite such a dire mess as they now face.

Second, if religions were more theocentric, open to the spiritual searcher who is struggling (*jihad*) through the dark night of the soul to an encounter with the numinous, then much of the modern spirituality revolution would be superfluous. These seekers could be accommodated within existing religious groups and would have little need or inclination to step outside of them.

Third, if every religion could abandon all claims to be the *only preferred* revelation of God, then all people could develop more harmonious relationships with those of other faiths. They might also be better understood and accepted by those who spurn religious faith and belief in God, and thereby create a more secure and peaceful world.

A New Vision?

The vision for religions that I am advocating is similar to that which Gretta Vosper recommends for individual churches: to be "open, welcoming, honest, self-critiquing, dogma-free, values-based, spiritually engaging communit(ies)"[24] The question remains whether they will have the vision and courage they will need to proceed along that path. For the fact is that they have a great deal invested in what Rachael Kohn insists is really a "political" agenda:

> After September 11 it is impossible not to seriously consider the political implications of religious beliefs. The women and girls who are cruelly abused by men and are forced into silence by tribal laws, the Church culture that

protects its own clerics when they are known to be perpetrators of crimes, the extremist religious communities
that believe critics should be "rubbed out" and different
religious communities subjugated, if not eliminated are
acting politically. Equally, the religious community that
refuses to either oppress women or protect criminals, that
refuses to preach and fund terrorism and fosters friendship and dialogue with other religious communities, that
examines honestly the social consequences of its beliefs
and opens its doors to a changing society is also acting
politically.[25]

By widening the classification of religion to include its political dimension, Kohn alerts us to the high stakes that are
involved in reforming religions and subjecting their beliefs
and values to critical review. Their political aspirations often
take them beyond the status of mere spiritual organizations
whose main concern is the contemplation of the Divine. To
erase or revise a religion's ancient text(s) in a way that frees
its believers from adherence to following edicts that today
may appear "offensive" is often perceived as an attack on
both the integrity of the religion itself and its ability to establish a particular kind of society. Those who dare to suggest
that a religion modify its social codes are viewed as a threat
to the stability (and continuance) of theocractic governments.
As I have shown in this book, however, courageous people
like Aslan and Manji have begun tentative steps in Islam,
and an increasing number of Christian writers have called for
new visions of that faith. Likewise, spirited reconstructionist
theologians like the late Sherwin Wine have dared to widen
the horizons of Judaism.

But, it is also true to say that the majority of religions still
remain exclusivist and unwilling to change. The sacking of
Bruce K. Waltke in 2010 reveals the deep-seated conservatism that still pervades much of Christianity. In a video clip

disseminated worldwide on the internet, this evangelical professor of Old Testament studies at the Reformed Theological Seminary in Orlando not only endorsed evolution, but said that evangelical Christianity could face a crisis for its failure to accept science. Waltke sensibly observed that "If the data [are] overwhelmingly in favor of evolution, to deny that reality will make us a cult . . . some odd group that is not really interacting with the world; and rightly so, because we are not using our gifts and trusting God's Providence that brought us to this point of our awareness." This forthright statement should, of course, should have been greeted with applause.[26] Instead, he was left with no option but to resign as the conservative vultures circled. One positive note was that a more liberal evangelical college subsequently offered Waltke an academic position, but it is clear that one must not underestimate the resistance of religions to even the most rational calls for change.

What I am advocating is obviously further along the liberal continuum than what John Hick in 1980 labeled a "Copernican revolution": one in which "the universe of faiths centers upon God, and not upon Christianity or upon any other religion."[27] Peter Carnley, the former primate of the Anglican Church of Australia has advocated a "theology of cross reference" in which religions lose their "tendency to introspective self-definition and self-reference" in favor of "mutual wrestling" by means of interrogating "one another's texts and beliefs." His rationale is radically **theological,** for he simply asserts that "we all worship the same God, and if God is in some way interested in what goes on this world, then the question that currently confronts us all in the context of our heightened awareness of religious pluralism today is: What is God doing in such a world?"[28]

Perhaps though, despite all the rhetoric and overtures of good-will, it is only when a catastrophic event overtakes us that the eyes of believers are opened to a new way of understanding God and their religion. In the wake of the 9/11 tragedy appeared the remarkable book *From the Ashes*. It united people of different faiths and spiritualities in their determination to proclaim that the God they worshipped *was not the same God* as those who had killed over three thousand people. Many of the responses were in tune with the sentiments expressed by Armstrong and Spong. One striking example from a Muslim gives hope that religions might yet muster up the will to change. It also indicates a theological shift that encompasses those outside its faith system and looks forward to a renewed humanity. These words offer hope that change may come:

> People have been gathering everywhere for prayer, but maybe prayer is not all that God wants. God is not waiting for us to beseech him [sic] to heal the world. God who is "nearer than our jugular vein" is within the anguish of the human race, pleading us to do good that only our hands and hearts can do. Spirituality is not about easing fear, not about mere consolation; it is about facing truth. *I will begin the struggle for a unified and healed humanity, breathe and remember God.*[29]

Notes

1. Leaves, "A Journey in Life" in Hedrick (ed.), *When Faith Meets Reason*, 37.

2. Holloway, *Doubts and Loves*, 15–16.

3. Cowdell, *God's Next Big Thing*, 65.

4. The five fundamentals of Christianity were formulated in 1910 by the Presbyterian Church of the USA. They are: belief in the inerrancy of scriptures; the virgin birth and deity of Jesus; the substitutionary understanding of the atonement; the bodily resurrection of Jesus and the authenticity of Jesus' miracles. However, not all Christians agree with these five fundamentals and they have been expanded by various denominations to include the following: belief in The Trinity, the total depravity of humankind, the pre-millennial return of Christ, and the necessity of being born again. Mainline churches have tended to affirm belief in the historic creeds—the

Nicene Creed, the Apostles' Creed and even the Athanasian Creed. The Roman Catholic Church includes as essential belief in such doctrines as the Assumption of Mary and the Transubstantiation. Interestingly, it has recently eliminated belief in Purgatory.

5. Gibbs and Bolger, *Emerging Churches*, 54.

6. The English theologian, C. H. Dodd (1884–1973) was the first theologian to propose "realized eschatology" in his books, *The Parables of the Kingdom* (1935) and *History of the Gospel* (1938). In *The Parables of the Kingdom* he writes: "[The parables] use all the resources of dramatic illustration to help men [sic] see that in the events before their eyes . . . God is confronting them in His kingdom, power and glory. This world has become the scene of a divine drama, in which the eternal issues are laid bare. It is the hour of decision. It is realized eschatology."

7. Gibbs and Bolger, *Emerging Churches*, 122.

8. McLaren, *A Generous Orthodoxy*, 264.

9. McLaren, *The Last Word and a Word After That*, 188–89.

10. Borg, *The Heart of Christianity*, 14.

11. Mark Driscoll, http://www.TheResurgence.com.

12. Richard Dawkins, "Haiti and the hypocrisy of Christian Theology," *The Washington Post*, 25 January 2010.

13. Ali, *Nomad,* 240 (my italics).

14. Armstrong, *The Battle for God*, 368.

15. Holloway, *Doubts and Loves*, x–xi.

16. Armstrong, *The Case for God*, 308 (my bold).

17. Cupitt, "Reforming Christianity," in Funk (ed.), *The Once and Future Faith*, 52.

18. Armstrong, *The Case for God*, 140.

19. Armstrong, *The Case for God*, 320–21.

20. Armstrong, *The Case for God*, xvii.

21. Armstrong, *The Case for God,* 330.

22. Spong, *A New Christianity*, 181 (my bold)

23. Robert John Russell, "Bridging Science and Religion: why it must be done. http://www.ctns.org/about_history.html#bridging.

24. Vosper, *With or Without God*, 307.

25. Kohn, *The New Believers*, 212–13.

26. http://www.youtube.com/watch?v=UdEr5DpA-gE. I have given this link as the original YouTube address was removed a few days after its screening at the insistence of the Reformed Theological Seminary.

27. Hick, *God has Many Names*, 52.

28. Carnley, *Reflections in Glass*, 312.

29. Kabir Helminski in *From the Ashes*, 35.

Conclusion

The "Boobquake" Phenomenon

In April 2010 a senior cleric, Ayatollah Hojatoleslam Kazem Sedighi, addressed the Islamic faithful in Tehran at Friday prayers. He railed against women who wear what he considered provocative clothing, arguing that their lack of female reserve precipitated seismic activity. He reasoned that there was a direct correlation between the incidence of earthquakes and the amount of female flesh on display:

> Many women who do not dress modestly . . . lead young
> people astray, corrupt their chastity and spread adultery
> in society, which (consequently) increases earthquakes.
> What can we do to avoid being buried under the rubble?
> There is no other solution but to take refuge in religion
> and adapt our lives to Islam's moral codes.

In any other era the Ayatollah's comments would have been heard only in Iran, but today's communication superhighway quickly disseminated his message to the entire globe. In the United States, a university senior and genetics major from Indiana named Jennifer McCreight decided to put his claim to the test. Being both scientist and atheist, she used an internet "social networking" site to enlist more than a hundred thousand women to test the hypothesis that the exposure of an unusual amount of female flesh would result in an increase in earthquakes. Cheekily labeling her day of action "Boobquake," she encouraged women to reveal as much cleavage as possible (or, if they preferred, uncovered legs) to see whether the presumed ire of the Almighty would unleash tremors around the world. If a noteworthy increase in seismic activity failed to occur, however, then the Ayatollah's claims would be proven false, the alleged influence of women's exposed chests and legs could be dismissed, and God's credibility would be diminished.

On the fateful day of "exposure," 26 April 2010, it was estimated that twice the anticipated number, that is, two hundred thousand females flaunted an abnormal expanse of presumably "titillating" flesh, and seismologists officially recorded 47 earthquakes. This, as McCreight notes: "fell well within the 95% confidence interval for the number of earthquakes (about 0 to 148) on any given day around the world." Indeed, on that particular day, the mean *magnitude* of the quakes was slightly **lower** than normal, a statistic that might be taken to suggest divine pleasure at the increased display of female breasts and legs! Some newspapers reported an earthquake in Taiwan with a magnitude of 6.5; but this is not unusual as earthquakes with a magnitude measuring from 6.0–6.9 occur on average 134 times a year. McCreight observes that "the Taiwan earthquake was good for headlines, but not statistically significant." It also occurred a few hours *prior* to the official commencement of the "Boobquake" experiment on 25 April at 10:59 PM, Indiana time.[1]

Though clearly a burlesque, this incident has serious implications and raises two important issues. First, it illustrates the changing attitude towards edicts uttered by religious leaders. Religions are no longer off-limits for ridicule, and ostensibly irrational statements by clerics are subject to close examination and even sharp criticism.

Second, it raises questions as to how those who heard the sermon in Tehran received the Ayatollah's pronouncements; and how do religious believers think that God acts in history (if at all)? Did any of the faithful gathered for prayer consider his statement absurd? Did *all* his hearers agree with the premise of a direct causal link between what women wear and earthquakes? How many believers (of any religion) actually think that God inflicts natural disasters on people? Or, are these incidents really "supernatural" events? And if so, are they unleashed by the Almighty because of human sinfulness or to teach people a lesson? How many religious people think that prayers addressed to God will affect climatic conditions either for good or ill? As a minister of religion I have been frequently asked to pray for seasonable weather for a forthcoming church event occurring out-of-doors. I wonder if these well-meaning parishioners actually think that I can affect the weather patterns in *a particular location*. Again, it is a deeply *theological* question: What kind of *God* do they believe in?

One need go back only as far as 6 July 1984 to recall that a number of Christians claimed a fire in York Minster, United Kingdom, was as a **direct result** of the consecration **three days earlier** of The Right Reverend David Jenkins as Anglican Bishop of Durham. The Christian God, they insisted, had been angered by Jenkins' liberal views concerning the virgin birth and resurrection of Jesus and had sent a lightning bolt to express the Deity's displeasure at this sacrilegious priestly elevation! Again, one need only ask such simple questions as why it took God three days to act or why he did not strike down Jenkins instead of harming the historic building to reveal the ludicrousness of the argument. Moreover, as the central thesis of this book has repeatedly asked, "What kind of theology is being promoted by such notions?"

I predict that what I shall call the "The Boobquake phenomenon," will become more commonplace as ordinary people grow increasingly skeptical about supernatural beliefs and claims. With more people more highly educated than ever before, to say nothing of being able to obtain a vast amount of information and debate issues on the internet, they are empowered to assess and critique all manner of social and religious ideas.

Information-gathering, conversation, dispute, and protest are going on every second of every day, and on a global scale. People in cities as diverse as San Francisco, Delhi, Jakarta and Auckland can (and do) discuss freely *with each other* every imaginable topic, including religion. The fact that in just a few hours over one million people visited the "Boobquake Blog," and that people from all corners of the globe engaged in intense debate about Islam and women's rights, reveals that no religion can escape intense worldwide scrutiny. Further "Boobquake" incidents will occur as thoughtful people challenge unfounded claims by institutions that are discussed openly and without restraint in the public domain. Indeed, as this book has shown, religions are already experiencing a very bumpy ride, and it seems certain that the bumps will increase in both frequency and magnitude in coming years.

It is not surprising that the first "Boobquake" event was orchestrated by a scientist who was also an atheist, for I have shown (chapters 1–3) that both scientists and atheists now have religion squarely in their sights. And I have argued that most of their attacks have been justified and that far from dismissing them as angry militants launching superficial and ill-informed invectives, we must address their contributions to the debate over the future of religion with utter seriousness.[2] Indeed, they should be congratulated for their honest free-thought and their healthy challenge that religions explain clearly what they believe and articulate how is it still possible to believe in God in the face of an indifferent and seemingly random universe. Supporters of religion can no longer retreat into a "holy huddle" claiming sacrosanct status for their beliefs; rather they must welcome and join the debate begun by atheism and science. Tom Frame's insights about the failure of the Australian churches to engage with secularism and its philosophical underpinning could with equal justification be applied to all religions:

> I agree with those who ask that theological claims be subject to philosophical scrutiny. I do not accept that religious convictions are either immune to, or quarantined from, such a critique, which implies that theology and philosophy have nothing to say to each other. Theology does not consist of private truths or insights accessible only to the initiated. It must also be conveyed in language that outsiders can understand. In the context of contemporary public debates in which nothing is above being questioned or criticized, the Church has been found wanting. Catechesis of individual believers is poor; apologetics is not a high priority. . . . Part of the problem is the Church's mistaken perception that belief needs to be sugar-coated and made culturally appealing if it is to be heeded by the rising generation of young Australians. Religion is depicted not as the quest for truth but a mere lifestyle option.[3]

A New (Non?) Religious Age

It is clear that whether people redefine religion by using inclusive terms like spirituality or whether they jettison it altogether, we are now entering a new religious era. I am uncertain as to whether this means that we are at the beginning of what some have termed a "Second Axial Age," but one cannot overlook the significant reappraisal of religion in the last few years.[4]

I have shown in chapter 5 that the spirituality revolution is now a significant part of the religious landscape; and has the potential to eclipse religion altogether. The recent increase of spiritual creativity has taken religion by surprise and many of its converts were once practitioners of mainstream religions. "The new believers," as Rachael Kohn famously describes them, have wrested the initiative from traditional religion with more appealing and less dogmatic ideas of faith. Not only the feminine principle, but also ecological and environmental concerns have been encompassed within the Godhead. The search for meaning is both popular and populist and is conducted beyond the walls of the church, synagogue, gurdwara, or mosque. Millions have joined this movement and its books sell extensively. Although its detractors often denounce it as individualistic, egotistic, self-serving and "me-centered," I am inclined to be much more positive towards the motives and intentions behind the spiritual search of ordinary people. To be sure, one must apply to any spiritual practice the caveat that applies to all religions: beware of unscrupulous operators and bogus claims. However, *for most people* the spiritual search is genuine, honest, and sincere. Moreover, I would assert that religions have much to learn from investigating what those in the spirituality revolution are seeking.

Along with the increase in those involved in the spiritual search has come a significant growth in the number of people who have taken leave of religion altogether (chapter 6). This is not a temporary sojourn into the wilderness of non-belief, but a permanent abandonment. Current sociological research has identified Western nations in which living *without* religion is now the norm. And this development does not reflect ignorance or lack of exposure to the messages of the various religions, but rather that people have consciously decided that religion does not help them to find meaning in their lives. Yet far from having descended into anarchy or moral decay, these societies have created highly successful, morally responsible, peaceful, equitable, and healthy social environments without recourse to religion.

Likewise, there are countless individuals for whom living without God or the alleged comforts of religion is commonplace. These are either "ex-believers" who have put away what they now view as their childish ways or those who have embraced atheism to rid themselves of supernaturalism and a non-existent god. They are quite content to face life without the props of religion, totally self-sufficient and spiritually fulfilled in atheism. We can do without God and religion, yet still live meaningful and worthwhile lives. Human goodness need not be divinely inspired and love, trust and ethical behavior can be achieved without supernatural endorsement.[5] Even the prospect of death, the supposed "final frontier" that makes some people fall on their knees before the Almighty holds no fear for them:

> We all live on in others in elemental ways, through our disposition, our example, our caring, our sense of humor, our way of solving problems, as well as through our consciousness and deliberate contributions. We live on through the memory of special moments in which we are present. And we live on through being a grain of sand in the vast social movements that we lived through and in which we participated. What we have done, and who we have been, remains part of the wider universe long after we are gone. This is only one of many things we might hope to affirm in the face of death.[6]

An Appropriate
Theological Response

My ultimate aim in writing this book has been to demonstrate the need for an appropriate theological response to the crisis of belief that has befallen the West and is slowly but surely infiltrating Islam (chapter 4). Indeed, I would go so far as to suggest that most religions are blithely but perilously unaware of the prevailing descent into unbelief, disdain for religion, and the growth of alternative spiritualities that has resulted from fundamentalism and dogmatism. The well-attested "information" explosion of recent years means that people are free to investigate and debate the merits or drawbacks of religious beliefs and practices, and this demands a more carefully orchestrated response by liberal Christians to those who make outrageous statements about (or even on behalf of!) God. Preposterous ideas concerning or offered in the name of the Almighty must be greeted with a loud chorus: **"That's not my God."** Religious leaders must be held accountable for their pronouncements in the same way that Gordon Kaufman prescribes for theologians:

> Theologians today must take responsibility for all the concepts they use and all the claims they advance. They may no longer evade accountability by advocating positions simply because they seem well grounded in tradition or what in earlier generations regarded as divine revelation. . . . Since much about the world (as we presently understand it) was completely unknown to our religious traditions, and this significantly affects the way in which God has been conceived, theologians dare not simply take over traditional ideas; we must be prepared to criticize every use and interpretation of the symbol "God" that has appeared to date.[7]

I have argued that without this necessary theological corrective, religions will become ever more conservative and sect-like. And this retreat from debate and dialogue will increasingly distance them not only from the world at large, but also from other religions and spiritualities whose adherents will fail to recognize the exclusivity of their pathway to God. That will in turn lead to more fundamentalist vitriol and the accompanying danger of intolerance that leads to fear, suspicion, and hostility. It also drives people into the arms of waiting atheists who are keen to persuade us that "a world without religion is indeed a better world."

At the heart of this book is a plea for religions to reinstate the apophatic tradition that affirms the mystery, transcendence, and unknowability of God. This long-revered view has been overshadowed by the modern quest for knowing what is "real," yet is ironically in tune with the postmodern recognition that things cannot be known in themselves. Instead, we can say only what "things are *for us*" and admit that our assertions reflect "only *our own* perspective." Classical theology similarly posits a limit to the human understanding of God: "God as God in God's self is an unsearchable mystery"; or, as Peter Carnley neatly expresses it, "the object of our religious conviction can only ever be perceived dimly, like reflections in glass."[8]

It is with this sense of humility and utter gratitude for our existence that we grapple with the God beyond the god that has been revealed to us in the religious tradition we find ourselves in, and whom we glimpse but fleetingly:

> We don't approach the practice of religion, therefore, as though it involved having all the answers, because we do not see life primarily as a problem to be solved. Rather, we see ourselves as being on an open-ended journey into a future to which we are called by God, a journey in faith and hope, in which there is always something new to learn, a mind-set to be expanded, a perception of things to be stretched, a deeper wisdom to be discerned.[9]

Notes

1. http://www.guardian.co.uk/commentisfree/belief/2010/apr/29/boobquake-earthquake-immodest-dress-iran.

2. For a good overview of those Christian critics who have contemptuously dismissed atheists see Frame, *Losing my Religion*, 212–19.

3. Frame, *Losing my Religion*, 294 (my bold).

4. For a discussion of Axial Age, see Leaves, *Surfing on the Sea of Faith*, 1ff. Among those who have championed the idea of a Second Axial Age are Don Cupitt, Lloyd Geering and Karen Armstrong.

5. Comte-Sponville, *The Little Book of Atheist Spirituality*.

6. Aronson, *Living without God*, 185.

7. Kaufman, *Mystery*, 28, 29 quoted in Funk (ed.), *The Once and Future Faith*, 87–88.

8. Carnley, *Reflections in Glass*, 29.

9. Carnley, *Reflections in Glass*, 50.

Bibliography

Ali, Ayaan Hirsi. *The Caged Virgin: an emancipation proclamation for women and Islam*. New York: Free Press, 2008.

_____. *Infidel*. New York: Free Press, 2008.

_____. *Nomad: From Islam to America: A personal journey through the clash of civilizations*. New York: Free Press, 2010.

Ali, Nujood. *I am Nujood, Age 10 and Divorced*. Sydney: Heinemann, 2010.

Al-Sadaawi, Nawal. *Walking through fire: a life of Nawal al-Sadaawi*. New York: Zed Books, 2002.

Antony, Louise. *Philosophers without Gods: meditations on atheism and the secular life*. New York: Oxford University Press USA, 2007.

Armstrong, Karen. *The Battle for God: Fundamentalism in Judaism, Christianity and Islam*. London: HarperCollins, 2000.

_____. *The Case for God*. New York: Knopf, 2009.

Aronson, Ronald. *Living without God: new directions for atheists, secularists and the undecided*. Berkeley CA: Counterpoint, 2008.

Aslan, Reza. *No god but God: the origins, evolution and future of Islam*. New York: Random Trade Paperbacks, 2006.

Ballis, Peter H. and Gary D. Bouma eds. *Religion in an Age of Change*. Victoria: Christian Research Association, 1999.

Barbour, Ian G. *Religion and Science: historical and contemporary issues*. New York: HarperCollins, 1997.

Barker, Dan. *Godless: how an evangelical preacher became one of America's leading atheists*. Berkeley CA: Ulysses Press, 2008.

Beattie, Tina. *The New Atheists: the twilight of reason and the war on religion.* New York: Orbis Books, 2008.

Beliefnet Editors. *From the Ashes: a spiritual response to the attack on America.* Emmaus PA: Rodale Inc., 2001.

Berger, Peter L. *The Desecularization of the World: resurgent religion and world politics.* Grand Rapids: Eerdmans Publishing, 1999.

Borg, Marcus. *The Heart of Christianity: rediscovering a life of faith.* San Francisco: HarperCollins, 2004.

Boulton, David. *Who on Earth was Jesus?: the modern quest for the Jesus of history.* Winchester UK: O Books, 2008.

Bowker, John. *Licensed Insanities: religions and belief in God in the contemporary world.* London: Darton, Longman and Todd, 1977.

Brooks, Geraldine. *Nine Parts of Desire: the hidden world of Islamic women.* New York: Anchor Books, 2006.

Brown, Andrew. *The Darwin Wars: the scientific battle for the soul of man.* London: Touchstone, 2000.

Browne, Janet. *Charles Darwin: Voyaging.* Princeton: Princeton University Press, 1995.

_____. *Charles Darwin: The Power of Place.* Princeton: Princeton University Press, 2002.

Bruce, Steve. *God is Dead: Secularization in the West.* Oxford: Blackwell, 2002.

Carnley, Peter. *Reflections in Glass: trends and tensions in the contemporary Anglican Church.* Sydney: HarperCollins, 2004.

Carrette, Jeremy and Richard King. *Selling Spirituality: the silent takeover of religion.* Oxford: Routledge, 2005.

Carrier, Richard. *Sense and Goodness without God: a defense of metaphysical naturalism.* Bloomington IN: Authorhouse, 2005.

Collins, Francis. *The Language of God: a scientist presents evidence for belief.* New York: Free Press, 2006.

Comte-Sponville, André. *The Little Book of Atheist Spirituality.* New York: Viking, 2007.

Cornwell, John. *Darwin's Angel: an angelic riposte to* The God Delusion. London: Profile Books, 2007.

Coyne, Jerry. *Why Evolution is True.* New York: Viking, 2009.

Cowdell, Scott. *God's Next Big Thing: discovering the future church*. Melbourne: John Garratt Publishing, 2004.

Craig, William Lane and Walter Sinnott-Armstrong. *God?: A debate between a christian and an atheist*. New York: Oxford University Press USA, 2004.

Crimp, Susan and Joel Richardson. *Why we left Islam: former Muslims speak out*. Los Angeles: WND Books, 2008.

Crowley, Vivianne. *Wicca: the old religion in the new millennium* (Revised Edition). Dorset UK: Element Books, 1996.

Cupitt, Don. *Taking Leave of God*. London: SCM Press, 1980.

_____. *The World to Come*. London: SCM Press, 1982.

_____. *The Sea of Faith*. 2nd ed. London: BBC SCM Press, 1994.

_____. *The Old Creed and the New*. London: SCM Press, 2006.

_____. *The Meaning of the West: an apologia for secular Christianity*. London: SCM Press, 2008.

_____. *Jesus and Philosophy*. London: SCM Press, 2009.

_____. *Theology's Strange Return*. London: SCM Press, 2010.

Darabi, Parvin. *Rage Against the Veil: the courageous life and death of an Islamic dissident*. New York: Prometheus Books, 1999.

Darwin, Charles. *The Autobiography of Charles Darwin with original omissions restored*. New York: Norton, 1969.

Dawkins, Richard. *The Blind Watchmaker: why the evidence of evolution reveals a universe without design*. London: Penguin, 1990.

_____. *Unweaving the Rainbow: science, delusion and the appetite for wonder*. Boston: Houghton Mifflin, 1998.

_____. *The Selfish Gene: 30th Anniversary Edition*. Oxford: Oxford University Press, 2006.

_____. *The God Delusion*. Boston: Houghton Mifflin, 2006.

_____. *The Greatest Show on Earth: the evidence for evolution*. London: Bantam Press, 2009.

Dennett, Daniel C. *Breaking the Spell: religion as a natural phenomenon*. New York: Penguin, 2007.

_____. *Darwin's Dangerous Idea: evolution and the meanings of life*. London: Penguin, 1995.

Desmond, Adrian and James Moore. *Darwin: the life of a tormented evolutionist*. New York: Norton, 1994.

_____. *Darwin's Sacred Cause: how a hatred of slavery shaped Darwin's views on human evolution.* Boston: Houghton Mifflin, 2009.

Ebadi, Shirin. *Iran Awakening: a memoir of revolution and hope.* New York: Random House, 2006.

Edis, Taner. *The Ghost in the Universe: God in light of modern science.* New York: Prometheus Books, 2002.

_____. *Science and Nonbelief.* New York: Prometheus Books, 2008.

Eliade, Mircea. *The Sacred and the Profane: the nature of religion* (trans. Willard R. Trask). New York: Harper Torchbooks, 1961.

Forman, Robert K. C. *Grassroots Spirituality: what it is, why it is here, where it is going.* Charlottesville: Imprint Academic, 2004.

Frame, Tom. *Losing my Religion: unbelief in Australia.* Sydney: UNSW Press, 2009.

Funk, Robert. *Honest to Jesus: Jesus for a New Millennium.* San Francisco: HarperSanFrancisco, 1996.

_____, ed. *The Once and Future Jesus.* Santa Rosa CA: Polebridge Press, 2000.

_____, ed. *The Once and Future Faith.* Santa Rosa CA: Polebridge Press, 2001.

_____. *A Credible Jesus: fragments of a vision.* Santa Rosa CA, Polebridge Press, 2002.

Geering, Lloyd. *God in the New World.* London: Hodder and Stoughton, 1968.

_____. *Faith's New Age.* London: Collins, 1980.

_____. *Fundamentalism: the challenge to the secular world.* Victoria: St Andrew's Trust for the Study of Religion and Society, 2003.

_____. *Wrestling with God: the story of my life.* Wellington: Bridget Williams Books, 2006.

_____. *Coming Back to Earth: from gods to God to Gaia.* Santa Rosa CA: Polebridge Press, 2009.

Gibbs, Eddie and Ryan K. Bolger. *Emerging Churches: creating Christian community in postmodern cultures.* Grand Rapids MI: Baker Academic, 2005.

Gingerich, Owen. *God's Universe.* Harvard: Harvard University Press, 2006.

Goodwin, Jan. *Price of honor: women lift the veil of silence on the Islamic world* (Revised Edition). New York: Plume, 2003.

Gould, Stephen Jay. *Rocks of Ages: Science and Religion in the Fullness of Life.* New York: The Ballantine Publishing Group, 1999.

Grafen, Alan and Mark Ridley, eds. *Richard Dawkins: how a scientist changed the way we think.* Oxford: Oxford University Press, 2007.

Hampson, Michael. *Last Rites: the end of the Church of England.* London: Granta, 2006.

Harris, Sam. *The End of Faith: Religion, Terror and the Future of Reason.* London: The Free Press, 2005.

_____. *The Moral Landscape: how science can determine human values.* New York: The Free Press, 2010.

_____. *Letter to a Christian Nation.* New York: Knopf, 2006.

Hedrick, Charles W., ed. *When Faith Meets Reason: religion scholars reflect on their spiritual journeys.* Santa Rosa CA: Polebridge Press, 2008.

Heelas, Paul and Linda Woodhead. *The Spiritual Revolution: why religion is giving way to spirituality.* Oxford: Blackwell, 2005.

Heligman, Deborah. *Charles and Emma: the Darwin's leap of faith.* New York: Henry Holt, 2009.

Hick, John. *God has Many Names.* London: Macmillan, 1980.

Hitchens, Christopher. *God is not Great: how religion poisons everything.* New York: Twelve, 2007.

_____. *The Portable Atheist: essential readings for the non-believer.* Philadelphia: Da Capo Press, 2007.

Holloway, Richard. *Dancing on the Edge: Faith in a post-Christian age.* London: Fount, 1997

_____. *Doubts and Loves: what is left of Christianity?* Edinburgh: Canongate, 2001.

_____. *Godless Morality: keeping religion out of ethics.* Edinburgh: Canongate, 1999.

_____. *Looking in the Distance: the human search for meaning.* Edinburgh: Canongate, 2005.

Howard, Jonathan. *Darwin.* Oxford: Oxford University Press, 1983.

Hume, Lynne. *Witchcraft and Paganism in Australia.* Melbourne: Melbourne University Press, 1997.

Hunter, Alastair G. *Christianity and Other Faiths in Britain.*
London: SCM Press, 1985.

Jacoby, Susan. *Freethinkers: a history of American secularism.*
New York: Metropolitan Books, 2004.

_____. *The Age of American Unreason.* New York: Vintage, 2009.

Jama, Afdhere. *Illegal Citizens: queer lives in the muslim world.*
USA: Salaam Press, 2008.

Joyce, James. *Portrait of the Artist as a Young Man.* St Albans:
Panther Books, 1977.

King, Max R. *The Spirit of Prophecy.* Colorado Springs CO:
Bimillennial Press, 2002.

Kohn, Rachael. *The New Believers: re-imagining God.* Sydney:
HarperCollins, 2003.

Krimsky, Sheldon. *Science in the Private Interest: has the lure of
profits corrupted biomedical research?* Maryland: Rowman
and Littlefield, 2004.

Kugle, Scott. *Homosexuality in Islam: Islamic reflection on
gay, lesbian, and transgender Muslims.* Oxford: Oneworld
Publications, 2010.

Kurtz, Paul. *Science and religion: are they compatible?* New York:
Prometheus Books, 2003.

LaHaye, Tim and Jerry B. Jenkins. *Left Behind: a novel of the
earth's last days.* Illinois: Tyndale House Publishers, 1996.

Latifa. *My Forbidden Face: growing up under the Taliban: a
young woman's story.* New York: Hyperion, 2003.

Leaves, Nigel. *Odyssey on the Sea of Faith: the life and writings
of Don Cupitt.* Santa Rosa CA: Polebridge Press, 2004.

_____. *Surfing on the Sea of Faith: the ethics and religion of
Don Cupitt.* Santa Rosa CA: Polebridge Press, 2005.

_____. *The God Problem: alternatives to fundamentalism.* Santa
Rosa CA: Polebridge Press, 2006.

Levin, Tanya. *People in Glass Houses: an insider's story of a life
in and out of Hillsong.* Melbourne: Black Inc., 2007.

Lobdell, William. *Losing My Religion: how I lost my faith report-
ing on religion in America-and found unexpected peace.* New
York: HarperCollins, 2009.

Loftus, John. *Why I became an Atheist: a former preacher rejects
Christianity.* New York: Prometheus Books, 2008.

Luongo, Michael T., ed. *Gay Travels in the Muslim World.* New
York: Harrington Park Press, 2008.

Maddox, Marion, *God Under Howard: the rise of the religious right in* Australia. NSW: Allen and Unwin, 2005.

Manji, Irshad. *The Trouble with Islam Today: a muslim's call for the reform of her faith.* New York: St Martin's Press, 2005.

McClaren, Brian. *A Generous Orthodoxy.* Grand Rapids MI: Zondervan, 2004.

_____. *The Last Word and the Word after That: A Tale of Faith, Doubt, and a New Kind of Christianity.* San Francisco: Jossey-Bass, 2005.

McGrath, Alister. *Dawkins' God: genes, memes and the meaning of life.* Oxford: Blackwell, 2005.

_____. *The Twilight of Atheism: the rise and fall of disbelief in the modern world.* New York: Galilee, 2006.

McGrath, Alister and Joanna Collicut McGrath. *The Dawkins Delusion: atheist fundamentalism and the denial of the divine.* London: SPCK, 2007.

Messaoudi, Khalida. *Unbowed: an Algerian woman confronts Islamic fundamentalism.* Philadelphia: University of Pennsylvania Press, 1998.

Miller, Robert M., ed. *The Apocalyptic Jesus: a debate.* Santa Rosa CA: Polebridge Press, 2001.

Mills, David. *Atheist Universe: why God didn't have a thing to do with it.* USA: Xlibris, 2006.

Morris, Simon C. *Life's Solution: inevitable humans in a lonely universe.* Cambridge: Cambridge University Press, 2003.

Murray, Stephen and Will Roscoe. *Islamic Homosexualities: culture, history and literature.* New York: New York University Press, 1997.

Nasr, Vali. *The Shia Revival: how conflicts within Islam will shape the future.* New York: Norton, 2006.

Nasrin, Taslima. *Shame.* New York: Prometheus Books, 1997.

_____. *Meyebela: My Bengali childhood: a memoir of growing up female in a Muslim world.* Trans. Gopa Majumdar. South Royalton, VT: Steerforth Press, 1998.

Nietzsche, Friedrich. *The Joyous Science.* London: Weidenfeld and Nicolson, 1965.

_____. *Twilight of the Idols and The Anti-Christ.* London: Penguin, 1990.

Onfray, Michel. *Atheist Manifesto: the case against Christianity, Judaism and Islam.* New York: Arcade Publishing, 2007.

Otto, Rudolf. *The Idea of the Holy*. Oxford: Oxford University Press, 1923.

Pataki, Tamas. *Against Religion*. Melbourne: Scribe, 2007.

Peters, Ted and Gaymon Bennett. *Bridging Science and Religion*. Minneapolis: Fortress Press, 2003.

Polkinghorne, John. *Exploring Reality: the intertwining of science and religion*. New Haven CT: Yale University Press, 2005.

Phillips, Melanie. *Londonistan*. New York: Encounter Books, 2006.

Price, Robert M. *The Reason Driven Life: what am I here on earth for?* New York: Prometheus Books, 2006.

Ruse, Michael. *The Evolution-Creation Struggle*. Cambridge MA: Harvard University Press, 2006.

Ruthven, Malise. *The Divine Supermarket: shopping for God in America*. New York: Morrow, 1990.

_____. *Fundamentalism: the search for meaning*. Oxford: Oxford University Press, 2005.

Saeed, Abdullah and Hassan Saeed. *Freedom of Religion, Apostasy and Islam*. Aldershot UK: Ashgate, 2004.

Safi, Omid. *Progressive Muslims: on gender, justice and pluralism*. Oxford: Oneworld Publications, 2003.

Sanghera, Jasvinder. *Shame*. London: Hodder and Stoughton, 2007.

Segerstråle, Ullica. *Defenders of the Truth: the battle for science in the sociology debate and beyond*. New York: Oxford University Press USA, 2001.

Shermer, Michael. *Why Darwin Matters: the case against intelligent design*. New York: Owl Books, 2006.

Shirer, William L. *The Rise and Fall of the Third Reich*. New York: Touchstone, 1981.

Spong, John Shelby. *Why Christianity must change or die: a bishop speaks to believers in exile*. San Francisco: HarperSanFrancisco, 1998.

_____. *Here I Stand: my struggle for a Christianity of integrity, love and equality*. San Francisco: HarperSanFrancisco, 2000.

_____. *A New Christianity for a New World: why traditional faith is dying and how a new faith is being born*. San Francisco: HarperSanFrancisco, 2001.

_____. *The Sins of Scripture: exposing the Bible's texts of hate to reveal the God of love*. San Francisco: HarperSanFrancisco, 2005.

Sproul, R.C. *The Last Days According to Jesus*. Grand Rapids MI: Baker Books, 2000.

Sulima and Hala. *Behind the Burqa: our life in Afghanistan and how we escaped to freedom*. Hoboken NJ: John Wiley & Sons, 2002.

Tacey, David. *ReEnchantment: The New Australian Spirituality*. Sydney: HarperCollins, 2000.

_____. *The Spirituality Revolution: the emergence of contemporary spirituality*. Sydney: HarperCollins, 2003.

Taussig, Hal. *A New Spiritual Home: progressive Christianity at the grassroots*. Santa Rosa CA: Polebridge Press, 2006.

Vosper, Gretta. *With or Without God: how we live is more important than what we believe*. Toronto: Harper Perennial, 2009.

_____. Walker III, Ethan. *The Mystic Christ: the light of non-duality and the path of love according to the life and teachings of Jesus*. Oklahoma: Devi Press, 2003.

_____. *Soft Moon Shining: Poems for the Mother of the Universe*. Oklahoma: Devi Press, 2003.

Warraq, Ibn. *Why I am not a Muslim*. New York: Prometheus Books, 2003.

_____. *Leaving Islam: apostates speak out*. New York: Prometheus Books, 2003.

Wertheim, Margaret. *Pythagoras' Trousers: God, physics and the gender wars*. New York: Norton, 1997.

Whitaker, Brian. *Unspeakable Love: gay and lesbian life in the middle east*. Berkeley CA: University of California Press, 2006.

White, Michael J. and John Gribbin. *Darwin: a life in science*. USA: Plume, 1997.

Wilson, A. N. *God's Funeral*. London: Abacus, 2000.

Wielenberg. Erik. J. *Value and Virtue in a Godless Universe*. Cambridge: CUP, 2005.

Wilson, David S. *Evolution for Everyone: how Darwin's theory can change the way we think about our lives*. New York: Delta Trade, 2008.

Wilson E. O. *Sociobiology: a new synthesis*. Harvard: Harvard University Press, 1975.

Young, Matt and Taner Edis. *Why intelligent Design Fails: a scientific critique of the new creationism*. Piscataway NJ: Rutgers University Press, 2004.

Zuckerman, *Society without God: what the least religious nations can tell us about contentment*. New York: New York University Press, 2008.

Index

CPSIA information can be obtained at www.ICGtesting.com
Printed in the USA
LVOW102023080113

314898LV00027B/1565/P